SPOKEN
STANDARD CHINESE

Volume One

by

Parker Po-fei Huang
Hugh M. Stimson

FAR EASTERN PUBLICATIONS
YALE UNIVERSITY

ACKNOWLEDGMENTS

The authors are deeply indebted to John Montanaro and the staff of Far Eastern Publications for seeing this difficult text through the press. We would also like to thank Mrs. Pao-chen Huang and Mrs. Sophia O'Neill for their patient labors over the manuscript in its various stages.

We would also like to thank Mrs. Hwei Li Chang, Mr. Wen-tao Cheng, Mrs. Cecilia Chiang, Mrs. Vivien Lu and Mr. S. Robert Ramsey for their helpful suggestions while they were teaching from an earlier version of this text, during 1974-75. Finally, we would also like to thank the thirty students of Chinese 25a and 26b, of the academic year 1974-75, who patiently submitted to the inaccuracies which we perpetrated on them in the first draft of these materials.

New Haven, Connecticut   Hugh M. Stimson
September, 1975   Parker Po-fei Huang

CONTENTS

ACKNOWLEDGEMENTS. iii
FOREWORD. ix
INTRODUCTION. xi

Lesson 1. Tones, descriptive sentences, and questions.   1
    Pronunciation.   1
    Dialogs.   5
    New words.   6
    Notes.   8
    Pyramid drills 12
    Questions and answers. 13
    Translation. 14

Lesson 2. The direct object. 15
    Pronunciation. 15
    Dialogs. 17
    New words. 19
    Notes. 20
    More notes on grammar. 22
    Pyramid drills 26
    Questions and answers. 27
    Translation. 28

Lesson 3. Specifiers and measures, and the indirect object . . 29
    Pronunciation. 29
    Dialogs. 31
    New words. 33
    Notes. 34
    More notes on grammar. 34
    Pyramid drills 40
    Questions and answers. 41
    Translation. 42

Lesson 4. The object as topic, numbers, modification by
          stative verbs, and auxiliary verbs 43
    Pronunciation. 43
    Dialogs. 45
    New words. 47
    Notes. 50
    More notes on grammar. 53
    Pyramid drills 62
    Exercises. 63
    Translation. 64

Lesson 5. Names and titles, embedded sentences, pronunciation
          and partial inclusion. 65
    Dialogs. 69
    New words. 72
    Notes. 74

Lesson 5. Names and titles, embedded sentences, pronunciation
           and partial inclusion [continued]
     More notes on grammar.   78
     Pyramid drills   86
     Exercise   87

Lesson 6. More numbers, prices and measurement, the imperative,
           and the pivot with yǒu and méiyǒu.   88
     Pronunciation.   88
     Dialogs.   92
     New words.   95
     Notes.   101
     More notes on grammar.   106
     Pyramid drills   115
     Exercise   115

Lesson 7. Eating, drinking and cooking   117
     Pronunciation.   117
     Dialogs.   119
     New words.   121
     Notes.   124
     More notes on grammar.   129
     Pyramid drills   131
     Exercises.   132
     Translation.   133

Lesson 8. Modification of nouns; stative verbs as fixed
           adverbs.   134
     Pronunciation.   134
     Dialogs.   136
     New words.   140
     Notes.   145
     More notes on grammar.   146
     Pyramid drills   153
     Exercises.   154

Lesson 9. Clauses modifying nouns, and change of status le . .   156
     Pronunciation.   156
     Dialogs.   158
     New words.   161
     Notes.   165
     More notes on grammar.   169
     Exercises.   176
     Review of modification of nouns.   177

Lesson 10. Location and existence, and continuative ne   178
     Pronunciation.   178
     Dialogs.   180
     New words.   184
     Notes.   193
     More notes on grammar.   197

Lesson 10. Location and existence, and continuative ne
            [continued]
    Review: Construction with de in sentences 204
    Exercises. 206

Lesson 11. Going and coming, purpose clauses and future
            change of status (with and without le). 208
    Pronunciation. 208
    Dialogs. 210
    New words. 213
    Notes. 221
    More notes on grammar. 224
    Pyramid drills 228
    Exercises, translation 229

Lesson 12. The past tense, completed action, the shi...de
            construction, and "when" clauses. 231
    Pronunciation. 231
    Dialogs. 233
    New words. 237
    Notes. 243
    More notes on grammar. 244
    Exercises. 254
    Translation. 255

Lesson 13. Time when and time spent. 256
    Pronunciation. 256
    Dialogs. 258
    New words. 263
    Notes. 269
    More notes on grammar. 271
    Exercises. 278

Lesson 14. Indefinites, "before and after" 280
    Pronunciation. 280
    Dialogs. 281
    New words. 288
    Notes. 296
    More notes on grammar. 300
    Exercises. 308
    Translation. 309

Vocabulary. 310

Index 326

FOREWORD

Chinese language teaching and language texts have changed considerably over the years. In addition, the nature of the student body in Chinese language classes has also steadily evolved. In a field once dominated by graduate students, many teachers are now finding classes populated more and more by undergraduate students. Another area of change, far more obvious perhaps, is the altered relationship between Americans and Chinese most notable, of course, in international affairs. As the nature of the student body alters, and as other changes occur, classroom texts must constantly be revised and updated to meet the needs of students. Thus it is with pleasure that Far Eastern Publications, Yale University, welcomes this new publication for the teaching of elementary level Chinese. It is published with the hope that it can assist in solving some of the learning problems of the modern college student.

The text presents several unique features. First of all, the authors bring to their task the talents of a professional linguist and teacher as well as a native Chinese with a great depth of experience both in teaching Chinese and in text compilation. Within the text itself, there is a constant concern for correct pronunciation. Indeed, the first task which confronts the student in each lesson is pronunciation. Pronunciation practice moreover is cleverly combined with vocabulary review in each lesson. Additionally, the nature of the pronunciation of standard Chinese is explained carefully. The rules and peculiarities of Chinese grammar, especially as they compare to English grammar, are fully explained. There is a conscious attempt to account for all grammatical points. The Chinese used in the text is also very natural and free-flowing. There has been also considerable effort to introduce new usages and new vocabulary prevalent in the People's Republic. However, as is appropriate for a beginning text, the relatively unchanging aspects of Chinese, such as phonology and basic structure, are strongly emphasized.

The spoken language series now comprises two volumes, both
entirely in _pinyin_ romanization. A two-volume series for reading and
writing Chinese characters is also available. In addition, supplementary
materials to practice both the spoken and written language have also been
prepared.

The entire series, as this first volume illustrates, will emphasize a close examination of what modern standard Chinese is, how it
works and how it should be learned.

John Montanaro

Yale University, New Haven, Conn.
September, 1975

Introduction

Spoken Standard Chinese, in two volumes, is a beginning and intermediate level textbook teaching the official spoken language of China, as used in the Republic of China (Taipei, Taiwan) and the People's Republic of China (Peking). Each volume provides enough material to be taught in one thirteen-week academic term with nine class-hours a week. It is assumed that no sooner than four weeks after a class has begun these spoken materials, it will begin learning to read in the standard Chinese orthographies, using both simplified and unsimplified forms of the characters, and that by the end of two terms it will have learned six hundred basic Chinese characters. This two-volume set for spoken Chinese is coordinated with the two-volume series, Written Standard Chinese.

The fourteen lessons of the first volume (SSC I) introduce five hundred and seventy-five vocabulary items and the most basic sentence patterns. As are all the lessons in both volumes, they are designed to be taught by the oral-aural method; that is, they are for a course where most of the instruction is conducted by native speakers of standard Chinese who use no language but Chinese in small classes of no more than twelve students, and where a minimum of class time is spent by a linguist explaining Chinese grammar to the class in English. The explanations of grammar and usage incorporated in the lessons are designed to eliminate the need for the linguist to use valuable class time to explain grammar; the student can read the explanations for himself outside of class.

Each lesson of SSC I begins with a section stressing pronunciation. This section is followed by dialogs and other spoken material. Next is a "New words" section. Explanations of grammar and usage appear in footnotes to the "New words" section and in the following section called "More notes on grammar", which stresses pattern displays and structural build-ups. The lesson ends with exercises of various types. The earlier lessons also have "Pyramid drills" to

help build up rhythm and fluency. All new words introduced in <u>SSC I</u>
are listed alphabetically after Lesson 14.

Pronunciation

The phonological structure of spoken standard Chinese and Pīnyīn
romanization are introduced gradually in the sections called "Pronunciation". A unified description of this structure and romanization
is <u>Introduction to Chinese pronunciation and the</u> Pīnyīn <u>romanization</u>,
by Hugh M. Stimson (Far Eastern Publications, 1975).

It is possible to teach spoken Chinese using materials written
in either (or both) of the standard native orthographies. We feel
that it is less of a burden on students whose native language is
written in roman letters to teach them Chinese with romanized materials. There are four common systems of romanizing Chinese. The
Wade-Giles romanization is normally used by scholars writing in
Western languages about China; it has a system of indicating tones
with superscript numerals, generally ignored except in dictionaries:
<u>Li</u>^{3}. The Yale romanization, widely used in language texts, uses
diacritics to indicate tones: <u>Lǐ</u>. Another widely used romanization
is the Guóyǔ Luómǎ Zì, or National Romanization, used by the Republic
of China; this romanization ingeniously "spells in" the tones: <u>Lii</u>.
The People's Republic uses a far simpler system, somewhat resembling
the Yale romanization, called Pīnyīn, which literally means "it
spells the sounds": <u>Lǐ</u>. Besides these four formal systems, there
are informal spellings that have arisen with custom; these often show
the influence of non-standard Chinese pronunciation and foreign spell-
ing practices: <u>Lee</u>; also <u>Peking</u> for <u>Běijīng</u>, <u>Chungking</u> for <u>Chóngqìng</u>,
and <u>lichee</u> for <u>lìzhī</u>. We use Pīnyīn in the Chinese portion of these
lessons; in the English parts, we usually use Wade-Giles and informal
spellings to transcribe Chinese.

In Lesson 1, intonation patterns, tones, stress, and the "break"
are introduced, using examples from material appearing later in the
lesson. Beginning with Lesson 2, the new words of each lesson are

grouped with a selection of words from previous lessons chosen because
of shared features of pronunciation.   In Lesson 3 we begin to introduce the structural features of the Chinese syllable in terms of
initial, final, and tone.   In Lesson 6 we introduce a way of grouping
syllables according to whether the finals are plain, frontalized,
labialized, or frontalized and labialized.   The new words of Lessons
6-14 are all introduced with appropriate old words according to this
format.   New words are given brief glosses; old words are not glossed.

Here is how we thought the pronunciation section might be used
most effectively.   First of all, we recommend that sound recordings
be made by a native speaker of all relevant examples and vocabulary
items in each pronunciation section.* Before working on this material
in class, the student should read through any explanatory material in
the section; if he has questions about this material, he should ask
the linguist (not the Chinese teacher, until the teacher and the student are able to discuss such matters in Chinese).   The student should
then go over the examples and vocabulary in the section, repeating
them after the recordings, if possible.   He should listen to them
several times; the first time through, he should have the printed
text in front of him so that he can begin to learn the meanings of
the new words.   He should also try to remember the meaning of the
old word with which the new word is associated; if he has forgotten
it, he should look it up in the word list at the back of the book.
After the first time through, he should avoid referring to the printed
text, as far as possible.

Before working with the students on this section, the teacher
should go over the examples and vocabulary so that he is thoroughly
familiar with them.   For the new words and the old words associated
with them, he should write out short phrases that will provide a
context familiar to the students.

In class, the teacher should drill the examples, and the old and
new words using both choral repetition and individual repetition
techniques.   In choral repetition, the teacher says the word once and

* Tapes are available from the publisher, Far Eastern Publications,
  Yale University.

the class repeats it in chorus; the teacher repeats each word once
or twice before going on to the next word. Occasionally, the teacher
may want to let each student pronounce the word individually; sometimes he will have a student who is mispronouncing a word try to
improve his pronunciation by repeating it four or five times (but no
more than five times). The teacher should use the text as a guide
to the particular aspect of pronunciation that should be stressed
at any given point in the text; but he should bear in mind that total
perfection of pronunciation is the goal. The teacher should use the
phrases he has made up whenever he thinks appropriate, but especially
when it is obvious that one of the students fails to recognize a word.
The teacher should refer to his written notes when necessary but
should avoid reading from them; the students should watch the teacher
at all times and should have their textbooks closed during this
section.

If these suggestions are followed, the students will not only
learn new general points about Chinese pronunciation, but they will
learn the meanings of new words and review old vocabulary.

Dialogs

The dialogs and other spoken materials in this section are
designed to present new words and grammatical patterns in a useful
context. These materials should be recorded by native speakers at
normal conversational speed and as naturally as possible.

Before going over them in class, the student should listen to
the recordings of them and repeat each sentence, following as closely
as possible the rhythm and intonation of the recording. Ideally, the
student should practice all the material in this section until he can
reproduce it all smoothly and from memory; he should approach this
ideal as closely as time permits.

In class, the teacher should say the sentences of the dialog and
the class should repeat them, chorally and individually. The teacher

should be sure that everyone in the class can say each sentence
smoothly before passing on to the next sentence. Here the emphasis
should be on rhythm and fluency, though other aspects of pronunciation
should not be overlooked. Long, difficult sentences can be drilled
pyramid fashion: the sentence is first reduced to its basic element
or elements; then the other words are gradually added, ending with
the original sentence. The teacher should anticipate which sentences
will be helpfully turned into pyramid drills, and he should write out
the drills beforehand so that he can refer to them in class without
breaking the rhythm of the drill work. In preparing these drills,
the teacher should take care that each phrase, from the smallest on,
is a possible complete sentence. When he utters each phrase, he
should be especially careful to maintain a normal speed and natural
intonation and rhythm.

The goal of this section is to provide the student with a mental
treasury of natural Chinese, which he can draw from, naturally and at
normal speed.

New words

New words introduced in the dialogs and new meanings for old
words that appear in the dialogs are given in this section. They are
grouped roughly according to part of speech, and then according to
the order in which they appear in the preceding section. Included in
every Chinese entry is an indication of part of speech; these indica-
tions are explained as they come up, in the notes to the "New words"
section. They are also listed at the end of this introduction.
English translations of the Chinese words suggest the semantic range
of the Chinese without giving all possible ways in which the Chinese
might be rendered in English. Where appropriate, examples are included in the entries; sometimes these examples are extended enough
to serve as the basis for a drill.

The student should keep some record of these vocabulary items so

that he knows at any point what words have been introduced so far.
One way is to keep a card file; lists arranged alphabetically, or by
the system introduced in Lesson 6, "Pronunciation", or according to
part of speech are also helpful. The time spent in keeping multiple
lists of this sort is repaid by reinforcing the oral work done while
in class and while listening to recordings, and by providing another
opportunity to associate new words with old ones that share features
of pronunciation or usage.

The new words and the examples should be recorded. The student
should practice the examples carefully before they are gone over in
class. The teacher should write out more examples before class,
making sure that these include only words and uses of words to which
the students have already been exposed.

Notes

The notes following the "New words" section include definitions
of grammatical terms, explanations of abbreviations and other conventions of notation followed in this series, and some further examples. The additional examples should also be recorded, and the
student should practice them before coming to class. The teacher
should write out further examples illustrating the same grammatical
points and drill them along with the examples given in the text.
Again, the teacher should avoid new uses of old words, and, of course,
any new words.

The content of grammatical explanations is not really the point
of the course, which is to teach people to speak Chinese, not to talk
about Chinese grammar. We include grammatical explanations here and
in the next section in the hope that they will help some students
understand the structure of the language they are learning. In these
explanations, we intend to describe the language as it is actually
spoken, and if somehow a description is wrong or inadequate, the
teacher should feel free to make corrections, bearing in mind that

natural speech is the target of description. As far as we know,
these explanations are accurate; we have been known to be wrong.

More notes on grammar

Whereas examples appearing in the notes on the "New words" section are chosen to clarify the usage of individual words and particles,
examples in the section called "More notes on grammar" are chosen to
make more general grammatical points. In the early lessons especially,
we have gone to the trouble of making rather elaborate pattern displays, which offer a visual reinforcement of the grammatical explanations. The teacher is encouraged to construct his own displays where
they are lacking in this text, and to use them in class.

The examples in this section should be recorded. Before going
over them in class, the student should practice them with the recording, until he can say them all fluently, and, if possible, from memory.
Some students will find the grammatical explanations and the displays
helpful in learning the sentences; however, the sentences themselves
should take precedence over the explanations and displays.

The teacher should understand thoroughly the grammatical explanations and the displays before using the material in class. Where appropriate, he should compose more examples for each grammatical point
being made and include them with the examples in the text. As usual,
he should write out his "script" before coming to class, and refer to
it in class, rather than read from it. The class should be drilled
chorally, for the most part, with some individual spot-checking.
Again, as usual, the students should be looking at the teacher during
the drills, not at the book.

Pyramid drills

Lessons 1-8 and Lesson 11 have pyramid drills. These are sets
of sentences where each set begins with a simple sentence and continues
by adding phrases and words to make longer sentences, or by making

other changes to form related sentences. They should be recorded
and the student should practice them carefully following the rhythm
and intonation of the recording. Faithful attention to these drills
should help improve speed and fluency.

As mentioned above, in the section on "Dialogs", the teacher
should be prepared to use the pyramid method in drilling long sentences, whether in the dialog section or among the examples included
in the notes to the "New words" section or in "More notes on grammar".
It is always best to write these drills out before class, and, as
far as possible, to refer to them during the drill, rather than read
from them directly.

Exercises

A variety of exercises is suggested at first. Translations
from English into Chinese should be done by the student at home and
should be corrected by the teacher outside of class. The teacher
is encouraged to write sets of appropriate short phrases in
English, for quick translation into Chinese at sight by the students.
Class time should never be used for translation from Chinese into
English, however.

Chinese answers to questions in Chinese can be written out at
home, but when these are gone over in class, it is better that the
student say his answer without reading his written notes. Composing
questions to answers which the text has provided can also be done
at home; in class the student is encouraged to refer to the questions
he has written out, but not to read from them; another student should
answer the question without referring to the text.

As the class progresses, the class will be more and more able to
engage in free conversation. One way of starting such an exchange is
for the teacher to describe a situation (in Chinese of course) and
then ask students questions about it. Also it is possible to ask one
student what another student thinks about the situation; usually the

first student will not know what the other student thinks, and so he has an opportunity to ask that student a question in Chinese.

This concluding part of each lesson is the one which requires the most ingenuity on the part of the teacher, who must go to considerable trouble outside of class to think up ways to start brief conversations in class, always using only Chinese and only materials that the students have studied. And during class, the teacher must always be on the alert for the students' errors, but he should wait until the end of the conversation or question-answer exchange before correcting them. Always, when correcting a mistake, the teacher should be sure that the student has repeated the corrected sentence.

Again, the teacher is encouraged to make more exercises than are found in this book, to repeat the format of an exercise from one lesson in a later lesson where it is not found, and to think of new kinds of exercises.

Pīnyīn and other romanizations

Pīnyīn, Yale, Wade-Giles, and the International Phonetic Alphabet signs for the sounds of Chinese are given below.

Tones

	Pīnyīn	Yale	Wade-Giles	IPA
High level:	‾	‾	1	˥
High rising:	´	´	2	˦
Low: before pause:	ˇ	ˇ	3	˧
elsewhere:	ˇ	ˇ	3	˨
Falling:	`	`	4	˩
Neutral:				·˩

Initials

	Pīnyīn	Yale	Wade-Giles	IPA
Labials: plain:	b-	b-	p-	b̥-
aspirated:	p-	p-	p'-	p'-
nasal:	m-	m-	m-	m-
spirant:	f-	f-	f-	f-
Apicals: plain:	d-	d-	t-	d̥-
aspirated:	t-	t-	t'-	t'-
nasal:	n-	n-	n-	n-
lateral:	l-	l-	l-	l-

Dorsals: plain:	g-	g-	k-	g̊-
aspirate:	k-	k-	k'-	k'-
spirant:	h-	h-	h-	χ -
Frontals: plain:	j-	j-	ch-	d̠ʑ̊ -
aspirate:	q-	ch-	ch'-	tɕ '-
spirant:	x-	sy-	hs-	ɕ-
Retracted: plain	zh-	j-	ch-	d̠ʐ̊-
aspirate:	ch-	ch-	ch'-	tʂ'-
spirant:	sh-	sh-	sh-	ʂ-
voiced:	r-	r-	j-	ʐ-
Apical affricates: plain:	z-	dz-	ts-, tz-	dz̊-
aspirate	c-	ts-	ts'-, tz'-	ts'-
spirant:	s-	s-	s-, sz-	s-

<u>Finals</u> (except those with the suffix <u>-r</u>)

	Pīnyīn	Yale	Wade-Giles	IPA
Plain:	(-)a	(-)a	(-)a	(-)A
	(-)e	(-)e	(-)ê, (-)o	(-)ɤ
zh-, ch-, sh-, r-:	-i	-r	-ih	-ɭ
z-, c-, s-:	-i	-z	-ŭ	-ɿ
	(-)ai	(-)ai	(-)ai	(-)ae̯
	(-)ei	(-)ei	(-)ei	(-)ei̯
	(-)ao	(-)au	(-)ao	(-)ao̯
	(-)ou	(-)ou	(-)ou	(-)ou̯

	(-)an	(-)an	(-)an	(-)an
	(-)en	(-)en	(-)en	(-)ən
	(-)ang	(-)ang	(-)ang	(-)ɑng
	(-)eng	(-)eng	(-)eng	(-)ə˒ng
	er	er	erh	ɛɹ
Frontalized:	-ia	-ya	-ia	-i̯A
	ya	ya	ya	i̯A
	-ie	-ye	-ieh	-i̯E
	ye	ye	yeh	i̯E
	-i	-i	-i	-i
	yi	yi	i	i̯i
	-iao	-yau	-iao	-i̯aǫ
	yao	yau	yao	i̯aǫ
	-iu	-you	-iu	-i̯ou̯
	you	you	you	i̯ou̯
	-ian	-yan	-ien	-i̯ɛn
	yan	yan	yen	i̯ɛn
	-in	-in	-in	-in
	yin	yin	yin	i̯in
	-iang	-yang	-iang	-i̯aŋ
	yang	yang	yang	i̯aŋ
	-ing	-ing	-ing	-ing
	ying	ying	ying	i̯ing

Labialized:	-ua	-wa	-ua	-u̯A
	wa	wa	wa	u̯A
b-, p-, m-, f-:	-o	-wo	-o	-u̯ɔ
sh-, g-, k-, h-:	-uo	-wo	-uo	-u̯ɔ
elsewhere:	-uo	-wo	-o	-u̯ɔ
	wo	wo	wo	u̯ɔ
	-u	-u	-u	-uʼ
	wu	wu	wu	u̯uʼ
	-uai	-wai	-uai	-u̯aę̣
	wai	wai	wai	u̯aę̣
	-uan	-wan	-uan	-u̯an
	wan	wan	wan	u̯an
	-un	-wun	-un	-u̯əʼn
	wen	wen	wen	u̯ən
	-uang	-wang	-uang	-u̯aŋ
	wang	wang	wang	u̯aŋ
	-ong	-ung	-ung	-oˀŋ
	weng	weng	weng	-u̯əˀŋ

Frontalized-labialized:	-ue	-ywe	-üeh	-ü̯E
	yue	ywe	yüeh	ü̯E
n-, l-:	-ü	-yu	-ü	-ü
elsewhere:	-u	-yu	-ü	-ü
	yu	yu	yü	ü̯ü
	-uan	-ywan	-üan	-ü̯an
	yuan	ywan	yüan	-ü̯an
	-un	-yun	-ün	-ün
	yun	yun	yün	ü̯ü̆n
	-iong	-yung	-iung	-ü̯oˇŋ
	yong	yung	yung	ü̯oˇŋ

Grammatical notations

Abbreviations for grammatical terms used in the vocabulary are given below. Explanations of the grammatical terms are located in the text by a code which gives first the lesson number, then the section or footnote that contains the explanation. "N" stands for "note to the 'New words' section".

A	adverb (fixed) 1.N5	MA	movable adverb 4.N12
AT	attributive 5.N3	N	noun 1.N3
AV	auxiliary verb 4.N9	NU	number 4.N3
BF	bound form 2.N5	P	particle 1.N7
C	conjunction 11.N8	PW	place word 10.N1
CA	conjunctive adverb 13.N2	SP	specifier 3.N2
CV	coverb 10.N3	SV	stative verb 1.N4
I	interjection 10.N11	TW	time word 9.N6, 12.N3
IE	idiomatic expression 1.N8	V	verb (functive) 2.N8
L	localizer 10.N2	VO	verb object 2.5, 7.N13
M	measure 3.N1	VS	verbal suffix 6.N17

Lesson 1

Tones, descriptive sentences, and questions

Pronunciation

1.1 <u>Intonation patterns and range.</u> Like English, Chinese uses
"intonation patterns" to distinguish meanings of sentences. In English,
for example, "It's a girl.", with a drop in pitch at the end of the
sentence, carries the declarative sentence intonation pattern, and this
pattern identifies the sentence as a simple statement of fact. But
when the same sentence is uttered with a rise in pitch at the end, as
in "It's a girl?", it carries the interrogative sentence intonation
pattern, identifying it as a question.

In Chinese, intonation patterns are best described in terms of
the "range" within which the various pitches of the pattern lie. The
Chinese "declarative" intonation pattern, much like the English one,
has a drop in range at the end of the sentence. The Chinese "interrogative" intonation pattern starts higher than the declarative pattern
and maintains that height throughout the sentence.

In this book, the declarative pattern is marked by placing a period at the end of the sentence; the interrogative pattern is marked with
a question mark.

shān gāo ma?	"Are the mountains high?"
shān hěn gāo.	"The mountains are very high."
hé cháng ma?	"Is the river long?"
hé hěn cháng.	"The river is very long."
lù jìn ma?	"Is the road nearby?"
lù hěn jìn.	"The road is very close."

1.2 <u>Tones.</u> Unlike English, Chinese uses differences in pitch
to distinguish words; these differences occur within the pitch range
established by the intonation pattern. Standard Chinese has five

"tones" including the neutral tone.

The following pronunciation build-up introduces the new words of the lesson, except for the idiomatic expressions. These new words are grouped according to tone. Practice them alone and in phrases, as indicated, paying special attention to the tones.

When carried by syllables followed by pause (i.e. at the end of a clause or sentence, or alone), the tones have the following shapes:

1.2.1 The "first tone" (indicated by a macron ⁻ over the vowel) starts on a relatively high pitch and stays at that pitch for the duration of the syllable.

shān   "mountain"
gāo   "high"
zhēn   "truly"

1.2.2 The "second tone" (indicated by an acute accent ´ over the vowel) starts at a lower pitch than the first tone, and rises to a higher pitch.

hé   "river"
cháng   "long"

1.2.3 The "third tone" (indicated by a haček ˇ over the vowel), when it occurs before pause, starts close to the bottom of the range. For some speakers, it then dips to an even lower pitch; for others it simply stays at the same low pitch. At the end of its duration, it rises quickly to a pitch near the middle of the range.

yuǎn   "far"
hǎo   "good"
hěn   "very"

1.2.4 The "fourth tone" (indicated by a grave accent ` over the vowel) starts at the top of the range and falls quickly, ending at a pitch near the bottom of the range.

lù   "road"

jìn   "near"
bù   "not"

1.2.5 <u>The "neutral tone"</u>,which is unmarked, has a pitch that is
determined by the pitches of neighboring syllables. The question
particle <u>ma</u> has the neutral tone. After a syllable carrying the first,
second, or fourth tone, and before pause, the pitch of this syllable
is slightly lower than the pitch at the end of the preceding tone.

gāo ma?   "Is it high?"
cháng ma?   "Is it long?"
jìn ma?   "Is it near?"

1.2.6 <u>The third tone before a first, second, fourth, or neutral</u>
<u>tone</u> omits the rise in pitch that it has before pause.

hěn gāo   "very high"
hěn cháng   "very long"
hěn jìn   "very near"

1.2.7 <u>A neutral tone, after a third tone, and before pause</u>, has
a pitch near the middle of the range.

yuǎn ma?   "Is it far?"
hǎo ma?   "Is it good?"

1.2.8 <u>In a succession of two third-tone syllables</u>, the tone of
the first syllable changes to the second tone.

hěn yuǎn   --⟩   hén yuǎn   "very far"
hěn hǎo   --⟩   hén hǎo   "very good"

In this book, the original third tone is written in these cases: <u>hěn</u>
<u>yuǎn</u>, not <u>hén yuǎn</u>.

1.2.9 <u>Tone realizations of the negative adverb</u> bu-. <u>bu-</u> has
tone realizations peculiar to itself. It has the fourth tone before
syllables carrying the first, second, or third tone:

bùgāo   "not high"   bùcháng   "not long"   bùyuǎn   "not far"

Before a syllable carrying the fourth tone, bu- has the second tone:
bújìn "not near".

Sometimes the tone on bu- is neutral. This realization tends to occur
in general when speaking in a rapid and relaxed way. It also occurs
associated with certain patterns (see below, 1.12.2).

'cháng bucháng?   "Is it long?"

1.3 Stress. Relative loudness of syllables is expressed in
terms of "stress" (sometimes called "accent").

1.3.1 Normal stress distribution. In Chinese, neutral-tone
syllables carry the weakest stress, and are said to be "stressless".
In phrases of two or more syllables carrying tones other than the
neutral tone, stress is normally distributed as follows: the last
syllable carries the strongest stress, the first syllable carries the
next strongest stress, and any intervening syllables carry stresses
that are weaker still, but not so weak as to obliterate their tones.
In the examples below, the syllable that is most strongly stressed is
marked by a raised tick ('); the syllable with the next strongest
stress is marked with a lowered tick (,); syllables with the weaker
and weakest stresses are unmarked.

,shān hěn 'gāo ma?   "Are the mountains very high?"
,hé hěn 'cháng ma?   "Are the rivers very long?"
,lù hěn 'jìn ma?   "Is the road very near?"

It is not necessary to mark stress in these normal situations.

1.3.2 Displaced stress. Sometimes, because of the requirements
of certain patterns (as in the last Chinese sentence of 1.2.9, above),
a strong stress is displaced from its normal position. A syllable that
carries a displaced stress will be marked with a single raised tick ('

1.4 The break. When a sentence slows down and then returns to
normal speed, without necessarily effecting a pause, a "break" in the
rhythm of the sentence occurs at the point where the slow-down ends.

A break is marked by a comma.

A pause affects the realization of tones, whereas a break does not. For example, a third tone before a pause rises to the middle of the range; before a break it stays low, or changes to the second tone, just as if the break were not there.

A break only occurs in the middle of a sentence. A pause may occur either in the middle or at the end of a sentence. A pause in the middle of a sentence will be marked by a semicolon. Compare:

'shān hǎo, 'hé hǎo?   "Which are better, mountains or rivers?"
'shān hǎo; 'hé hǎo?   "Are mountains better, or are rivers?"

Dialogs

I

A: shān gāo ma?   Are the mountains high?
B: shān bùgāo.   No, they're not.

II

A: hé 'cháng bucháng?   Is the river long?
B: hé hěn cháng.   Yes, it is.

III

A: hé bùyuǎn ma?   Isn't the river far away (from
                                      here)[1]?
B: hé bùyuǎn; hěn jìn.   No, it isn't; it's quite near.

IV

A: 'lù jìn, 'hé jìn?   Which is nearer, the road or the
                                      river? /[2] Which way is shorter,
                                      by the road or by the river?
B: 'lù jìn.   The road. / By the road.
A: lù 'hǎo buhǎo?   Is it a good road?
B: hěn hǎo.   It's very good.

A: 'zhēn hǎo ma?   Is it really good?
B: 'zhēn hǎo.   Yes, it's very good indeed.

New words

shān N[3]	mountain, hill
hé N	river
lù N	road; route, way
gāo SV[4]	high
cháng SV	long
yuǎn SV	far; long (of a route)
jìn SV	near, nearby; short (of a route)
hǎo SV	good
bù (bú- `) A[5]	not
hěn A	very
zhēn A	truly[6]
ma P[7]	(sentence particle, indicating that the sentence is a question)
nǐ tīng. IE[8]	(You listen:)[1] Listen.
nǐ shuō. IE	(You say:) You say it.
nǐ wèn. IE	(You ask:) Ask the question.
nǐ huídá. IE	(You answer:) Answer.
gēnzhe wǒ shuō. IE	(Following me, say:) Say after me.
zài shuō. IE	(Again say:) Say it again.
hǎo. IE	(Good:) Fine.

Notes

[1]Parentheses enclose supplementary material. In the English
version of the dialogs, words in parentheses either have no corresponding words in the Chinese and are added for the sake of smoothness or
clarity of the English; or they have corresponding words in the Chinese
and are best omitted in the English. In the English of the dialogs
and of the "New words" sections, if the material in parentheses ends
in a colon, this material is a more literal translation of the

corresponding Chinese than the following smooth translation.

[2] Alternate translations are separated by a diagonal (/).

[3] "N" stands for "noun". Chinese nouns (other than certain nouns referring to persons) are intrinsically ambiguous as to number and specificity. Thus, shān is translated "a mountain", "the mountain", "mountains", or "the mountains", depending on context.

[4] "SV" stands for "stative verb", which is a verb that expresses a state or condition. It is like the English adjective, except that an English adjective requires a form of the verb "be" when it occurs as the main word in a sentence (i.e. when it does not modify a noun), whereas the Chinese stative verb does not require such a verb. In Chinese, verbs (including stative verbs) are intrinsically ambiguous as to time, person, and number. Thus, gāo is translated "is high", "are high", "were high", and so on, depending on context.

[5] "A" stands for "adverb". See below, 1.6.

[6] In the "New words" section of each lesson, English meanings are chosen to suggest, rather than to specify exhaustively, the range of the meaning of the Chinese word. Thus gāo is "high" when it refers to mountains, but in other contexts it should be translated "tall". Sometimes the English meanings given in this section are different from those given elsewhere in the lesson. For example, yuǎn "far" appears in the dialogs as "far away"; zhēn "truly" appears there as "very...indeed". These differences arise from an effort to bring some naturalness to the English version of the dialog. The same goal of naturalness dictates the omission of some words that would appear in a word-for-word version of the Chinese. Thus, shān bùgāo "(Mountains: not high:) The mountains aren't high." is more naturally rendered in the context of the dialog as "No, they're not."

It should be mentioned at this point that there are words for "Yes." and "No." in Chinese, but they are considered somewhat abrupt, so they are not introduced for the time being. Far more frequent and smooth-sounding is a repetition of the verb for "Yes.", and a repetition of the verb preceded by a negative adverb for "No."

[7]"P" stands for "particle". See below, 1.8.

[8]"IE" stands for "idiomatic expression", which is an expression
that for the time being is to be learned by heart without attention
to its internal construction or to the meanings of its parts. The
idiomatic expressions introduced in this lesson are useful in classroom situations. They are not included in the pronunciation build-up.

More notes on grammar

1.5 The "topic-comment" relationship. A Chinese sentence consists of a lone comment, or a topic followed by a comment. The regular
order is fixed: first the topic (if any), then the comment.

The topic expresses old or shared information. Here appear words
that have come up earlier in the conversation, or words that indicate
something that the speaker assumes the hearer knows about. The English
definite article, "the", often appears with the translation of a
Chinese noun in topic position. There is an optional break (,)
after a topic. In these lessons, a break after a topic is marked
only when it is especially likely to occur, as when the topic is long.

The comment contains new information which the speaker wants to
bring to the hearer's attention. When a Chinese sentence consists of
a lone comment (with no preceding topic), there is a tendency in the
English translation to supply a pronoun to fill the topic position.

(Topic)	Comment	
shān	gāo ma?	The mountains: are they high? --> Are mountains high?
hé	hěn cháng.	The river: it's very long. --> The river is very long.
	hěn jìn.	(It)'s quite nearby.

1.6 The "modifier-modified" relationship. With a few exceptions,
the modifier precedes the modified, in Chinese. An adverb always precedes the stative verb that it modifies. Sometimes two or more adverbs
occur in sequence. In such cases, the first adverb modifies the second

the second modifies the third, and so on.

    1.7   The simple descriptive sentence.

(Topic)	Comment.			
	(Modifier)			Modified.
(N)	(A)	(A)	(A)	SV
shān		bù	hĕn	gāo.
hé			zhēn	cháng.
lù	hĕn			yuăn.
	zhēn	bú		jìn.
				hăo.

    The above display illustrates the simple descriptive sentence.
Such displays will be used, especially in the early lessons, to give
visual clarity to the grammatical patterns. In this and subsequent
displays, certain conventions will be used. Words are arranged in
columns which are headed by abbreviations for the parts of speech;
these headings are in turn grouped under names suggesting the particular relationship that obtains among the various parts of the
pattern. To make a sentence from the words in the display, one word
is chosen from each "required" column, identified by a label that is
not enclosed in parentheses; from each "optional" column, with pa-
renthesized labels, one word may be chosen, as desired. The patterns
illustrated by the displays are generally valid, but not all the
logical possibilities suggested in the displays result in Chinese
sentences that are possible or likely to occur.

    In the above display, a sentence that combines shān and cháng,
or one that combines hé or lù with gāo, would be semantically far-
fetched. Furthermore, not all combinations of adverbs are possible.
Permitted are: bùhĕn, bùzhēn, hĕn bù-, zhēn bù-, and zhēn bùhĕn.
Note: zhēn and other such intensive adverbs optionally take displaced
stress ('), which will not usually be marked in these lessons.

    The labels in the display specify the structure of the pattern.
Here, a simple descriptive sentence has a structure which the labels

specify as consisting of a stative verb, optionally preceded by from
one to three modifying adverbs, constituting a comment, which is in
turn optionally preceded by a noun topic.

1.8 **Particles.** A particle (P) at the end of a sentence modifies
the sentence, thus reversing the usual modifier-modified relationship.

1.9 **Simple questions with** ma. A question which asks simply for
agreement or disagreement is made by adding the sentence particle ma
to the end of the corresponding declarative sentence, and by changing
the intonation pattern from declarative to interrogative (see above,
1.1) Thus: shān hěn gāo. "The mountains are very high." becomes
shān hěn gāo ma? "Are the mountains very high?" There is no change
in the Chinese word order when ma is added. Note that ma modifies
the sentence that precedes it.

Question?				Answer:		
(Topic)	Comment?			(Topic)		
(N)	(A...)	SV	ma?	(N)	(A...)	SV.
shān	bù	gāo	ma?	shān	bù	gāo.
hé	hěn	cháng		hé	hěn	cháng.
lù	zhēn	yuǎn		lù	zhēn	yuǎn.
		jìn				jìn.
		hǎo				hǎo.

"(A...)" means that adverbs are optional, and more than one
adverb may be chosen. Permitted sequences of adverbs are listed in 1.7.

1.10 hěn **and comparison.** A stative verb without hěn is ambiguous,
in a simple descriptive sentence (or question with ma). It may be a
simple comment describing a quality of the topic, or it may imply a
comparison. For example, hé cháng, means either "The river is long."
or "The river is longer (than, say, the road)." But hé hěn cháng.
only means "The river is (very) long." hěn thus blocks comparison
here; it is also weaker than the English equivalent "very", so "very"
may be omitted in a free translation.

1.11 The "co-ordinate" relationship. Two elements are in a
"co-ordinate" relationship if their grammatical relationships to other
elements in the sentence are identical. In English, there is usually
a co-ordinate conjunction between the two elements, such as "and" or
"or". Such conjunctions exist in Chinese, but they are used less
often than in English.

1.12 The choice-type question. A choice-type question presents
two elements in a co-ordinate "or" relationship, between which the
speaker is asked to choose. Choice-type questions occur in two
patterns, so far.

1.12.1 Choose the noun. The first is one where the hearer is
asked to choose which of two nouns has more of the quality specified
by a stative verb. The question consists of two simple descriptive
sentences, each of which consists of a noun and an unmodified stative
verb. Between the two sentences there is usually a break or a pause.
The nouns of the two sentences are different, whereas the stative verbs
are the same. (In the pattern displays, sameness and difference of
elements will be indicated by subscript numerals.) The comparative
meaning of the stative verb is definitely implied. Thus: 'lù jìn,
'hé jìn? "Is the road nearer, or is the river nearer?" --> "Which
is nearer, the road or the river? / Which route is shorter, by road
or by river?"

The answer is simply one or the other of the two sentences in the
question: lù jìn. "The road (is nearer). / By road."

Question?				Answer.	
Sentence$_1$,	or	Sentence$_2$?		Sentence$_{1/2}$*	
Topic$_1$	Comment$_1$,	Topic$_2$	Comment$_1$?	Topic$_{1/2}$	Comment$_1$
N$_1$	SV$_1$,	N$_2$	SV$_1$?	N$_{1/2}$	SV$_1$.
'shān	yuǎn	'hé	yuǎn?	'shān	yuǎn.
'hé	jìn,	'lù	jìn?	'hé	jìn.
'lù	hǎo,	'shān	hǎo?	'lù	hǎo.
	cháng,		cháng?		cháng.

Notice: no optional elements.

*"1/2" means "1 or 2".

1.12.2 '<u>V</u> bu-<u>V</u>? The second choice-type question pattern consists
of an optional topic noun, followed by a two-part comment: the first
part is an unmodified stative verb; the second part is the same stative
verb preceded by <u>bù-</u>. These two parts are in a co-ordinate "or" relationship. The first part has a displaced strong stress, and the <u>bù</u>
tends to lose its tone. Thus: hé 'cháng <u>bucháng</u>? "Is the river long
or not long?" --> "Is the river long?"

The answer consists of a repetition of the SV for the equivalent
of "Yes.", or of the SV preceded by <u>bù-</u> for the equivalent of "No."

Question?				Answer.	
(Topic)	Comment	<u>or</u>	Comment?	(Topic)	Comment.
(N_1)	'SV$_1$		<u>bu-SV$_1$</u>?	(N_1)	(<u>bu-</u>)SV$_1$.
shān	'gāo		bugāo?	shān	(bù-)gāo.
hé	'cháng		bucháng?	hé	(bù-)cháng.
lù	'yuǎn		buyuǎn?	lù	(bù-)yuǎn.
	'jìn		bujìn?		(bú-)jìn.
	'hǎo		buhǎo?		(bù-)hǎo.

This pattern is extremely common. It is slightly more abrupt
than the <u>ma</u> questions, but not nearly as abrupt as the English "Is the
river long or not?" In the Chinese, the topic noun is usually omitted
in the answer.

Pyramid drills

gāo ma?

hěn gāo ma?

bùhěn gāo ma?

zhēn bùhěn gāo ma?

shān zhēn bùhěn gāo ma?

bùgāo.

bùhěn gāo.

zhēn bùhěn gāo.

shān zhēn bùhěn gāo.

          'gāo bugāo?

     shān 'gāo bugāo?

          gāo.

        hěn gāo.

        zhēn gāo.

     shān zhēn gāo.

Substitute cháng, yuǎn, jìn, and hǎo for gǎo; and hé and lù for shān. Remember to change bù- to bú- before jìn, and to change hěn to hén before yuǎn and hǎo. Avoid sentences with shān together with cháng, and sentences with hé and lù together with gāo.

Questions and answers

Answer the following questions.

shān gāo ma?

lù bújìn ma?

'hé yuǎn, 'lù yuǎn?

lù 'cháng bucháng?

shān hěn yuǎn ma?

'hé hǎo, 'shān hǎo?

hé bùhěn jìn ma?

shān 'yuǎn buyuǎn?

lù bùhǎo ma?

shān 'zhēn bújìn ma?

Make questions to which the following would be likely answers.

shān hěn yuǎn.

'lù jìn.

bújìn.

hén gāo.

bùcháng.

'zhēn bùhěn hǎo.

'zhēn bùgāo.

shān yuǎn.

hěn cháng.

'zhēn hǎo.

Translate the following into Chinese:

1. The mountain was not so high.
2. The roads were really close.
3. It's long.
4. The road was longer.
5. We're far from the mountains.
6. Which is closer, the river or the mountain?
7. Is it a good road? -- No.
8. Was the river really long? -- Yes, it really was.
9. We're not at all close to the river.
10. It's really not so good.
11. Is the river longer, or the road? -- The river.
12. Which way is longer, by the road or by the river? -- By the river.

Lesson 2

The direct object

Pronunciation

Review the tones of words introduced in Lesson 1 and compare them with the tones of words introduced in this lesson.

1: (first tone): tā "he"; gāo; zhēn; Zhōngguo "China"; shān; shū "book".

2: máng "busy"; nín "you"; hé; cháng.

3: mǎi "buy"; nǐ "you"; hǎo; hěn; zǎo "early"; yě "also"; wǒ "I"; yuǎn.

4: bù; bào "newspaper"; tài "excessively"; lù; guì "expensive"; kàn "read"; jìn; xièxie "thanks".

2.1 The neutral tone at the end of a sentence has a pitch that depends on the intonation pattern (1.1) carried by the sentence, and on the tone (1.2) of the preceding syllable. At the end of a sentence with question intonation, the neutral tone is higher than it is at the end of a sentence with declarative intonation:

gāo ma?	Zhōngguo. "China."
	tāmen. "They."
yuǎn ma?	Měiguo. "America."
hǎo ma?	nǐmen. "You (plural)."
zǎo ma? "Is it early?"	wǒmen. "We."
jìn ma?	xièxie. "Thanks."
guì ma? "Is it expensive?"	

2.2 Stress (1.3) in two-syllable phrases, where neither syllable carries the neutral tone, is louder on the second syllable than on the first:

zhēn gāo.   nín gāo. "You're tall."

15

shān gāo.

tā gāo. "She's tall."

hěn gāo.   bùgāo.

nǐ gāo. "You're tall."   tài gāo. "Too high."

yě gāo. "(He's) tall, too."   kàn shū. "To read a book."

wǒ gāo. "I'm tall."

mǎi shū. "To shop for some
    books."

zhēn cháng.   hé cháng.

zhēn máng. "(She's) really   nín máng. "You're busy."
    busy."

tā máng. "He's busy."

hěn cháng   bùcháng.

hěn máng. "(He's) very busy."   lù cháng.

yě cháng. "It's long, too."   tài cháng. "It's too long."

nǐ máng. "You're busy."   bùmáng. "(I'm) not busy."

yě máng. "(She's) busy, too."

zhēn hǎo.   hé hǎo.

shān hǎo.   hé yuǎn.

zhēn yuǎn.   nín hǎo. "You're fine."

shān yuǎn.   nín zǎo. "You're early."

zhēn zǎo. "It's really early."

tā hǎo. "She's fine."

shū hǎo. "Books would be fine."

tā zǎo. "He's early."

hěn hǎo. (1.2.8)   bùhǎo.

hěn yuǎn.   lù hǎo.

hěn zǎo. "It's very early."   bùyuǎn.

yě hǎo. "That'll be fine, too."   lù yuǎn.

wǒ hǎo. "I'm fine."   bùzǎo. "It's not early."

nǐ zǎo. "You're early."   bào hǎo. "Newspapers are fine."

yě zǎo. "It's early, too."   tài hǎo. "It's too good."
wǒ zǎo. "I'm early."   tài yuǎn. "It's too far away."
                                     tài zǎo. "It's too early."

zhēn jìn.   bújìn. (1.2.9)
shān jìn.   hé jìn.
zhēn guì. "It's really   nín jìn. "You're nearby."
  expensive."   búguì. "It's not expensive."
tā jìn. "He's nearby."
shū jìn. "The book is nearby."
shū guì. "Books are expensive."

hěn jìn.
hěn guì. "It's expensive."
nǐ jìn. "You're nearby."
yě jìn. "It's nearby, too."
wǒ jìn. "I'm nearby."
yě guì. "It's expensive, too."
yě kàn. "(I) read them, too."

    2.3 The "half-fourth" tone. When it appears before another
fourth tone, a fourth tone drops in pitch only about half as far as
it does before other tones:

lù jìn.
tài jìn. "It's too nearby."
kàn bào. "Read a newspaper."
bào guì. "Newspapers are more expensive."
tài guì. "It's too expensive."

Dialogs

I

A: nǐ kàn bào ma?   Do you read newspapers?
B: wǒ kàn bào.   Yes, I do.

A: nǐ kàn shū ma?   Do you read books?

B: wǒ yě kàn shū.   Yes, I read books, too.

A: nǐ mǎi 'shū bumǎi?   Do you buy books?

B: wǒ 'bùmǎi shū; shū tài guì.   No, I don't; they're too expensive.

                          II

A: nǐmen 'mǎi bumǎi Zhōngguo   Do you buy Chinese books?
   shū?

B: mǎi.   Yes.

A: nǐmen mǎi 'Měiguo shū bumǎi?   Do you buy American books?

B: wǒmen 'bùmǎi.   No, we don't.

A: tāmen yě bùmǎi Měiguo shū   (Do they not buy American books,
   ma?   too?:) Don't they buy American
                                        books either?

B: tāmen yě bùmǎi.   No, they don't, either.

A: tāmen búkàn Měiguo shū ma?   Don't they read American books?

B: tāmen búkàn; tāmen tài máng.   No; they're too busy.

                          III

A: tā máng ma?   Is she busy?

B: tā hěn máng.   Yes, she is.

A: tāmen 'máng bumáng?   Are they busy?

B: tāmen 'yě hěn máng.   Yes, they are, too.

                          IV[1]

A: nín hǎo?[2]   How do you do?

B: hǎo.[2] nín hǎo ma?   I'm fine. How are you?

A: hěn hǎo, xièxie.   I'm fine, thanks.

B: 'máng bumáng?   (Are you busy?:) Have you got a
                                        moment?

A: bùmáng.   (No, I'm not.:) Of course.

V^1

A: zǎo?[2]   Good morning.
B: zǎo, zǎo?[2]   Good morning.

VI^1

A: nín zǎo?[2]   Good morning, sir / madam.
B: zǎo, zǎo?[2]   Good morning.

VII

A: nǐ kàn shū, kàn bào?   Which do you read, books or news-
                                        papers?

B: wǒ kàn shū.   I read books.

A: kàn 'Měiguo shū, kàn   American or Chinese?
    'Zhōngguo shū?

B: kàn 'Zhōngguo shū.   Chinese. Are Chinese books ex-
    Zhōngguo shū 'guì buguì?   pensive?

A: bútài guì.   Not too.

B: 'Zhōngguo shū guì, 'Měiguo   Which are more expensive, Chinese
    shū guì?   books or American?

A: 'Měiguo shū guì.   American ones are.

New words

wǒ N[3]   I
nǐ N[3]   you (singular)
nín N[3,4]   you (singular, polite)
tā N[3]   he, she
-men BF[5]   (suffix to nouns that denote humans,
                                        indicating plural)

wǒmen N[3]   we
nǐmen N[3]   you (plural)
tāmen N[3]   they

bào N	newspaper
shū N	book
Zhōngguo N	(Central guó Nation:) China
Měiguo N	(Beautiful Nation:) America, the United States
gāo SV	high (1)[6]; tall
hǎo SV[7]	good (1); well, healthy
guì SV	expensive
máng SV[7]	busy
zǎo SV[7]	early
kàn V[8]	read
mǎi V	shop for, buy
yě A	also, too, either[9]
tài A	too, excessively
xièxie. IE	Thanks.

Notes

[1]Dialogs IV, V, and VI are "socially charged". This means that the sentences in them tend to be formulaic, and that certain changes in their wording which in uncharged situations would be grammatically correct would here signal a refusal on the part of the speaker to enter into ordinary polite conversation with the hearer. Such a refusal is rude when the two participants in the dialog are strangers; it may be startling and confusing when the participants are slightly acquainted but not completely at ease with each other socially; even among friends it is uncommon, and when it occurs it is apt to be regarded as playful, if slightly irritating, banter. The phrase bùhǎo is available as a judgment in uncharged situations, as a comment to shān, hé, or lù, for example. But as a response to the question nín hǎo? in Dialog IV, it is unexpected. Similarly, máng in the same dialog implies not simply "busy", which is its ordinary meaning in uncharged situations, but more "too busy to spare even a moment to

speak with someone". <u>hěn máng.</u> as a response to (<u>nǐ</u>) <u>'máng bumáng?</u>
would be unexpected. On the other hand, when the conversation is
about a third person or persons, as in Dialog III, the situation is
uncharged, and all grammatically possible combinations may occur
without causing embarrassment or irritation.

[2]In Dialogs IV, V, and VI, <u>nín hǎo?, zǎo?</u>, and <u>nín zǎo?</u> are
questions simply by virtue of their intonation pattern. The use of
the interrogative question pattern alone, without the question particle
<u>ma</u> or any other device to show that the sentence is a question, is
mostly limited to greetings.

In the excitement that often accompanies a greeting or parting
dialog, even the responses may carry interrogative intonation,
especially if they are said twice. Thus: <u>nín zǎo? -- zǎo, zǎo?</u>, and
<u>nín hǎo? -- hǎo, hǎo?</u> Bear in mind that the term "interrogative in-
tonation" is a convenient label for a specific intonation pattern
which usually occurs with questions, but which sometimes occurs elsewhere.

[3]The Chinese words corresponding to the English personal pronouns
are nouns, uninflected as to case. Thus <u>wǒ</u> means not only "I", but
also "me" and "my". So also with the other pronouns.

[4]<u>nín</u> is used to address an older person or a superior in polite
conversation. A student may use this form in addressing his teacher,
but the teacher will ordinarily use <u>nǐ</u> in addressing a student.

[5]"BF" stands for "bound form", which means a form that always
occurs in construction with another form and never stands alone as a
complete sentence. Adverbs and particles are bound forms in Chinese.
The abbreviation "BF" will be used to mark bound forms that are otherwise unclassified (are not classed as "A" or "P", for example). Sometimes a hyphen is added to a bound form, showing whether the form is
usually prefixed or suffixed to the other form with which it is in
construction. Thus the hyphen in <u>-men</u> shows that it is a suffix.

[6]When an old word appears in a new meaning, the old meaning is
given first, followed by a number in parentheses that gives the lesson
where the word was introduced in that meaning.

[7]In addition to their ordinary usages, hǎo, máng, and zǎo occur
in greetings and other socially charged situations, where appropriate
English translations within the context of the situation may diverge
considerably from the usual translations of the Chinese words.

[8]"V" stands for "(functive) verb", which is a verb that denotes
an action or an event. A functive verb is thus different from a
stative verb, which denotes a state or condition.

[9]Translations for yě are "also, too" in positive sentences, and
"either" in negative ones, but notice that whereas the English words
"too" and "either" come after the verb, yě strictly follows the rule
applying to Chinese adverbs, that they always precede the verb.

More notes on grammar

2.4 The N_1-N_2 construction. The first noun modifies the second:
Zhōngguo shū "(China book:) book made in China, Chinese book"

2.5 The "verb-object" relationship. In some sentences, a functive verb occurs in conjunction with a word that denotes the person
or thing affected by the action of the verb. This word is the
"(direct) object"-- "O" -- of the verb. The order which is considered
basic is first the verb, then the object.

2.6 The functive sentence is a sentence the main word of whose
comment is a (functive) verb.

(Topic)	Comment ?/.			
(N)	(A...)	V	(O)	ma? / .
tā		kàn	bào	ma?
wǒ	yě bu-	mǎi	shū	.
nín				
nǐ				
wǒmen				

nǐmen

tāmen

In making sentences according to this pattern, avoid $\underset{\smile}{wo}$ in questions: they would be far-fetched.

The first question of a dialog is likely to include both the topic and the direct object, and the answer may leave these words out, especially if they are common to both the question and the answer:

A: nǐ kàn bào ma?   Are you reading a newspaper?
B: wǒ kàn.   Yes.

A: tā mǎi shū ma?   Is she buying a book?
B: mǎi.   Yes.

2.7 The functive sentence in choice-type questions. Four patterns are available so far.

2.7.1 Choose the noun topic.

Question?				Answer.	
$Topic_1$	$Comment_1$,	$Topic_2$	$Comment_1$?	$Topic_{1/2}$	Comment.
'N_1	V_1 O_1,	'N_2	V_1 O_1?	'$N_{1/2}$	V_1 O_1
'nǐ	kàn bào,	'tā	kàn bào?	'wǒ	kàn bào.
...	mǎi shū,	...	mǎi shū?	...	mǎi shū.

Notice that the entire comment is repeated in the second half of the question, and in the answer. Thus:

A: 'nǐ mǎi bào, 'tā mǎi bào?   Who'll buy a newspaper, you or he?
B: 'wǒ mǎi bào.   I will.

2.7.2 Choose the object.

Question?   Answer.

(Topic)   Comment$_1$,   Comment$_2$?   (Topic)   Comment$_{1/2}$.

(N) V_1 O_1, V_1 O_2?   (N) V_1 $O_{1/2}$.

nǐ   kàn bào,   kàn shū?   wǒ   kàn shū.

...   mǎi shū,   mǎi bào?   ...   mǎi bào.

Notice that the verb is always present. Thus:

A: nǐ mǎi bào, mǎi shū?   Which are you going to buy, some
                                  newspapers or some books?

B: wǒ mǎi shū.   Some books.

2.7.3 Choose the modifying noun.

Question?   Answer.

(Topic) Comment?   (Topic) Comment.

(N) V_1 'N$_1$ O_1, V_1 'N$_2$ O_1? (N) V_1 'N$_{1/2}$ O_1.

nǐ   kàn 'Měiguo bào,   kàn 'Zhōngguo bào? wǒ kàn 'Zhōngguo bào.

... mǎi 'Zhōngguo shū, mǎi 'Měiguo   shū? ... mǎi 'Měiguo   shū.

Again, notice that the entire comment is present in both the second
half of the question and in the answer. Thus:

A: tā kàn 'Měiguo shū, kàn   Which does she read, American books
    'Zhōngguo shū?   or Chinese ones?

B: kàn 'Zhōngguo shū.   Chinese books.

2.7.4 Choose V or bu-V. There are two patterns for making choice-
type questions with functive verbs that take objects. These patterns
correspond to the single one used when the verb is stative: 'SV bu-SV?
Notice that the adverb yě occurs in neither of these patterns.

2.7.4.1 'V bu-V O?

Question?			Answer.			
(Topic)	Comment?		(Topic)	Comment.		
(N)	'V_1 bu-V_1 O?		(N)	(bu)	V_1	(O)
tā	'kàn bukàn bào?		tā	bú-	kàn bào.	
...	'mǎi mǎi shū?		...	bù-	mǎi shū.	

Thus:

A: nǐmen 'mǎi bumǎi shū?   Do you buy books?
B: wǒmen mǎi.   Yes, we do.
A: nǐmen 'mǎi bumǎi bào?   Do you buy newspapers?
B: wǒmen bùmǎi bào.   No, not newspapers.

2.7.4.2 V 'O bu-V?

Question?				Answer.				
(Topic)	Comment?			(Topic)	Comment.			
(N)	V_1	'O	bu-V_1?	(N)	(A)	(bu-)	V_1	(O).
tā	kàn	'shū	bukàn?	tā	yě	bú-	kàn shū.	
...	mǎi	'bào	mǎi?	...		bù-	mǎi bào.	

2.8 The simple descriptive sentence: choice-type questions: choose the modifying noun.

Question?						Answer.		
Topic$_1$		Comment$_1$,	Topic$_2$		Comment$_1$?	Topic $_{1/2}$		Comment
'N$_1$	N$_2$	SV$_1$,	'N$_3$	N$_2$	SV$_1$?	'N$_{1/3}$	N$_2$	SV$_1$.
'Měiguo	shān	gāo,	'Zhōngguo	shān	gāo?	'Zhōngguo	shān	gāo.
'Zhōngguo	hé	cháng,	'Měiguo	hé	cháng?	'Měiguo	hé	cháng.
	lù	jìn,		lù	jìn?		lù	jìn.
		yuǎn,			yuǎn?			yuǎn.
	bào	hǎo,		bào	hǎo?		bào	hǎo.
	shū	guì,		shū	guì?		shū	guì.

Pyramid drills

kàn shū ma?

nǐ kàn shū ma?

nǐ kàn Zhōngguo shū ma?

nǐ yě kàn Zhōngguo shū ma?

kàn.

kàn shū.

wǒ kàn shū.

wǒ kàn Zhōngguo shū.

wǒ 'yě kàn Zhōngguo shū.

mǎi 'bào bumǎi?

mǎi Zhōngguo 'bào bumǎi?

nǐmen mǎi Zhōngguo 'bào bumǎi?

mǎi bumǎi bào?

mǎi bumǎi Zhōngguo bào?

nǐmen 'mǎi bumǎi Zhōngguo bào?

                                bùmǎi.

                                bùmǎi bào.

                    wǒmen 'bùmǎi bào.

                    wǒmen 'bùmǎi Zhōngguo bào.

               wǒmen 'yě bùmǎi Zhōngguo bào.

                    Questions and answers

Answer the following questions.

nǐ kàn Zhōngguo shū ma?

nǐ mǎi 'bào bumǎi?

nǐ hěn máng ma?

'Zhōngguo shū hǎo, 'Měiguo shū hǎo?

nǐ hǎo?

tāmen 'máng bumáng?

'tā gāo, nǐ gāo?

Měiguo shū 'guì buguì?

nǐmen 'mǎi bumǎi Měiguo shū?

     Make questions to which the following would be likely answers.

kàn 'Zhōngguo bào.

'Zhōngguo shū guì.

'yě hěn guì.

bùmǎi.

wǒ 'yě kàn shū.

bútài hǎo.

'wǒmen bùmǎi.   'tāmen mǎi.

zǎo, zǎo.

'nín jìn.

Translation

Translate the following into Chinese:

1. I read books, not newspapers.
2. Does he read books, or do you? -- I do.
3. Do you read American newspapers? (3 ways) -- Yes.
4. Which are higher, American mountains or Chinese? -- Chinese
    mountains.
5. Which shall we buy, the books or the newspapers? -- The books.
    Won't we buy the newspapers, too? -- No.
6. Books aren't too expensive, either.
7. They're tall, and so are we.
8. Chinese roads are not too long.
9. He's too busy.
10. Have you got a moment, sir? (2 ways) -- (Give appropriate
    response)

Lesson 3

Specifiers and measures, and the indirect object

Pronunciation

Practice the tones on old and new words.

<u>1:</u> tā; gāo; zhēn; shān; shū.

<u>2:</u> máng; nín; hé; qián "money"; cháng.

<u>3:</u> bǐ "pen(cil)"; biǎo "watch"; mǎi; nǐ; gěi "give"; hǎo; hěn;
    qǐng "request"; zǎo; yě; yǒu "have"; wǒ; yuǎn.

<u>4:</u> bào; bù; tài; lù; guì; kàn; jìn; yào "want".

<u>1-0:</u> gāo ma?

<u>1-1:</u> tā gāo.

<u>1-2:</u> tā máng.

<u>1-3:</u> gāngbǐ "pen"; qiānbǐ "pencil"; zhēn hǎo.

<u>1-4:</u> shū guì.

<u>2-0:</u> piányi "inexpensive"; méiyou "not have"; máng ma?

<u>2-1:</u> nín gāo.

<u>2-2:</u> hé cháng.

<u>2-3:</u> méiyǒu "not have"; hé yuǎn.

<u>2-4:</u> búguì.

<u>3-0:</u> něige? "Which?"; xǐhuan "like"; yuǎn ma?

<u>3-1:</u> 'něizhǐ? "Which (sticklike object)?"; 'yě gāo.

<u>3-2:</u> 'něitiáo? "Which (long object)?"; 'yě máng.

<u>3-3:</u> fěnbǐ "chalk"; hěn hǎo.

<u>3-4:</u> hǎokàn "good-looking"; hěn guì.

<u>4-0:</u> nèige "that"; zhèige "this"; guì ma?

<u>4-1:</u> nèizhǐ "that (sticklike object)"; zhèizhǐ "this (sticklike
    object)"; tài gāo.

<u>4-2:</u> nèitiáo "that (long object)"; zhèitiáo "this (long object);
    tài máng.

29

4-3: bùmǎi.

4-4: kàn bào.

3.1 b-, d-, g- <u>vs.</u> p-, t-, k-: <u>plain vs. aspirate stop initials.</u> A Chinese syllable consists of an "initial", a "final", and a "tone". Tones were discussed in 1.2 and in 2.1-2.3. A final may here be defined informally as what follows an initial in a syllable that has one, and as the entire syllable when the syllable has no initial; finals will be discussed in 6.1.1. Initials are "defined" simply by listing them, as in 5.6. <u>b-, d-, g-, p-, t-,</u> and <u>k-</u> are on the list of initials, so <u>-iao</u> is the final in <u>biǎo</u> "watch", and the whole syllable (minus the tone), <u>yao</u>, is the final in <u>yào</u> "want".

The six initials that are the subject of this section are "stops". This means that during their production the passage of air coming from the lungs and going out the mouth is completely blocked. Furthermore, <u>p-, t-,</u> and <u>k-</u> are "aspirate stops" in Chinese. A stop is said to be aspirate if it is held strongly enough so that pressure builds up behind the point of its articulation, resulting in an explosive "pop" when the stop is released. In Chinese, <u>b-, d-,</u> and <u>g-</u> are not aspirate such stop initials are called "plain".

At the beginning of a neutral-tone syllable that follows close after another syllable, a plain stop initial is "voiced" in Chinese, which means that during its production the vocal cords vibrate, producing their own characteristic humming sound. Thus the <u>-g-</u> in the following words is like the <u>-g-</u> in English "wiggle":

něige?   "Which?"
nèige.   "That."
zhèige.   "This."

Otherwise, the Chinese sounds written <u>b-, d-,</u> and <u>g-</u> are different from the English sounds usually written with the same letters in th the Chinese sounds are "voiceless" (i.e. produced without any vibratio of the vocal cords), whereas the English sounds are voiced. English

has other sounds that are more like Chinese b-, d-, and g- than
English b-, d-, and g-: these are the sounds that follow s- in words
like spade, stake, and skate. The English sounds spelled -p-, -t-,
and -k- are voiceless (and thus different from the sounds spelled b-,
d-, and g- in bay, day, and gay, which are voiced) and unaspirated (and
thus different from the sounds spelled p-, t-, and K- in paid, take,
and Kate, which are aspirated).

The aspiration of the Chinese sounds spelled with p-, t-, and k-
is stronger than the corresponding English aspirate stops.

Pay attention to the initials of the following words, which are
all the words in Lessons 1-3 beginning with b-, d-, g-, or p-, t-, k-:

Plain:	Aspirate:
bào	
bǐ "pen(cil)"	
biǎo "watch"	piányi "inexpensive"
bù	
	tā
	tài
gěi "give"	
gāo	
gāngbǐ "pen"	kàn
guǐ	

Dialogs

I

A:	'něige shān gāo?	Which mountain is higher?
B:	'zhèige shān gāo.	This one is.
A:	'nèige shān bùgāo ma?	Isn't the other one high?
B:	nèige, 'yě hěn gāo.	That one is high, too.

II

A: hé 'cháng bucháng?   Are the rivers long?

B: 'nèitiáo hé bùcháng;   That one isn't, but this one is.
   'zhèitiáo cháng.

III

A: 'něige biǎo hǎokàn?   Which watch is better looking?

B: 'zhèige hǎokàn.   This one is.

A: zhèige biǎo búguì ma?   Isn't this watch expensive?

B: búguì; hěn piányi.   No; it's cheap.

IV

A: nǐ yǒu Zhōngguo 'qián meiyǒu?   Do you have any Chinese money?

B: méiyǒu. wǒ méiyou 'Zhōngguo   No. I have no Chinese money;
   qián; wǒ yǒu 'Měiguo qián.   I have some American money.
   nǐ yào ma?   Do you want some?

A: búyào, xièxie. wǒ 'yě yǒu   No, thanks. I have American
   Měiguo qián.   money, too.

V

A: nǐmen yǒu bǐ ma?   Do you have pens-and-pencils?

B: yǒu. wǒmen yǒu 'gāngbǐ,   Yes. We have pens, pencils, and
   'qiānbǐ, yě yǒu 'fěnbǐ.   chalk, too.

A: 'něige piányi?   Which is cheapest?

B: 'fěnbǐ piányi. nín yào ma?   Chalk is. Do you want some?

A: búyào; wǒ yào 'qiānbǐ.   No; I want some pencils.

B: nín xǐhuan 'něizhǐ qiānbǐ?   Which pencil do you like?

A: wǒ xǐhuan 'něizhǐ. nèizhǐ   I like that one. Is that pencil
   'guì buguì?   expensive?

B: búguì; hěn piányi.   No, it's quite cheap.

A: qǐng nǐ gěi wǒ nèizhǐ bǐ.   Please give me that pencil. Do
    nǐ yào 'Zhōngguo qián, yào   you want Chinese money or
    'Měiguo qián?   American?

B: 'Zhōngguo qián hǎo.   Chinese money would be better.

New words

-ge M[1,3]	(gè; single person or object)
nèi- SP[2]	which?
nèige? N	which?
zhèi- SP	this
zhèige N	this
nèi- SP	that
nèige N	that
-tiáo M[3]	(long objects: hé, lù)
bǐ N (M: -zhǐ)	pen, pencil[4]
-zhǐ M[3]	(sticklike objects: bǐ)
gāngbǐ N (M: -zhǐ)	(steel writing implement:) pen
qiānbǐ N (M: -zhǐ)	(lead writing implement:) pencil
fěnbǐ N (M: -zhǐ)	(powder writing implement:) chalk
	(for writing)
biǎo N	watch
qián N	money
yǒu V	have
méiyǒu, méiyou A V	not have
yào V	want
xǐhuan V	like
qǐng V	request, invite
gěi V	give
hǎokàn SV	(easy to look at:) good-looking
piányi SV	inexpensive

Notes

[1]"M" stands for "measure", which is a noun-like bound form that denotes the unit of measurement or classification applying to the noun with which it is associated. A Chinese measure is a word like "cup" in English, as in "a cup of coffee", or like "herd" in "a herd of cattle", or "dozen" in "two dozen eggs", but in Chinese measures are far more widely used: every Chinese noun has a measure conventionally associated with it.

[2]"SP" stands for "specifier", which is another noun-like bound form that points to a definite thing or person, or things or persons, or asks "Which thing(s) or person(s)?"

[3]In other contexts tiáo and zhī mean "a strip" and "a stick", respectively, but in this lesson they are introduced as measures conventionally associated with certain nouns, usually indicating singular number.

-ge is the most generally used measure. Furthermore, it is often possible to substitute -ge for the more particular measures, like -tiáo and -zhī, especially in sentences where the focus of attention is somewhere other than on the noun so measured. In Dialog V, compare 'něige piányi? "Which is cheapest?", where the focus is on piányi, with nín xǐhuan 'něizhī qiānbǐ? "Which pencil do you like?", with the focus on 'něizhī qiānbǐ?

[4]bǐ alone is ambiguous in Chinese. It means either pen or pencil; prefixing gāng or qiān clears up the ambiguity. Another compound made with bǐ is fěnbǐ "chalk", but this word does not participate in the ambiguity when bǐ is used by itself: "pen" is bǐ or gāngbǐ, "pencil" is bǐ or qiānbǐ, but "chalk" is generally only fěnbǐ.

More notes on grammar

3.2 Specification. As has been stated before (Lesson 1, "New words", nt. 3) a Chinese noun standing alone gives no indication of number or specificity. Some of this ambiguity is removed when a noun

is preceded and modified by a "specific" noun phrase, that is, a noun
phrase that consists of a specifier followed by a measure: SP-M.
Most measures are intrinsically singular in number; when such a
measure is used in the SP-M phrase, the following noun is marked as
singular. The noun is also marked as definite, by the specifier:
něi- asks "which (particular thing or person is being referred to)?";
zhèi- specifies "this", and něi- "that".

A noun forms a "noun phrase" with its preceding modifiers, and
in Chinese a noun or noun phrase may stand alone as a complete sentence
only when the context of the dialog is right. Each construction
generated by the following pattern is perhaps best thought of as
lifted from the larger context of a sentence.

The construction SP-M-N may be shortened to SP-M alone; this
SP-M construction stands for the larger SP-M-N construction and is
hence pronominal. Thus zhèige shān "this mountain" may be replaced
by zhèige "this one", with "mountain" understood.

One or more modifying nouns may precede the main noun.

...zhèizhǐ bǐ...   "this pen"
...zhèizhǐ Měiguo bǐ...   "this American pen"
...zhèizhǐ...   "this one"

Noun phrase

SP-	-M	(N_1)	(N_2)
něi-	-tiáo		hé
zhèi-			lù
něi-	-ge		shān
		Zhōngguo	bǎo
		Měiguo	biǎo
	-zhǐ		bǐ
			gāngbǐ
			qiānbǐ
			fěnbǐ

Here, the specifiers combine with any measure. -tiáo combines
only with hé and lù (or replaces a noun phrase whose main word is hé
or lù); -ge is associated similarly with shān, bào, and biǎo, and
sometimes with bǐ and its derivatives. -zhī is associated only with
bǐ and its derivatives. Avoid combining Zhōngguo and Měiguo with hé
lù and shān in these specifying phrases.

The placement of the words in the pattern display is intended to
suggest the restrictions on combination just mentioned.

3.3 <u>Specific phrases in simple descriptive sentences.</u> The following pairs of questions and answers are examples of specific phrases
inserted into the descriptive sentence patterns introduced earlier.
The sections in which they were introduced are given in parentheses.

A: něige shān gāo?   Which mountain is higher?

B: 'zhèige gāo.   This one is. (1.7)

A: nèitiáo hé hěn cháng ma?   Is that river (very) long?

B: nèitiáo hé, bùhěn cháng.   Not very. (1.9)

A: 'zhèige shān gāo, 'nèige   Which mountain is higher, this
   shān gāo?   one or that one?

B: 'nèige gāo.   That one is. (1.12.1)

A: nèige Zhōngguo biǎo,   Is that Chinese watch cheap?
   'piányi bupiányi?

B: bùhěn piányi.   Not very. (1.12.2)

A: nèige 'Měiguo bào guì,   Which is more expensive, the
   nèige 'Zhōngguo bào guì?   American newspaper or the
                                         Chinese one?

B: nèige 'Zhōngguo bào guì.   The Chinese one. (2.8)

3.4 <u>Specific phrases as objects in functive sentences.</u>

A: nǐ kàn 'něige bào?   Which newspaper are you going to read

B: wǒ kàn 'zhèige bào.   This one. (2.6)

A: 'tā kàn nèige bào, 'nǐ kàn   Which of you is going to read that
   nèige bào?   newspaper, he or you?

B: 'wǒ kàn nèige bào.   I'm going to. (2.7.1)

A: nǐ kàn zhèige, kàn nèige?   Which are you reading, this one
                                    or that one?

B: wǒ kàn zhèige.   This one. (2.7.2)

A: nǐ kàn 'zhèige bào, kàn   Which newspaper are you going to
   'nèige bào?   read, this one or that one?

B: wǒ kàn 'zhèige bào.   This one. (2.7.3)

A: nǐ kàn nèige 'Zhōngguo bào,   Which newspaper are you going to
   kàn nèige 'Měiguo bào?   read, the Chinese one or the
                                    American one?

B: wǒ kàn nèige 'Měiguo bào.   The American one. (2.7.3)

A: nǐ 'kàn bukàn nèige bào?   Are you going to read that newspaper?

B: búkàn.   No. (2.7.4.1)

A: nǐ kàn nèige 'bào bukàn?   Are you going to read that newspaper?

B: kàn.   Yes. (2.7.4.2)

    3.5 The special negative adverb méi-. The verb yǒu "have" takes
méi- as its negative adverb. The tone of yǒu in méiyǒu is often neutral,
especially in the middle of a sentence. The sentence patterns involving
negative comments are the same with méiyǒu as they are with bù- prefixed
to other verbs. Compare:

A: nǐ yǒu bào ma?   Have you any newspapers?

B: wǒ 'méiyou bào?   No, I haven't.

A: nǐ mǎi bào ma?   Do you buy newspapers?

B: wǒ 'bùmǎi bào.   No, I don't.

A: nǐ méiyou bào ma?   Don't you have any newspapers?

B: méiyou bào.   No.

A: nǐ bùmǎi bào ma?   Don't you buy newspapers?

B: bùmǎi bào.   No.

A: nǐ 'yǒu meiyǒu bào?   Have you any newspapers?

B: 'méiyǒu.   No.

A: nǐ 'mǎi bumǎi bào?   Do you buy newspapers?

B: bùmǎi.   No.

A: nǐ yǒu 'bào méiyǒu   Have you any newspapers?

B: yǒu.   Yes.

A: nǐ mǎi 'bào bumǎi?   Do you buy newspapers?

B: mǎi.   Yes.

    3.6 The pivot. Certain verbs take an object that is in turn
the topic of a following comment. A noun functioning as both object
and topic in this way is called a "pivot".

    3.7 Sentences with qǐng "request". The person whom someone
else requests to do something is expressed as a pivot. The action
requested to be done is expressed as the comment of a functive
sentence. Thus:

wǒ qǐng tā mǎi shū.   I'm asking her to buy some books.

tā qǐng nǐ mǎi shū.   He's asking you to buy some books.

qǐng nǐ mǎi shū.   (I'm) asking you to buy some
                                       books. / Please buy some books.

    Notice that "Please..." is expressed as qǐng nǐ...

(Topic)	Comment ?/.			
(N)	<u>qǐng</u> O			
		Topic	Comment ?/.	
(N)	<u>qǐng</u>	N	V O	<u>ma?</u>/.
nǐ	qǐng	tā	mǎi bǐ	ma?
tā		wǒ	gěi qián	.
wǒ		nǐ	kàn bào	
...		...	shū	

3.8 <u>The indirect object.</u> Some Chinese verbs take two objects.
One such verb is <u>gěi</u> "give", which has one object, the "direct object",
denoting the thing given, and a second object, the "indirect object",
("IO") denoting the person to whom the thing is given. When both
indirect and direct object are present in a Chinese sentence, the
order is the same as it is in the English sentence, "I'm giving him
the books.": first the indirect object, then the direct.

tā gěi wǒ qiānbǐ	He's giving me a pencil.
tāmen gěi nǐ nèige Měiguo biǎo.	They're giving you that American watch.

Notice that there is another way to express the indirect object
in English, namely to incorporate it in a prepositional phrase
governed by the preposition "to": "He's giving a pencil to me." and
"They're giving that American watch to you." The resulting order,
first the direct object, then the indirect, is not available in Chinese.

It is of course possible to combine sentences that have <u>gěi</u> and
an indirect object with ones that have <u>qǐng</u> and a pivot:

qǐng nǐ gěi wǒ qiānbǐ.	Please give me some pencils.
wǒ qǐng tāmen gěi nǐ nèige Měiguo biǎo.	I'm asking them to give you that American watch.

(Topic)   Comment ?/.
            (qǐng)   O
                      (Topic)   Comment ?/.
(N)   (qǐng)   (N)   gěi   IO   (SP-   -M)   (N)   O   ma

wǒ   qǐng   tā   gěi   nǐ   Zhōngguo   qián   ma
nǐ   wǒ   gěi   tā   Měiguo   shū   .
...   . něi-   -ge   bào ?
                                        zhèi-   biǎo
                                        nèi-   -zhī   bǐ
                                                                 gāngbǐ
                                                                 qiānbǐ
                                                                 fěnbǐ

                         Pyramid Drills

                         mǎi biǎo ma?
                         mǎi.
                   mǎi biǎo, mǎi bào?
                         mǎi biǎo, bùmǎi bào.
                         mǎi 'něige biǎo?
                         mǎi 'zhèige biǎo.
                         mǎi 'nèige biǎo ma?
                       bùmǎi 'nèige biǎo.
            mǎi 'zhèige biǎo, mǎi 'nèige biǎo?
                   mǎi 'zhèige biǎo, bùmǎi 'nèige biǎo.

     In this drill, switch biǎo and bào, substitute yào or xǐhuan for
mǎi, and make other changes that result in likely sets of sentences.

yǒu shū ma?

yǒu.

nǐ yǒu shū ma?

wǒ yǒu shū.

'nǐ yǒu shū, 'tā yǒu shū?

'wǒ yǒu shū; tā 'méiyǒu

nǐ yǒu Zhōngguo shū ma?

wǒ yǒu Zhōngguo shū.

nǐ yǒu 'Zhōngguo shū, yǒu 'Měiguo shū?

wǒ yǒu 'Zhōngguo shū; méiyou 'Měiguo shū.

In this drill, substitute various appropriate nouns for shū.

Questions and answers

Answer the following questions.

1. nǐ xǐhuan 'shān buxǐhuan?
2. nǐ yǒu fěnbǐ ma?
3. zhèizhǐ gāngbǐ, hǎo'kàn buhǎokàn?
4. nǐ 'xǐhuan buxǐhuan Měiguo qiānbǐ?
5. nǐ yào 'qián buyào? yào 'Zhōngguo qián, yào Měiguo qián?
6. zhèige biǎo, 'guì buguì?
7. tā hǎokàn ma?
8. Zhōngguo fěnbǐ, 'piányi bupiányi?

Make questions to which the following would be likely answers.

1. 'Zhōngguo shān hǎokàn.
2. wǒ méiyou qián.
3. xièxie, wǒ búyào nèizhǐ bǐ.
4. nèizhǐ, buhǎokàn.
5. wǒ qǐng 'nǐ mǎi, wǒ bùqǐng 'tā mǎi.
6. gěi 'wǒ qián.
7. wǒ xǐhuan 'Zhōngguo shān.

8. wǒ méiyou fěnbǐ.

9. Zhōngguo shū, bùhěn piányi.

10. wǒ méiyou qiānbǐ; tāmen yě méiyǒu.

Translation

Translate the following into Chinese.

1. Which do you prefer, Chinese pens or American? -- Chinese.

2. Chinese rivers are very pretty indeed.

3. The other watch is cheaper.

4. That road isn't too long.

5. Which do you prefer, pens or pencils? -- I like them both.

6. I'm giving him some chalk.

7. Please give me the money.

8. Don't you want this book? -- No, thank you.

9. Have you any pencils? (3 ways) -- No, we don't.

10. Are you asking him to give me some American books? -- (I'm not
    asking him to give you some American books:) No; I'm asking
    him to give you some Chinese ones.

Lesson 4

The object as topic, numbers,

modification by stative verbs, and auxiliary verbs

Pronunciation

Review tones: old and new words.

1: bā "eight"; dōu "in all cases"; tā; gāo; qī "seven"; xīn "new";
zhēn; shuō "speak"; shū; shān; sān "three"; yī "one".

2: máng; tiáo; nín; hé; qián; xíng "acceptable"; cháng; shí "ten".

3: biǎo; mǎi; dǒng "understand"; nǐ; gěi; hǎo; hěn; jiǔ "nine";
qǐng; zǎo; yě; yǒu; wǒ; wǔ "five"; yuǎn.

4: bù; bào; tài; liù "six"; lù; guì; kàn; huà "language"; jiù₁ "old";
jiù₂ "only"; jìn; sì "four"; èr "two"; yào.

1-0: gāo ma?; zhuōzi "table"; Yīngguo "England".

1-1: bāzhī "eight; bāzhāng "eight (flat objects)"; dōu gāo "all are
tall"; dōu shuō "all speak"; gāo shān "high mountains"; qīzhī
"seven"; qīzhāng "seven"; xīn shū "new books"; sānzhī "three";
sānzhāng "three".

1-2: bātiáo "eight"; bāshí "eighty"; dōu máng "all are busy"; dōu xíng
"all are acceptable"; dōu cháng "all are long"; tā máng; qītiáo
"seven"; qīshí "seventy"; Zhōngwén "Chinese language"; sāntiáo
"three"; sānshí "thirty"; Yīngwén "English language".

1-3: bābǎ "eight (objects with handles or arms)"; bāběn "eight
(bound volumes)"; gāngbǐ; qībǎ "seven"; qīběn "seven"; qiānbǐ; xīn
biǎo "new watches"; sānbǎ "three"; sānběn "three".

1-4: xīn bào "new newspaper"; xīn lù "new roads"; shū guì.

2-0: báge "eight"; piányi; péngyou "friend"; qíge "seven"; shíge
"ten"; yíge "one".

2-1: nín gāo; shíbā "eighteen"; shíqī "seventeen"; shízhī "ten";
shízhāng "ten"; shísān "thirteen"; shíyī "eleven".

2-2: hé cháng; cháng hé "long rivers"; shítiáo "ten".

<u>2-3:</u> méiyǒu; shíbǎ "ten"; shíběn "ten"; shíjiǔ "nineteen"; shíwǔ
"fifteen".

<u>2-4:</u> bùguì; cháng lù "long roads"; shíliù "sixteen"; shísì "fourteen";
shíèr "twelve".

<u>3-0:</u> něige?; liǎngge "two"; kěshi "but"; jǐge "several"; jiǔge "nine";
xǐhuan; yǐzi "chair"; wǔge "five".

<u>3-1:</u> něizhǐ?; něizhāng "which one?"; hǎo shū "good books"; jǐzhǐ
"several"; jǐzhāng "several"; jiǔzhǐ "nine"; jiǔzhāng "nine"; wǔzhǐ
"five"; wǔzhāng "five"; yuǎn shān "distant mountains".

<u>3-2:</u> něitiáo?; jǐtiáo "several"; jiǔtiáo "nine"; jiǔshí "ninety";
wǔtiáo "five"; wǔshí "fifty"; yuǎn hé "distant rivers".

<u>3-3:</u> fěnbǐ; něibǎ? "which one?"; něiběn? "which one?"; hǎo bǐ "good
pens"; hǎo biǎo "good watches"; jǐbǎ "several"; jǐběn "several";
jiǔbǎ "nine"; jiǔběn "nine"; wǔbǎ "five"; wǔběn "five".

<u>3-4:</u> hǎo bào "good newspapers"; hǎokàn; yuǎn lù "distant roads".

<u>4-0:</u> nèige; liùge "six"; zhèige; sìge "four".

<u>4-1:</u> nèizhǐ; nèizhāng "that one"; liùzhǐ "six"; liùzhāng "six"; guì
shū "expensive books"; jiù shū "old books"; zhèizhǐ; zhèizhāng
"this one"; sìzhǐ "four"; sìzhāng "four"; yìzhǐ "one"; yìzhāng "one".

<u>4-2:</u> nèitiáo; liùtiáo "six"; liùshí "sixty"; zhèitiáo; sìtiáo "four";
sìshí "forty"; yìtiáo "one".

<u>4-3:</u> bùmǎi; nèibǎ "that one"; nèiběn "that one"; liùbǎ "six"; liùběn
"six"; guì biǎo "expensive watches"; jiù biǎo "old watches"; zhèibǎ
"this one"; zhèiběn "this one"; sìbǎ "four"; sìběn "four"; yìbǎ
"one"; yìběn "one".

<u>4-4:</u> kàn bào; jiù lù "old roads"; jìn lù "nearby roads".

   4.1 -i <u>representing three different sounds.</u> Notice that "<u>-i</u>",
when it spells a whole final, represents different sounds, depending
on the initial.

   After most initials, <u>-i</u> sounds like the <u>-ee</u> in English "lee"; <u>yi</u>
sounds like English "ye".

nǐ   "you"

jǐge   "several"

qī   "seven"

yī   "one"

yǐzi   "chair"

Notice that in yǐzi, yǐ- is like the other four examples here, but -zi
is not.

    After zh-, ch-, sh-, and r-, -i sounds quite different to English
ears: it is like the "-ir-" in English "bird", or the "-ur-" in "churn",
but sometimes there is a slight buzzing sound, like the "-s-" in
"pleasure". This is a syllabic American "r" sound.

yìzhī   "one"

shí   "ten"

    After z-, c-, and s-, -i is again different. Here it is a
syllabic "z" sound, occurring in English only in certain onomato-
poetic words, like "zz" (imitating a snore), and "bzz" (imitating
the buzzing of a bee).

yǐzi   "chair"

zhuōzi   "table"

sì   "four"

Dialogs, etc.

I

yī èr sān; sān èr yī;	One, two three; three, two, one;
yī èr sān sì wǔ liù qī.	One, two, three, four, five, six, seven.
qī bā jiǔ; qī bā jiǔ;	Seven, eight, nine; seven, eight, nine.
'jiǔběn xīn shū wǒ méiyǒu.	I don't have (as many as) nine new books.

II

A: Zhōngguo huà, nǐmen 'dǒng   Do you understand Chinese?
   budǒng?

B: 'tā bùdǒng, 'wǒ dǒng.   He doesn't, but I do.

A: nǐmen dōu yào mǎi shū ma?   Do you both want to buy books?

B: wǒmen dōu yào mǎi jǐběn   We both want to buy a few English
   Yīngwén shū.   books.

A: nǐmen yào mǎi 'něijǐběn?   Which ones do you want to buy?

B: wǒ yào mǎi 'zhèishíběn;   I'll buy these ten, and my friend
   wǒ péngyou yào mǎi 'nèiwǔběn.   will buy those five. Please
   qǐng nǐ gěi tā nèiwǔběn.   give him those five.

III

A: nǐ nèiliǎngge Zhōngguo   Do those two Chinese friends of
   péngyou, shuō Yīng'wén bushuō?   yours speak English?

B: tāmen dōu bùshuō.   Neither of them does.

A: tāmen yě bù'dǒng Yīngwén ma?   And they don't understand English
                                    either?

B: yíge dǒng, yíge bùdǒng.   One does, and the other doesn't.

A: tā 'nèige Zhōngguo péngyou,   And that Chinese friend (i.e. a
   yě bùdǒng ma?   third friend of B's): doesn't
                                    he understand either?

B: 'tā nèige péngyou, Yīngwén,   He understands both English and
   Zhōngwén, dōu. dǒng.   Chinese.

IV

A: wǒ hěn xǐhuan zhèizhāng jiù   I like this old table a lot. It's
   zhuōzi. zhēn hǎokàn.   really beautiful.

B: zhèizhāng zhuōzi hěn piányi.   This table is very inexpensive.
   nín 'yào buyào?   Would you like it?

A: wǒ yào, kěshi wǒ méiyou   I would like it, but I haven't any
   Zhōngguo qián. tā yào; tā yǒu   Chinese money. He'd like it,
   Zhōngguo qián.   and he has Chinese money.

V

A: wǒ hěn xǐhuan nǐ zhèige xīn   I like this new watch of yours
   biǎo. 'guì buguì?   very much. Is it expensive?

B: búguì. nǐ yào mǎi yige ma?   No. Do you want to buy one?

A: wǒ yě yào mǎi yige.   Yes, I'd like to buy one, too.

VI

A: nǐ yǒu zhuōzi yǐzi ma?   Have you any tables and chairs?

B: wǒ yǒu zhuōzi, kěshi méiyou I have some tables, but no chairs.
   yǐzi.

A: nǐ péngyou yǒu yǐzi ma?   Does your friend have any chairs?

B: yǒu. tā yǒu bābǎ yǐzi,   Yes. He has eight chairs, and no
   méiyou zhuōzi.   tables.

A: wo[1] jiù yào yìzhāng zhuōzi. I only want one table. Please
   qǐng nǐ gěi wǒ yìzhāng zhuōzi; give me a table; and (would you)
   qǐng nǐ péngyou gěi wǒ sānzhāng ask your friend to give me three
   yǐzi, 'xíng buxíng?   chairs, OK?

B: xíng.   Fine.

New words

huà N	speech
Zhōngguo huà N[2]	Chinese language
Yīngguo N	(Heroic Nation:) England
Yīngwén N[2]	English language
Zhōngwén N[2]	Chinese language
péngyou N	friend
zhuōzi N (M: -zhāng)	table
yǐzi N (M: -bǎ)	chair
-běn M	(bound volumes, books)
-zhāng M	(flat objects, tables)
-bǎ M	(objects with handles or something for the hands to grip, chairs)

yī NU$^{3, 4}$ one

yìzhāng NU-M^4

yìtiáo NU-M^4

yìběn NU-M^4

yíge NU-M^4

èr NU^5 two

liǎngzhāng NU-M^5

liǎngge NU-M^5

sān NU   three

sì NU   four

wǔ NU   five

liù NU   six

qī NU^6 seven

qīzhāng NU-M^6

qītiáo NU-M^6

qīběn NU-M^6

qíge NU-M^6

bā NU^6 eight

bāzhāng NU-M^6

bātiáo NU-M^6

bāběn NU-M^6

báge NU-M^6

jiǔ NU   nine

shí NU   ten

shíyī NU$^{4, 7}$ eleven

shíyīzhāng NU-M$^{4, 7}$

shíyíge NU-M$^{4, 7}$

shíèr NU$^{5, 7}$ twelve

shíèrzhāng NU-M$^{5, 7}$

shíèrge NU-M$^{5, 7}$

shísān NU...^{7} thirteen...

shíqī NU$^{6, 7}$ seventeen

shíqīzhāng NU-M$^{6, 7}$

shíqíge NU-M$^{6,\ 7}$	seventeen
shíbā NU$^{6,\ 7}$	eighteen
shíbāzhāng NU-M$^{6,\ 7}$	
shíbáge NU-M...$^{6,\ 7}$	
'èrshí (NU-M) NU$^{5,\ 8}$	twenty
èrshiyī (NU-M-NU) NU$^{4,\ 7}$	twenty-one
èrshiyīzhāng NU-M$^{4,\ 7}$	
èrshiyíge NU-M$^{4,\ 7}$	
èrshièr (NU-M-NU) NU$^{5,\ 7}$	twenty-two
èrshièrzhāng NU-M$^{5,\ 7}$	
èrshièrge NU-M^{5}	
èrshisān (NU-M-NU) ...^{7}	twenty-three...
'sānshí (NU-M) NU^{8}	thirty
'sìshí (NU-M) NU^{8}	forty
'wǔshí (NU-M) NU^{8}	fifty
'liùshí (NU-M) NU^{8}	sixty
'qīshí (NU-M) NU$^{6,\ 8}$	seventy
'bāshí (NU-M) NU$^{6,\ 8}$	eighty
'jiǔshí (NU-M) NU^{8}	ninety
jǐ NU^{3}	several (ten or under), a few
yào AV^{9}	want to
xīn SV	new
jiù SV	old (referring to objects)
dōu A^{10}	in all cases
hěn A^{11}	very (1), very much
jiù A	only
kěshi MA^{12}	but
xíng IE	acceptable, OK
bùxíng IE	not acceptable, not OK
'xíng buxíng? IE	Would it be all right? / OK?
'dǒng budǒng? IE	Do (you) understand?
dǒng. IE	(I) understand.
shuō V	speak

Notes

[1]Notice how in A's last speech in this dialog, in the first
sentence, wo is written without a tone mark. This represents a weakening of the tone of the word wǒ "I", because of the special focus on
the word jiù "only". In general, when pronouns or other words are
not emphasized, they tend to be pronounced with a weakened tone, or
with a neutral tone; when this is likely to happen, the word will be
written without a tone mark.

[2]Zhōngguo huà is the usual informal word for "Chinese language".
It follows a pattern, which is almost universal for Chinese names of
languages, of being formed by the name of the country followed by huà
"speech". Another pattern is to replace any -guo with -wén. Both
forms are used for the names of the languages of most countries. Thus:
both Zhōngguo huà and Zhōngwén mean "Chinese language". But in the
case of Yīngguo, only Yīngwén is used in the meaning of "English
language". Yīngguo huà means "English as spoken in England"; similarly,
Měiguo huà is "American English". Zhōngwén is used in contrast to
Yīngwén (see Dialog III, last sentence).

[3]"NU" stands for "number", which is a form that may occur between
a specifier and a measure. A number is different from a "numeral",
which may be loosely defined as a form roughly corresponding to an
English numeral. Thus, in zhèiliǎngtiáo lù "these two roads", which
is a SP-NU-M N expression, -liǎng- is a number; and in zhèijǐtiáo lù
"these (few) roads", -jǐ- is also a number, because it occurs between
a specifier and a measure.

Four of the numbers from one to ten have alternate forms; see
notes 4-6 below.

[4]yī has the first tone when no measure follows, as in counting;
it is also yī in long NU-M expressions, between syllables carrying a
tone other than the neutral tone: shíyīzhāng.

Before a measure, it has the second or fourth tone, depending
on the tone of the measure. In this respect it is like the negative

adverb, bu- (see above, 1.2.9). The form is yí-, with the second
tone, if the measure carries the fourth tone, or if the measure is
-ge (which carries the fourth tone in certain contexts). The form
is yì-, with the fourth tone, otherwise (that is, if the measure
carries the first, second, or third tone).

The combination of yi- with a measure often corresponds to the
English indefinite articles "a, an". In this usage, the tones of
yi- and the measure are usually weakened.

[5]èr is the most general form of the word for "two". It occurs
in counting; as part of a larger number, even when a measure follows;
and with -shí "ten" to make èrshí "twenty". But alone before other
measures, a completely different form is used: liǎng-, which is a
bound form.

[6]qī "seven" and bā "eight" have the same tonal change. They
have the first tone everywhere except before a measure that carries
a fourth tone or before -ge, in which case they optionally carry the
second tone, no matter whether they are alone or part of a larger number.

[7]Numbers between tens (i.e. between ten and twenty, between twenty
and thirty, and so on) are all formed in the same way in Chinese. yī
(yì-, yí-), èr, sān, sì, wǔ, liù, qī (qí-), bā (bá-), jiǔ are added
to shí or to a larger number ending in -shí.

[8]shí "ten" is sometimes a number and sometimes a measure. In
forms for the tens (i.e. twenty, thirty, and so on), its function as
a measure is apparent: a "unit" number precedes it directly. Compare
sāntiáo "three (long objects)" with sānshí "thirty". èrshí "twenty"
is thus a NU-M expression, which we may call a "numeral", to distinguish
it from a "number", as defined above in note 3.

[9]"AV" stands for "auxiliary verb", somewhat corresponding to
English auxiliary verbs, like "can" and "would". An auxiliary verb
is a functive verb that takes as its direct object another verb or
verb-object expression. Many auxiliary verbs function also as ordinary

functive verbs and take a noun object. For example, yào shū (V O)
"want some books" occurs alongside of yào mǎi shū (AV V O) "want to
buy some books".

   [10]dōu "in all cases" is an adverb. The term "adverb" is applied
to three classes of words in Chinese, all bound forms, and all occurring earlier in the sentence than the main word of the comment. All
adverbs introduced so far belong to the first of these three classes
of adverb: "fixed adverb" ("A"). A fixed adverb is not only limited
to a position before the main word of the comment, but it is also
limited to a position after the topic, if the sentence has one.

   dōu often corresponds to English adjectives like "all" and "both"
in positive sentences, and "no" and "neither", in negative ones. But
the Chinese word is a fixed adverb: it comes before the verb and
after any topic.

   [11]hěn is another fixed adverb. It often precedes a stative verb
and means "very", though it need not be translated at all (see 1.10).
But it also occurs before certain functive verbs (including auxiliary
verbs), where it is sometimes translated "very much". Thus:

wǒ hěn xǐhuan zhèizhāng zhuōzi.   I very much like this table. ->
                                    I like this table a lot.

wǒ hěn xǐhuan, nǐ zhèige xīn biǎo. I like this new watch of yours
                                    very much.

   [12]"MA" stands for "movable adverb", the second of the three
kinds of adverb. A movable adverb is one that occurs before or after
the topic of a sentence, with no discernible difference in meaning.
Thus:

shū guì, keshi bào búguì   Books are expensive, but not
                                    newspapers.

shū guì, bào kěshi búguì.

The tone of kěshi is often weakened.

More notes on grammar

4.2 **The "topic-comment" comment.** Sometimes a comment is itself composed of a topic and a comment (which may in turn be composed of a topic and another comment, and so on).

Topic$_1$	Comment	
	Topic$_2$	Comment
Zhōngguo huà,	nǐmen	'dǒng budǒng?
'tā nèige péngyou,	Yīngwén, Zhōngwén,	dōu dǒng.
'jiùběn xīn shū,	wǒ	méiyǒu.

4.3 **The object as topic.** When an object appears after its verb, in the basic order (see 2.5), it is part of the comment, and as such receives part of the focus of attention, expressing what is new and interesting (see 1.5). Sometimes this V O order is disturbed, and the noun or noun phrase that denotes the person or thing affected by the action of a functive verb appears before that verb, in a topic position. Here, the object is away from the focus of attention of the sentence; it is a "given", about which something "new" is said in the comment.

In some sentences where the object is in topic position, the "subject" ("S") is also expressed. The order is determined in part by number of syllables: the longer phrase is more likely to come before the shorter one than the other way around. In part the order is determined by how the speaker feels about the relative topicality of the phrases: the more "given" (less interesting, less "new") phrase will come first.

In the first and third sentences in 4.2 above, the order is O S; in the second sentence, it is S O.

4.4 **The use of** dōu. The adverb dōu "in all cases" is translated in three ways, depending on whether a negative adverb (bu- or méi-) follows or precedes it.

With no negative adverb, dōu says, "(Of the things or persons expressed in the topic,) both or all (partake of the quality expressed
by the stative verb, or participate in or are affected by the action
of the functive verb)."

lù dōu hěn cháng.	Both/all the roads are long.
wǒmen dōu yào shū.	Both/all of us want some books.
shū, bào, wǒ dōu yào.	I want both the book(s) and the
	newspaper(s).

Followed by a negative adverb, dōu says, "(Of the things or
persons expressed in the topic,) neither or none (partakes of the
quality expressed by the stative verb, or participates in or is
affected by the action of the functive verb)."

lù dōu bùcháng.	Neither/none of the roads is long.
wǒmen dōu búyào shū.	Neither/none of us wants any books.
shū, bào, wǒ dōu búyào.	I want neither the book(s) nor the
	newspaper(s).

Preceded by a negative adverb, dōu says, "(Of the things or
persons expressed in the topic,) either but not both, or some but not
all (partake of the quality expressed by the stative verb, or are
affected by the action of the functive verb)."

lù bùdōu cháng.	Not both/all of the roads are long.
wǒmen bùdōu yào shū.	Not both/all of us want books.
shū, bào, wǒ bùdōu yào.	I don't want both the book(s) and
	the newspaper(s) (i.e. I'll
	settle for either).

It is important to remember that dōu (1) is a fixed adverb and
comes in the verbal phrase before the verb and after any topic, and
(2) refers backward to a word or words expressed in the topic, or
understood as the topic.

4.4.1 dōu <u>with a stative verb</u>. dōu marks the topic as plural in number. The choice-type question pattern is not used.

nǐmen dōu hěn máng ma?	Are all of you busy?
wǒmen dōu bútài máng.	None of us is too busy.
Zhōngguo shān, dōu zhēn gāo ma?	Are Chinese mountains all really high?
dōu zhēn gāo.	Yes, they all really are.
Měiguo shū, dōu hěn guì ma?	Are all American books expensive?
bùdōu guì.	Not all of them are.
bào yě bùdōu guì ma?	And are not all newspapers expensive either?
bào dōu búguì.	No newspapers are expensive.
gāngbǐ, qiānbǐ, dōu hěn piányi ma?	Are both pens and pencils inexpensive?
hěn piányi.	Yes.

(Topic)		Comment					
(S)		(A)	(A)	(A)			
(N$_1$)	(N$_2$)	(yě)	(bù-)	(dōu)	(A...)	SV	ma?/.
	nǐmen	yě		dōu	zhēn bu- hěn	máng	ma?
	wǒmen		bu-		tài	hǎo	.
	tāmen						
Zhōngguo	shān				hěn	gāo	
Měiguo	hé					cháng	
	lù					yuǎn	
						jìn	
	shū					hǎokàn	
	bào					guì	
	biǎo					piányi	
	bǐ...						

4.4.2 dōu <u>with a V O expression</u>. Again the topic, which is
the subject, is plural.

tāmen dōu bùmǎi Zhōngguo bào ma?	Are none of them buying Chinese newspapers?
dōu bùmǎi.	No.
tāmen yě dōu bùmǎi Zhōngguo shū ma?	Are none of them buying Chinese books, either?
yě bùmǎi.	No.
nǐmen dōu dǒng Yīngwén ma?	Do you all understand English?
wǒmen dōu dǒng.	Yes.
nǐmen dōu yǒu Měiguo qián ma?	Do you both have American money?
wǒmen bùdōu yǒu. wǒ yǒu, tā méiyǒu.	One of us has, but not the other.

Notice in the last answer <u>bùdōu yǒu</u> not <u>*méidōu yǒu</u>. (Expressions that are not acceptable Chinese are marked by a preceding
asterisk.)

(Topic)	Comment							
(S)	(yě)	(bu-)	(dōu)	(bu-)	V	(N)	(O)	ma?/.
tāmen	yě		dōu	bu-	mǎi	Zhōngguo	bào	ma?
nǐmen		bu-			kàn	Měiguo	shū	.
wǒmen					yào		biǎo	
							bǐ...	
					shuō		huà	
					dǒng		Yīngwén	
							Zhōngwén	
				méi-	yǒu		qián	

4.4.3 dōu <u>with a transposed object.</u> In order for <u>dōu</u> to apply
to the object of a verb-object construction, the object must be

transposed to a topic position. This transposition is a logical
result of the backward application of dōu to the topic.

This object is plural, if it is alone. When both object and
subject are present in this pattern, and when they are both otherwise
marked as plural, the application of dōu is ambiguous. Nèisānběn
shū, tāmen dōu yǒu. may mean "They have all three of the books." or
"They all have the three books." or even "They all have all three of
the books." In the sentences below, any subject is singular.

Měiguo biǎo, nǐ dōu yào mǎi ma?	Are you buying all the American watches?
dōu yào mǎi.	Yes.
'Zhōngguo shū, 'Měiguo shū, tā dōu kàn ma?	Does he read both Chinese and American books?
bùdōu kàn. tā jiù kàn 'Měiguo shū; búkàn 'Zhōngguo shū.	No. He only reads American books, not Chinese.
bǐ, biǎo, nǐ dōu yǒu ma?	Do you have both pens and watches?
dōu méiyǒu.	I have neither.
shū, bào, yě dōu méiyǒu ma?	Have you also neither books nor newspapers?
yě dōu méiyǒu.	No.

(Topic)		Comment						
(O)		(S)	Comment					
(N$_1$)	(N$_2$)	(N$_3$)	(yě)	(bu-)	(dōu)	(bu-)	V	./ma?
Zhōngguo	bào	nǐ		bu-	dōu		kàn	ma?
Měiguo	shū,	wǒ				bu-	mǎi	
	biǎo,	tā	yě				yào	
	bǐ...,							
	huà,						shuō	
	Yīngwén,						dǒng	
	Zhōngwén,							
	qián,					méi-	yǒu	

4.5 <u>The SV-N construction.</u> A stative verb that is one syllable
long may directly precede a noun and modify it. (Cf. 2.4.)

xīn shū	new books
jiù zhuōzi	old tables
gāo shān	high mountains

SV	N
gāo	shān
cháng	hé
jìn	lù
yuǎn	
xīn	shū
jiù	bào
hǎo	biǎo
	bǐ...
	zhuōzi
	yǐzi

4.6 <u>The NU-M (N) construction.</u> For a noun to be counted, it
must be preceded by a number, and between the number and the noun
there must be the measure which is appropriate to the noun. The
NU-M N combination is a noun phrase and may appear wherever a noun
appears. Between the measure and the noun other elements may occur
which modify the noun.

NU-M (without the following noun) stands for NU-M N.

These constructions are non-specific; often included in their
English equivalents are such English non-specific or indefinite words
as "a, an, any, some".

jǐběn xīn shū	a few new books
sānběn xīn shū	(any) three new books
sānběn shū	(any) three books
sānběn	(any) three (books)

wǒ yào shū.   I want some books.
wǒ yào xīn shū.   I want some new books.
wǒ yào sānběn xīn shū.   I want three new books.
wǒ yào sānběn.   I want three (books).

NU-	-M	(Mod.)	(N)
jǐ-	-zhāng	Zhōngguo	zhuōzi
yì- (yí-)	-bǎ	Měiguo	yǐzi
liǎng-	-ge	gāo	shān
sān-	-tiáo	cháng	hé
sì-		jìn	lù
wǔ-	-běn	xīn	shū
liù-		jiù	bào
qī- (qí-)		hǎo	biǎo
bā- (bá-)	-zhī		bǐ...
jiǔ-			
shí-			
shíyì- (-yí-)			
shíèr-...			
shíqī- (-qí-)			
shíbā- (-bá-)...			
'èrshí-			
èrshíyì- (-yí-)			
'èrshíèr-...			
èrshíqī- (-qí-)			
èrshíbā- (-bá-)...			
'sānshí-			
'sìshí-			
'wǔshí-			
'liùshí-			
'qīshí-			
'bāshí-			
'jiǔshí-			

4.7 zhèi- and nèi- with the neutral tone. When zhèi- and nèi-
are pronounced with a weakened or neutral tone, their meanings change
from "this" and "that" to something more like "the".

4.8 The SP-NU-M (N) construction. Adding a specifier to an
NU-M (N) construction makes it specific.

'nèisānběn xīn shū?	Which three new books?
'nèisānběn xīn shū.	Those three new books.
neisānběn xīn shu	the three new books
neisānběn shu	the three books
neisānběn	the three (books)
wǒ yào 'nèisānběn xīn shū.	I want those three new books.
wǒ yào neisānběn xīn shū.	I want the three new books.
wǒ yào neiběn xīn shū.	I want the new book. (N.B. "book"
	is singular.)
wǒ yào 'nèiběn.	I want that one.
wǒ yào neiběn.	I want it.

(SP-)	(NU-)	-M	(Mod.)	(N)
něi-	jǐ-	-zhāng	Zhōngguo	zhuōzi?
zhèi-	yì-(yí-)	-bǎ	Měiguo	yǐzi
nèi-	liǎng-	-ge	gāo	shān
.	.	.	.	.
.	.	.	.	.
.	.	.	.	.

(and so on, as in 4.6)

In this pattern, SP-, or NU-, or both, must be present.

In slow or emphatic speech, yi "one" occurring after zhèi-, nèi-,
or něi- often results in the forms zhèiyi-, nèiyi-, or nǎyi-, with a
changed vowel in the last form.

4.9 <u>The AV V (O) construction.</u> The auxiliary verb always
precedes the verb or verb-object construction. Choice-type questions
are formed thus: 'AV-<u>bu</u>-AV V(-O)? and AV-'V <u>bu</u>-AV?, AV-V-'O bu-AV?

nǐ yào mǎi shū ma?	Do you want to buy some books?
búyào.	No.
nǐ 'yào buyào mǎi bǐ?	Do you want to buy some pens?
búyào. wǒ búyào mǎi, jiù yào kàn.	No. I don't want to buy anything; I just want to look.
nǐ yào shuō Zhōngguo 'huà buyào?	Do you want to speak Chinese?
yào.	Yes.
nǐ yào 'kàn buyào?	Do you want to look?
yào.	Yes.

4.10 zhèi- <u>and</u> nèi- <u>phrases after pronouns.</u> The personal pronouns (wǒ, nǐ, tā, etc.) may precede and modify noun phrases beginning
with zhèi- or nèi-. The English translation of such an expression
follows the model: <u>nǐ zhèi- X</u> "this X of yours".

nǐ zhèige xīn biǎo	this new watch of yours
wǒmen nèige hǎo péngyou	that good friend of ours
tā nèige péngyou	that friend of his (but see below)

4.11 <u>The appositive relationship.</u> Two nouns or noun phrases
are said to be "in apposition" if one is the explanatory equivalent
of the other. In Chinese, nouns or noun phrases that are in apposition
are placed next to each other. In Dialog III, fifth sentence, <u>tā</u>
<u>nèige Zhōngguo péngyou...</u>, the N <u>tā</u> and the noun phrase <u>nèige péngyou</u>
are in apposition: "he, that other Chinese friend (of yours)". So
an expression like <u>tā nèige péngyou</u> may be ambiguous: "that friend
of his", or "he, that other friend (of yours)"; context, or placement
of stress, will usually make the expression unambiguous.

Pyramid drills

```
                          hěn cháng.
                      dōu hěn cháng.
                  hé dōu hěn cháng.
         Zhōngguo hé, dōu hěn cháng.

                          hěn gāo.
                        bùhěn gāo.
                    dōu bùhěn gāo.
                shān dōu bùhěn gāo.
        Měiguo shān, dōu bùhěn gāo.

                       'zhēn    hǎokàn.
                       'zhēn bùhǎokàn.
                   dōu 'zhēn bùhǎokàn.
              shū, dōu 'zhēn bùhǎokàn.
          xīn shū, dōu 'zhēn bùhǎokàn.
  zhèijǐběn xīn shū, dōu 'zhēn bùhǎokàn.
nǐ zhèijǐběn xīn shū, dōu 'zhēn bùhǎokàn.
tā nèijǐběn xīn shū, yě dōu 'zhēn bùhǎokàn.

                       mǎi jǐběn shū.
                       mǎi jǐběn Zhōngguo shū.
                       mǎi sìběn Zhōngguo shū.
                       mǎi sìshíběn Zhōngguo shū.
                       mǎi sìshí'sìběn Zhōngguo shū.
                   yào mǎi sìshí'sìběn Zhōngguo shū.
             tāmen yào mǎi sìshí'sìběn Zhōngguo shū.
         tāmen dōu yào mǎi sìshí'sìběn Zhōngguo shū.
```

                                wo dōu yào.

                                ni dōu yào ma?

                            wo yě dōu yào.

                        biǎo, wo yě dōu yào.

            Zhōngguo biǎo, wo yě dōu yào.

    zhèijǐge Zhōngguo biǎo, wo yě dōu yào.

    zhèisìge Zhōngguo biǎo, wo yě dōu yào.

    zhèisìge Zhōngguo biǎo, wo bùdōu yào.

    zhèisìge Zhōngguo biǎo, wo dōu búyào.

                                kàn shū.

                                kàn xīn shū.

                                kàn 'wǔběn xīn shū.

                            kàn nèi'wǔběn xīn shū.

                        yào kàn nèi'wǔběn xīn shū.

                    wǒ yào kàn nèi'wǔběn xīn shū.

        nèi'wǔběn xīn shū, wǒ dōu yào kàn.

    'zhèiwǔběn jiù shū, wǒ 'yě dōu yào kàn.

                            Exercises

    Add dōu to the following sentences, making any changes necessary
so that it applies to the underlined N. Example:

wǒ yào mǎi zhèishíběn shū.   Zhèishíběn shū, wǒ dōu yào mǎi.

wǒmen yào kàn bǎo.

Zhōngguo lù yě hěn cháng.

nǐ yě yào biǎo ma?

wǒ yào mǎi jiǔběn Zhōngguo shū.

wǒ méiyou 'Zhōngguo qián, yě méiyou 'Měiguo qián.

tā yào mǎi neisānzhī Měiguo qiānbǐ.

tāmen yào shuō Zhōngguo huà.

tāmen bùshuō Yīngwén.

tā bùshuō 'Yīngwén, yě bùshuō 'Zhōngwén.

Answer the following questions.

Zhōngguo hé bùdōu cháng ma?

nǐ yào kàn zhèijǐzhāng Zhōngguo zhuōzi ma?

wǒ zheibǎ yǐzi, hǎo'kàn buhǎokàn?

nǐ yào kàn 'něiběn shū?

nèijǐběn Yīngwén shū, nǐ dōu yào mǎi ma?

nǐ 'yǒu meiyǒu xīn gāngbǐ?

zhèijǐzhī qiānbǐ dōu hěn xīn ma?

nǐ hěn xǐhuan Měiguo ma?

nǐ neijǐge péngyou, dōu shuō Zhōngguo huà ma?

        Counting exercises. Using the counting forms of the numbers,
count from 1 to 30. Count by tens from 10 to 90. Count by fives
from 30 to 95. Count backwards from 99 to 70.

        Now add measures: zhāng, tiáo, běn, and ge. Remember to change
yī, èr, qī, and bā when necessary.

        (Rather than use English to start the students on these exercises
in class, the teacher might begin by saying "yī" to prompt the first
exercise; "shí" for the next; "sānshí"; "jiǔshíjiǔ"; then "yìzhāng";
"shízhāng"; and so on, through the measures.)

Translate the following into Chinese:

1. Which Chinese book do you want to buy? -- I want to buy them all.

2. Do you want all the chairs? -- No, I only want the Chinese ones.

3. Would it be all right if I gave that English friend of yours some
     money? -- No.

4. I wanted to give you those four Chinese tables, but they're too
     expensive, and I haven't the money.

5. I like rivers a lot, but I really dislike mountains.

Lesson 5

Names and titles, embedded sentences,

and partial inclusion

Pronunciation

5.1 <u>Spirant initials.</u> The Chinese initials spelled <u>f-</u>, <u>h-</u>, <u>x-</u>, <u>sh-</u>, and <u>s-</u> are all "spirants", which means that during their production air from the lungs is constricted in the mouth, tightly enough to cause a hissing sound, but not so tightly as to stop the passage of air completely.

<u>f-</u> is like the <u>f-</u> in English <u>fun</u>: fēnbǐ.

<u>s-</u> is like the <u>s-</u> in English <u>sand</u>: sān.

<u>h-</u> is made with the tongue moving the same way as it does for <u>g-</u> and <u>k-</u>. Thus it is less like the <u>h-</u> of English <u>how</u>, and more like the <u>ch</u> in Scottish <u>loch</u> and German <u>machen</u>: hǎo.

<u>sh-</u> is made with the tip of the tongue, like <u>s-</u>, but during the production of <u>sh-</u> the tongue tip is drawn back to a position behind the alveolar ridge (which is the bony ridge behind the upper front teeth). The result of this retraction is that a small cup-like depression is formed in the front part of the tongue, behind the tip, and the extra resonance provided by this depression accounts for the peculiar American <u>r-</u> like quality of <u>shr-</u>. It is thus less like <u>sh-</u>. in English <u>shank</u> and more like the <u>shr-</u> of English <u>shrank</u>: shān.

<u>x-</u> is made with the front part of the tongue, which moves toward the alveolar ridge. It is important to keep the tip of the tongue lowered during the production of this sound; the tip should touch the back of the lower teeth. <u>x-</u> is therefore like the <u>s-</u>'s in English <u>suit</u> and <u>sure</u>, but with the tongue tip down; it is also something like the <u>-ch</u> of German <u>ich</u>, but with the front of the tongue moving farther forward, toward the alveolar ridge: xīn.

5.2 <u>Affricates.</u> The initials spelled <u>j-</u> <u>q-</u>, <u>zh-</u> <u>ch-</u>, and <u>z-</u> <u>c-</u> are "affricates", which means that there are two audible phases during

65

their pronunciation: a stop phase (see 3.1), followed by a spirant
phase (see above).

j-, zh-, z- are plain initials (like b-, d-, g-): voiceless
(except in neutral-tone syllables) and unaspirated.

q-, ch-, c- are aspirated initials (like p-, t-, k-): voiceless
and with a strong puff of breath or a loud hiss following the stop
phase of their production.

j- and q- are made with the tongue at the same position in the
mouth as for x-: the tongue tip is down; the front of the tongue
touches the alveolar ridge briefly for the stop phase of the affricates, then breaks contact for the spirant phase: jìn, qī (cf. xīn).

zh- and ch- are made with the tongue in the same position as
for sh-: the tongue tip is up, briefly touching the roof of the mouth
just behind the alveolar ridge for the stop phase, then breaking
contact for the spirant phase: yìzhāng, cháng (cf. shān).

z- and c- are made with the tongue in the same position as for
s-: the tongue tip is again up, briefly touching the alveolar ridge
for the stop phase (exactly as for the stops d- and t-), then breaking contact for the spirant phase: zǎo, Cáo "Ts'ao (a surname)" (cf.
sān).

5.3 Nasals. The initials m- and n- are "nasals", which means
that during their production the passage from the pharynx to the
nasal cavity is open, and the air from the lungs is allowed to pass
through the nose.

m- is like the m- of English my: mǎi.

n- is like the n- of English name: nèige.

5.4 The lateral. l- is a "lateral" initial, which means that
during its production the air from the lungs is diverted from its
median axis.

l- is like the l- of English Lou: lù.

5.5 Initial r-. r- is a voiced initial made with the tongue
in the same position as for sh-: the tongue tip is up and retracted,

and there may be a slight buzzing sound during its production. It
is thus like the r- in American English run: rén "person". Notice,
however, that unless the Chinese r- is followed by a u (or by -ong),
it is pronounced with the lips spread, and not rounded, as it is in
many versions of American English.

5.6 Below are listed the Chinese initials, grouped according
to articulation of the lower lip or tongue:

Labials: lower lip touches upper lip: b-, p-, m-; lower lip
moves toward upper teeth: f-.

Apicals: tongue tip, or "apex", moves toward alveolar ridge:
d-, t-, n-, l-.

Dorsals: tongue back, or "dorsum", moves toward soft palate,
or "velum": g-, k-, h-.

Frontals: tongue front, or "frontum", moves toward alveolar
ridge; tongue tip down: j-, q-, x-.

Retracted initials: tongue tip moves to a retracted position,
behind the alveolar ridge: zh-, ch-, sh-, r-.

Apical affricates and spirant: tongue tip as for the other
apicals: z-, c-, s-.

Some syllables have none of the initials listed above. These
syllables are considered to consist of a final and a tone, and are
called "free-standing finals".

Old and new words are listed below according to initial, in the
order just given, with free-standing finals appearing last.

Labials:

bā; yìbǎ; bào; bǐ; biǎo; bù; bùzhidào "not know".
péngyou; piányi.
mǎi; méiyou; Měiguo; Měishēng "(proper name)"; Máo "(surname)"; máng;
  míngzi "name".
Fàguo "France"; fěnbǐ.

Apicals:

dà "big"; Jiānádà "Canada"; Déguo "Germany"; dōu; dǒng.

tā; tài; Tàitai "Mrs."; Tài Shān "(mountain)"; yìtiáo; Tóngxué
   "Student"; Tóngzhì "Comrade".

Jiānádà "Canada"; nà "that"; něige; nèige; nánháizi "boy"; nǐ; nín;
   nǚháizi "girl".

lù; Lù "(surname)"; Lǐ "(surname)".

Dorsals:

gěi; gāo; Gāo "(surname)"; gāngbǐ; 'něiguó? "which nation?"; Guóxiān
   "(proper name)"; Guóxīn "(proper name)"; guì.

kěshi; kàn.

hé; háizi "child"; hǎo; Hánguo "Korea"; hěn; xiǎohár "child"; Huá Shān
   "(mountain)"; Huáng "(surname)"; Huáng Hé "Yellow River".

Frontals:

Jiānádà "Canada"; jǐge"; jiào "be called"; Jiàoshòu "Professor";
   Jiāng "(surname)"; Jiǎng "(surname)"; jiǔ; jiù₁; jiù₂; jìn.

qǐ, qiānbǐ; qián; qǐng.

xǐhuan; Xiáojie "Miss"; xiǎo "small"; Xiānsheng "Mr."; xīn; xíng;
   xìng "surname".

Retracted initials:

zhè "this"; yìzhǐ; zhǐdao "know"; Zhào "(surname)"; zhēn; Zhēnzhēn
   "(proper name)"; yìzhāng₁; Zhāng₂ "(surname)"; Zhèng "(surname)";
   zhuōzi; Zhū Jiāng "Pearl River"; Zhōngguo; Zhōngwén.

Chén "(surname)"; cháng; Cháng Jiāng "Yangtze River".

shí; shì "be"; shéi "who?"; shān; shémma? "what?"; shuō; shū.

Rìběn "Japan"; rén "person".

Apical affricates and spirant:

yízuò "one (large, immovable object)"; zàijiàn "goodbye"; zǎo "early".
Cáo "(surname)".
Sītú "(surname)"; sì; sān.

Free-standing finals:

Èguo "Russia"; èr.
yě; yī; yào; yǒude "some"; yǒurén "some people"; Yīngguo; Yīngwén.
wǒ; wǔ; wèn "ask"; Wáng "(surname)".
yuǎn.

Dialogs

I

A: nèige rén shi shéi?	Who is that person?
B: nà shi wǒ péngyou, Zhāng Xiansheng.	That's my friend, Mr. Chang.
A: nèiwei shi ta tàitai ma?	Is that his wife?
B: shì. ...	Yes. ...
A: Zhāng Xs, Zhāng Taitai, nǐmen hǎo?	How do you do, Mr. and Mrs. Chang?
C: 'hǎo, hǎo. nín shì...?	Fine. And you are...?
A: wǒ xìng Cáo.	I'm Ts'ao.
C: Cáo Xs hǎo? zhè shi nín háizi ma?	How do you do, Mr. Ts'ao. Is this your child?
A: shì.	Yes.
C: ta jiào shémma míngzi?	What is her name?
A: ta jiào Zhēnzhēn. ...	Her name is Chen-chen. ...
B: Zhāng Xs, Zhāng Tt, tamen liǎngwèi, yǒu sāngge háizi; liǎngge 'nánháizi, yíge 'nǚháizi.	Mr. and Mrs. Chang have three children: two boys and one girl.

A: 'nǚháizi jiào shémma?

B: ta jiào Měishēng. Nèiliǎngge nánháizi, yíge jiào Guóxīn,
yíge jiào Guóxiān.

What's the girl's name?

Her name is Mei-sheng.

The two boys are called Kuo-
hsin and Kuo-hsien.

II

A: nín nèiliǎngwèi péngyou,
guìxìng?

B: zhèiwei xìng Zhāng; nèiwei
xìng Gāo.

A: tamen liǎngwèi shi 'něiguó
rén?

B: Zhāng Xiaojie shi 'Yīngguo
rén; Gāo Xj shi 'Měiguo rén.

A: tamen liǎngwèi yào mǎi
'něiguó shū?

B: tamen liǎngwèi dōu yào mǎi
'Rìběn shū.

A: wo méiyou 'Rìběn shū; jiù
yǒu 'Zhōngguo shū. tamen
'yào buyào?

B: wo wènwen tamen. ... Zhāng
Xj, ni mǎi Zhōngguo 'shū
bumǎi?

C: wo bùmǎi Zhōngguo shū;
kěshi wo yào mǎi Zhōngguo
bào.

B: Zhāng Xj shuō, ta yào mǎi
Zhōngguo bào.

A: women yě yǒu Zhōngguo bào.

C: nimen yě yǒu 'Rìběn bào ma?

A: 'Zhōngguo bào, 'Rìběn bào,
women dōu yǒu.

What are the surnames of those
two friends of yours?

This one's name is Johnson;
that one's name is Gordon.

What countries are they from?

Miss Johnson is from England; Miss
Gordon from America.

They want to buy books of what
country?

They both want to buy Japanese
books.

I don't have any Japanese books,
just Chinese. Would they like
some of those?

I'll ask them. ... Miss Johnson,
are you buying Chinese books?

I'm not buying Chinese books, but
I would like to buy some Chinese
newspapers.

Miss Johnson says she would like
to buy some Chinese newspapers.

We have Chinese newspapers, too.

Do you have Japanese newspapers, too?

Yes, we have both Chinese and
Japanese newspapers.

III

(Looking at a picture book)

A: nǐ 'zhīdao buzhidào, zhèizuò   Do you know what this mountain
shān jiào shémma?   is called?

B: zhèizuò shān, jiào 'Tài   This mountain is called Mount T'ai.
Shān.

A: nèitiáo 'hé jiào shémma?   What is that river called?

B: nèitiáo hé, jiào 'Huáng Hé.   That river is called the Yellow
River.

A: 'zhèitiáo ne?   What about this one?

B: 'zhèitiáo, jiào Cháng Jiāng.   This one is called the Yangtze.

IV

A: nèijǐzuò shān, jiào shémma   What are the names of those
míngzi?   mountains?

B: nèizuò 'dà shān, wǒ zhīdao,   I know that the name of that big
jiào 'Huá Shān. nèijǐge   one is Hua Mountain. Not all of
'xiǎo shān, bùdōu yǒu míngzi.   the small ones have names:
yǒude yǒu; yǒude méiyǒu.   some have, and some haven't.

A: nèitiáo hé ne?   And that river?

B: nǐ shuō 'nèitiáo hé?   Which one are you talking about?
shi nèitiáo 'xiǎo hé bushi?   Is it that small one?

A: búshi. shi nèitiáo 'dà hé.   No. It's that big one.

B: neitiao dà hé, jiào 'Zhū   The big river is called the Pearl
Jiāng.   River.

V

A: wǒ méiyou Zhōngguo xìng.   I don't have a Chinese surname.
qǐng nǐ gěi wǒ yige, 'xíng   Please give me one, OK?
buxíng?

B: xíng. xìng 'Gāo hǎo buhǎo?   OK. How about "Kao"?

A: nà hěn hǎo. wǒ yě yào   That would be fine. I'd also like
   yǒu yige Zhōngguo míngzi.   to have a Chinese name.

B: jiào Měi'zhēn hǎo buhǎo?   How about "Mei-chen"?

A: hǎo. Gāo Měizhēn, hěn hǎo.   Fine. "Kao Mei-chen" is very good.

<u>New words</u>

rén N	person
shéi? N	who?, whom?
shémma? N	what?
zhè N	this (as a topic only)
nà N	that (as a topic only)
Zhāng BF[1]	Chang (a surname; other surnames:)
Wáng BF	Wang, Wong
Lǐ BF	Lee
Zhào BF	Chao
Jiāng BF	Chiang
Jiǎng BF	Chiang
Máo BF	Mao
Lù BF	Lu
Zhèng BF	Cheng
Huáng BF	Huang, Wong
Cáo BF	Ts'ao
Gāo BF	Kao
Sītú N	Szu-t'u, Seeto
xiānsheng N	gentleman, husband
Xiānsheng N (abbr. Xs)[2]	Mr.
tàitai N	wife, lady
Tàitai N (abbr. Tt)[2]	Mrs.
Xiáojie N (abbr. Xj)[2]	Miss
Tóngxué N	(same school:) Fellow Student
Tóngzhì N	(same aim:) Comrade
Jiàoshòu N	Professor

háizi N	child
nán- AT[3]	male
nánháizi N	boy
nǚ- AT[3]	female
nǚháizi N	girl
míngzi N	name; given name
Zhēnzhēn N[4]	Chen-chen (a given name)
Měishēng N[4]	Mei-sheng (a given name)
Guóxīn N[4]	Kuo-hsin (a given name)
Guóxiān N[4]	Kuo-hsien (a given name)
Měizhēn N[4]	Mei-chen (a given name)
'něiguó N[5]	which nation?, what country?
Rìběn N[6]	Japan
Hánguo N[6]	Korea
Déguo N[6]	Germany
Fàguo N[6]	France
Jiānádà N[6]	Canada
Èguo, Éguo N[6]	Russia
Tài Shān N	Mount T'ai (a famous mountain in Shantung Province)
Huáng Hé N	Yellow River
Cháng Jiāng N	(Long River:) Yangtze River
Huá Shān N	Hua Mountain (in Shensi Province)
yǒude N[7]	some
Zhū Jiāng N	Pearl River (in Kwangtung Province)
xìng N[8]	surname
--- V[8]	be surnamed
-wèi[9]	(respected persons)
-zuò	(large, immovable objects; mountains)
shì V[10]	be
jiào V[11]	be named
wèn V[12]	ask, inquire of
wènwen V[13]	make a few inquiries of

shuō	speak (4); say
zhīdao V[14]	know
bùzhīdào[14]	not know
dà SV	big
xiǎo SV	small, little
xiǎoháizi, xiǎohár N	(small) child
ne? P	(interrogative particle, directly follows a noun: "What about N?")
guìxìng? IE[15]	(honorable surname:) What is your surname, please?
zàijiàn. IE	(again meet:) See you later.
'hǎo buhǎo? IE	How about it?
hǎo. / bùhǎo. IE	Fine. / No.

Notes

[1]Theoretically, there are an infinite number of Chinese surnames. Practically, there are only a few common ones, about fifty in all. Most of these common surnames consist of one syllable and are bound. Thus, a one-syllable surname occurs only after xìng "be surnamed", after certain affectionate prefixes like Lǎo "old" (Lǎo Zhāng "(old) Chang", see Lesson 16), and before titles, such as Xiānsheng (see below). Much rarer are two-syllable surnames, which are "free" forms-- they can stand alone as a complete sentence, given the right context.

The Chinese have ways of coping with polysyllabic foreign surnames, as a glance at any newspaper will confirm. But it is customary to assign a Chinese surname to a foreigner, usually on the basis of similarity of sound. Thus, in Dialog II, Zhāng and Gāo are given as the Chinese surnames of two foreigners whose English surnames are respectively Johnson and Gordon.

[2]The titles Xiānsheng, Tàitai, and Xiáojie are widely used among overseas Chinese and on Taiwan. In mainland China they are avoided, especially Tàitai and Xiáojie, because they have honorific

overtones which are objectionable in an anti-elitist society.

In addition to these three titles, there are many other titles
which indicate the rank or occupation of the person addressed, like
Jiàoshòu "Professor", Tóngxué "Fellow Student, Student"; Tóngzhì
"Comrade". In mainland China, such titles are widely used.

Titles are used alone, or with surnames; when used with surnames,
they appear after the surname. After surnames, Xiānsheng, Tàitai,
and Xiáojie tend to weaken their tones: Zhāng Xiansheng, Zhāng Taitai,
Zhāng Xiaojie.

The surname-title combination often appears where in English
"you" would occur, or "you" plus a title-surname combination. Thus
in Dialog I: Cáo Xs hǎo? "How do you do, Mr. Ts'ao?"

[3]"AT" stands for "Attributive", which is a noun-like bound form
used to modify following nouns.

[4]Given names in Chinese are one or two syllables long, and the
list of names is virtually infinite, both in theory and in practice.
There is no list of commonly used given names. They are given to
children according to a variety of principles. For example, the
brothers or male cousins of the same generation may all have two-
syllable given names, the first syllable of which is the same in all
names; thus the names of the Chang boys are Guóxīn and Guóxiān. Sometimes the names mean something, sometimes not. Usually one can tell
from a name whether the bearer is male or female. The given names
introduced in this lesson are:

Zhēnzhēn from zhēn "true, pure" (cf. its adverbial use "truly").
The reduplication makes the name intensive: "very true, very pure".
The quality described by zhēn is regarded as especially appropriate
to females, so Zhēnzhēn is easily spotted as the name of a woman.

Měishēng from měi "beautiful" and shēng "be born": "beautifully
born" is likely to be a woman's name, because of měi.

Guóxīn from guó "nation, country" and xīn "new": "The nation is
made new" is a man's name, because of guó.

Guóxiān from guó and xiān "first": "The nation comes first",
again a man's name.

Měizhēn: "Beautiful and true", doubly marked as a woman's name.

[5] -guó ("nation, country") is a measure in the question word
'něiguó "what country?". 'něiguó N means either "N of what country?"
or "N in the language of what country?". In context, it is often
extremely difficult to render it in smooth English. Usually, resort
has to be made to an awkward "quizmaster" style: ...yào mǎi 'něiguó
shū in Dialog II is perfectly smooth Chinese, but the quizmaster style
seems unavoidable in the English version: "... want to buy books of
what country?"

[6] Names of countries are of various sorts. Rìběn, from rì "sun"
and běn "origin" is an epithet: "Origin of the sun". Hánguo, from
Hán "(name of an ancient Chinese state, adopted by the Koreans as the
name of their state when they became independent from China in 1894)"
and guó: "Nation of Hán". Some of the names of other foreign countries are composed of -guo (which is of course guó with the tone
neutralized) preceded by a syllable that sounds like a syllable in
the name of the country; this syllable usually has a complimentary
meaning: Měiguo, from měi "beautiful"; Yīngguo, from yīng "heroic";
Déguo "Germany, Deutschland", from dé "virtue"; Fàguo "France", from
fǎ, fà "law". Sometimes the name is a syllable-by-syllable rendition
into Chinese of the foreign name; so: Jiānádà for "Canada" (the
syllables gā and kā occur in Chinese, but, where they might be expected
to occur in renditions of foreign names, as for the first syllable of
"Canada", jiā or chiā usually occurs instead). Èguo or Éguo "Russia"
is made up of È or É which is short for Éluósī, intended to render
"Rossiya", plus -guo.

[7] This is a "noun of partial inclusion" and is limited to preverbal position. It may stand alone or modify another noun. yǒude
rén "some people" may be shortened to yǒurén.

[8]The etymological connection between the noun xìng "surname"
and the verb xìng "be surnamed" is obvious. As a verb, it may take
the negative adverb bú-: ta 'búxìng Wáng; ta xìng Zhāng. "His surname isn't Wang, it's Chang." But there is a tendency to limit choice-
type questions to the form tā xìng 'Wáng buxìng Wáng? "Is his surname
Wang?", or to use shì: tā 'shì bushì xìng Wáng? (same meaning).

[9]-wèi is the measure for any noun denoting a human being, when
showing respect to that person. Thus it occurs as an measure for
xiānsheng, tàitai, xiáojie, and péngyou. Note: nèiwèi xiānsheng
"that gentleman", but nèige rén "that man": -wèi is not used with rén.

[10]shì has as its object a noun or nominal expression denoting
something that is the equivalent of the subject (e.g. tā shi wǒ péngyou.
"He is my friend."), or denoting the class of which the subject is a
member (e.g. tā shi Měiguo rén. "He is an American.")

shì, when it occurs as part of a sentence, usually carries the
neutral tone; alone, as an entire sentence, it carries the fourth tone.
Notice that the negative adverb is bú-, with the second tone, even
when the tone of shi is neutral.

[11]The verb jiào is often preceded by míngzi, functioning as its
noun topic. Then this topic-comment construction may also be preceded
by another topic:

(Topic)	Comment.	
	(Topic)	Comment.
(N)	(míngzi)	V O
tā	míngzi	jiào Zhēnzhēn.

[12]The verb wèn takes two objects of which the first is obligatory
and the second optional. The first object names the person to whom
the question is asked, and the second states the question asked. Thus:
wǒ wèn tā,'něige hǎo? "I'll ask him which is better." Notice that

there is question intonation beginning with the question part of the
Chinese sentence.

Sometimes the person asked and the subject of the question are
the same. In such cases one pronoun or noun may be deleted.
Thus: wǒ yào wèn (tā), tā xìng shémma? "I want to ask him what
his name is."

[13] wènwen is the reduplicated form of wèn. The reduplication of
a verb adds a flavor of informality to its meaning. wènwen differs
from wèn in that it optionally takes the first object, naming the
person asked, but it seldom takes the second object, stating the
question asked: wǒ wènwen ta. "I'll ask him."

[14] zhīdao has a different form after bù-: bùzhīdào; also after
shéi: shéi zhīdào? "Who knows?" zhīdao (or bùzhīdào) takes as its
object a sentence or a question. Thus: wǒ zhīdao ta xìng Zhāng,
kěshi wǒ bùzhīdào, ta míngzi jiào shémma. "I know that his surname
is Chang, but I don't know what his personal name is."

Sometimes bùzhīdào, before questions, has the force of "I wonder":
wǒ bùzhīdào ta míngzi jiào shémma? "I wonder what his name is."

[15] The idiomatic expressions in this lesson do not appear in the
pronunciation build-up. guìxìng? is a bit old-fashioned, but it is
still heard, even in the People's Republic. Now considered distinctly
quaint are the related expressions bìxìng "humble surname" preceding
one's surname as an answer to guìxìng?, and dà míng? "great name"
inquiring about a person's personal name.

More notes on grammar

5.7 Indirect statement. Certain verbs, like shuō "say" and
zhīdao "know", take whole sentences as direct object. The choice of
words and the word order in these "embedded sentences" are the same
as in the corresponding sentences in isolation.

Zhāng Xj shuō shémma?	What does Miss Johnson say?
ta shuō ta yào mǎi Zhōngguo bào.	She says she wants to buy Chinese newspapers.
wo zhīdao ta yào mǎi Zhōngguo bào.	I know she wants to buy Chinese newspapers.
ta shuō ta bùdǒng.	He says he doesn't understand.
wo zhīdao ta bùdǒng.	I know he doesn't understand.
ta shuō ta yào kàn bào.	She says that she wants to read a newspaper.
wo zhīdao ta yào kàn bào.	I know that she wants to read a newspaper.
ta shuō ta yào 'qǐng nǐ mǎi shū.	He says he wants to ask you to buy some books.
wo zhīdao ta yào 'qǐng wǒ mǎi shū.	I know he wants to ask me to buy books.
ta shuō ni bùgěi ta qián.	He says you're not giving him any money.
wo zhīdao ta shuō wǒ bùgěi ta qián.	I know that he says that I'm not giving him any money.

5.8 <u>Question words</u>. The specifier <u>něi-</u> "which?" and the nouns <u>shéi</u> "who?" and <u>shémma</u> "what?" occur in questions that ask information about content.

An important difference between Chinese question words and the corresponding English interrogative pronouns is that the Chinese words occupy the same position in the sentence as the words they replace, whereas the English words are regularly shifted to the front of the sentence:

<u>shéi</u> yào mǎi shū?	<u>Who</u> wants to buy books?
nǐ yào mǎi <u>shémma</u>?	<u>What</u> do you want to buy?

nǐ yào mǎi 'něiběn shū?   Which book do you want to buy?
tā shì shéi?   Who is she?

Sometimes it is impossible to shift the interrogative pronoun
in English; then it is necessary to resort to the awkward "quizmaster" style mentioned in note 5 in the "New words" section above.
This order either follows the Chinese word order exactly, or is
slightly different; in either case, the pronoun is still near the
position of the word it replaces:

nǐ yào mǎi 'něiguó shū?   You want to buy what country's
                                  books? / ...books of what country?
wǒ yào mǎi 'Rìběn shū.   I want to buy Japanese books.

    5.9 Questions introduced so far are of three main kinds: "yes-
no" questions ask for assent or dissent to an underlying statement.
Such questions end in the sentence particle ma.

nǐ yào mǎi shū ma? -- wǒ yào   Do you want to buy some books? --
    mǎi shū.   Yes.
tā shi 'Yīngguo rén ma? -- shì.   Is he an Englishman? -- Yes.

    "Choice-type" questions ask the hearer to choose between
alternatives in his answer.

nǐ yào mǎi shū, mǎi bào? --   Which do you want to buy, books or
    mǎi shū.   newspapers? -- Books.
nǐ 'yào buyào mǎi shū? -- yào.   Do you want to buy some books? -- Yes.
tā shi 'Yīngguo rén bushì? --   Is he an Englishman? -- No.
    'búshì.

    "Content" questions ask the hearer to supply missing information:

'shéi yào mǎi shū. -- 'wǒ yào   Who wants to buy some books? -- I do.
    mǎi shū.
nǐ yào mǎi shémma? -- wǒ yào   What do you want to buy? -- Books.
    mǎi shū.

nǐ yào mǎi 'shémma shū? -- wǒ yào mǎi 'Měiguo shū.	What books do you want to buy? -- I want to buy American books.
nǐ yào mǎi 'něiběn? -- wo yào mǎi 'zhèiběn.	Which do you want to buy? -- This one.
tā shi shéi? -- tā shi 'Zhāng Tt.	Who is she? -- It's Mrs. Chang.
zhèige shi shémma? -- zhèige shi yǐzi.	What's this? -- It's a chair.
'něiwèi shi Fàguo rén? -- 'něiwèi shi Fàguo rén.	Which one is from France? -- That one is.

5.10 _Indirect questions_. Choice-type questions (especially V_1-_bu_ V_1 questions) and content questions (but usually not questions with _ma_) both occur as clauses embedded in larger sentences. Such clauses are "indirect questions". A typical position for an indirect question in a sentence is after a verb like _wèn_ "ask" or _zhīdao_ "know". The words and the word order of an indirect question are the same as those of the corresponding question. If it is embedded in a declarative sentence, the indirect question carries the declarative intonation pattern when it is the object of _zhīdao_, but it sometimes keeps its interrogative intonation when it is the object of _wèn_.

wǒ yao wèn ta, 'yào buyào mǎi shū?	I want to ask him whether he wants to buy books.
wǒ bùzhidào, ta shi 'Yīngguo rén bushi.	I wonder if he's an Englishman.
wǒ zhīdao shéi yào mǎi shū.	I know who wants to buy books.
wǒ yao wèn tā, yào mǎi 'shémma shū?	I want to ask him what books he wants to buy.
wǒ bùzhidào shéi shi Fàguo rén.	I don't know who are from France.

5.11 _Indirect questions embedded in questions_. It is possible to make questions of sentences that include an indirect question.

Two useful patterns involve zhīdao. The first pattern is used when
there is a question word in the indirect question, and is simply to
make a yes-no question by adding ma. The second pattern is to make
a choice-type question by adding buzhidào between 'zhīdao and the
indirect question. The meanings of the two patterns are virtually
the same.

nǐ zhīdao, shéi yào mǎi shū ma?	Do you know who wants to buy books?
nǐ zhīdao, tā yào mǎi 'shémma shū ma?	Do you know what books he wants to to buy?
nǐ zhīdao, shéi shi Fǎguo rén ma?	Do you know who are from France?
nǐ 'zhīdao buzhidào, tā mǎi 'shū bumǎi?	Do you know whether he wants to buy books?
nǐ 'zhīdao buzhidào, tā 'shì bushi 'Yīngguo rén?	Do you know whether he's an Englishman or not?
nǐ 'zhīdao buzhidào, shéi yào mǎi shū?	Do you know who wants to buy books?
nǐ 'zhīdao buzhidào, tā yào mǎi 'shémma shū?	Do you know what books he wants to buy?
nǐ 'zhīdao buzhidào, shéi shi Fǎguo rén?	Do you know who are from France?

     5.12 Questions of the form "N ne?" comprise a fourth type of
question, a follow-up question, asking "And what about N?"

nèitiáo hé jiào shémma?	What is that river called?
nèitiáo hé jiào 'Huáng Hé.	That river is called the Yellow River.
'zhèitiáo ne?	What about this one?
'zhèitiáo, jiào Cháng Jiāng.	This one is called the Yangtze.

nǐ yào mǎi zhèiběn shū ma?	Do you want to buy this book?
wǒ yào mǎi.	Yes.
'zhèijǐběn ne?	And what about these?
zhèijǐběn, wǒ dōu buyào mǎi.	I don't want to buy any of them.
nǐ neige 'nánháizi, míngzi jiào shémma?	What's your boy's name?
jiào Guóxīn.	Kuo-hsin.
'nǚháizi ne?	What about the girls?
yíge jiào Měishēng, yíge jiào Zhēnzhēn.	One is Mei-sheng, one is Chen-chen.

Questions of this type do not form indirect questions.

5.13 <u>Polite questions of the form</u> guì-N? A limited number of nouns may be preceded by <u>guì</u> to form polite questions.

nín guìxìng? -- xìng Cáo.	May I know your surname? -- It is Ts'ao.
guìguó shi...? -- wǒ shi 'Měiguo rén.	And what country are you from? -- I'm an American.
nín 'péngyou guìxìng? -- tā xìng Lǐ.	What is your friend's surname? -- It is Lee.

5.14 <u>Naming</u>. See "New words", notes 8 and 11.

tā xìng Cáo ma?	Is his last name Ts'ao?
tā 'búxìng Cáo; tā xìng Wáng.	No, it isn't; it's Wang.
nín 'péngyou guìxìng?	May I know your friend's last name?
tā xìng Zhāng.	It is Chang.
tā jiào shémma míngzi?	What is his name?
tā jiào Guóxīn.	It's Kuo-hsin.
zhèizuò shān, míngzi jiào shémma?	What's the name of this mountain?
jiào Huá Shān.	It's Hua Mountain.

zhèige, Zhōngguo huà jiào shémma?   What do you call this in Chinese?
jiào "gāngbǐ".   "gāngbǐ".

"pen", Zhōngguo huà jiào shémma?   What do you call a pen in Chinese?
"pen", jiào "gāngbǐ".   "Pen" is "gāngbǐ".

5.15 Partial inclusion. A "noun of partial inclusion" tells
what part of a whole group is under discussion in the sentence.
yǒude "some" is indefinite as to the amount of the part; expressions
with numbers give more precise information: liǎngge "(of the whole
group, exactly) two".

Nouns of partial inclusion resemble adverbs in that they are
limited to preverbal position in a sentence. In order for a noun
of partial inclusion to apply to the object of a V O construction,
the object must be transposed to a topic position. This is because,
like dōu, nouns of partial inclusion have backward application (see
4.4.3).

Thus the first element in the sentence is the main topic, a
noun expression naming the whole group to be described. This main
topic is optional.

The comment to this topic usually consists of two clauses in a
co-ordinate "and" relationship. The first of these comment clauses
itself consists of a topic and a comment; the topic consists of a
noun of partial inclusion followed optionally by the noun that it
modifies; the comment may be of various constructions, including
topic-comment, A-SV, V, and so on. The second comment clause tells
about the rest of the whole group. For the most part it is grammatically parallel to the first comment clause.

(Topic)

(Topic)	Comment. / Topic	Comment, (Topic)	Comment,	+ Topic	Comment. (Topic)	Comment.
1. zhèisìge rén,	yíge		shuō 'Yīngwén,	sānge		shuō 'Zhōngwén.
2. nèiliǎngge biǎo,	yíge		hǎo,			bùhǎo.
3. zhèiliǎngběn shū,	yìběn	wo	yào kàn,	yìběn		bùyào kàn.
4. tā neisìge háizi,	liǎngge		hǎokàn,	liǎngge		bùhǎokàn.
5. zhèijǐge rén,	yǒude		kàn bào,	yǒude		kàn shū.
6. nèijǐge xiǎo shān,	yǒude		yǒu míngzi,	yǒude		méiyǒu.
7.	yíge rén		shuō 'Yīngwén,	yíge rén		shuō 'Zhōngwén.
8.	sìzhī bǐ		guì,	yìzhī bǐ		piányi.
9.	yǒude qián	wo	gěi ta,	yǒude qián		bùgěi ta.
10.	yǒude rén	wo	xǐhuan,	yǒude rén		bùxǐhuan.
11.	yǒurén		xǐhuan ta,	yǒurén		bùxǐhuan ta.
12.	yǒude		dǒng,	yǒude		bùdǒng.

Translations of the sentences in the pattern display are given below:

1. Of these four people, one speaks English, three speak
   Chinese.
2. Of those two watches, one is good, and one isn't.
3. I want to read one of these two books, and one I don't.
4. Two of his four children are good-looking and two aren't.
5. Some of these people are reading newspapers; some, books.
6. Some of those small mountains have names; some don't.
7. One man speaks English; one, Chinese.
8. Four pens are expensive; one, inexpensive.
9. I'll give him some of the money, and some I won't.
10. Some people I like, and some I don't.
11. Some people like him, and some don't.
12. Some (I) understand, some (I) don't.

Pyramid drills

Guóxiān.

Wáng Guóxiān.

shi Wáng Guóxiān.

tā shi Wáng Guóxiān.

tā shi wǒ péngyou, Wáng Guóxiān.

tā shi wǒ péngyou, xìng Wáng.

tā shi wǒ péngyou, xìng Wáng, jiào Guóxiān.

tā shi wǒ péngyou, xìng Wáng, míngzi jiào Guóxiān.

tā shi wǒ péngyou, Wáng Xs.

                        mǎi shémma?

                    ta mǎi shémma?

                ta yào mǎi shémma?

            wo bùzhidào, ta yào mǎi shémma.

        wo bùzhidào, Zhāng Xj yào mǎi shémma.

    ni 'zhīdao buzhidào, Zhāng Xj yào mǎi shémma?

        nǐ zhīdao, Zhāng Xj yào mǎi shémma ma?

            Zhāng Xj shuō, ta yào mǎi shémma?

            Zhāng Xj shuō, ta yào mǎi shū ma?

                ta shuō ta yào mǎi shū.

        wo zhīdao, ta shuō, ta yào mǎi shū.

    wo bùzhidào. wo wènwen ta.

Exercise

Answer the following questions to make connected dialogs.

nèiwei tàitai shi shéi?

'Zhāng Tt shi něiwèi?

búshi nèiwei ma?

Zhāng Xs ne?

tāmen liǎngwèi yǒu háizi ma?

jiù yǒu liǎngge?

míngzi dōu jiào shémma?

dōu shi 'nǚháizi ma?

ni 'zhīdao buzhidào tamen yào yige 'nánháizi?

Tài Shān, Huá Shān, nèiliǎngzuò shān, ni zhīdao něizuò dà ma?

Huá Shān hěn xiǎo ma?

'něizuò yuǎn?

Cháng Jiāng, Zhū Jiāng dōu hěn cháng ma?

Zhāng Xs zhīdao buzhidào 'něitiáo cháng?

qǐng nǐ wènwen ta.

Lesson 6

More numbers, prices and measurement, the imperative,
and the pivot with yǒu and méiyǒu

· Pronunciation

6.1 Further analysis of the syllable. A preliminary analysis
of the Chinese syllable which underlies the spelling system used in
this text has been given above, in 3.1. This analysis divides the
syllable first of all into an initial, a final, and a tone. The
initials were listed in 5.6, where it was also stated that a syllable that does not have an initial is a "free-standing final".

6.1.1 Analysis of the final. The structure of the final is
best observed in the free-standing finals. Every final has a "nuclear vowel": the first syllable of Èguo, è-, consists of a lone
nuclear vowel (plus a tone).

The nuclear vowel may be preceded by one or two "medials":
the y- of yě and the w- of wǒ are examples of one medial preceding
the nuclear vowel; the yu- of yuǎn is an example of two overlapping
medials preceding the nuclear vowel. In syllables with initials,
these medials are spelled -i- (corresponding to y-) and -u- (corresponding to w-), as in biǎo and guó.

The nuclear vowel may be followed by one or two "endings":
the -n of yuǎn and the -ng of cháng are examples of one ending
following the nucleus. (N.B. -ng is a digraph representing a
single sound.) No word having two endings has appeared so far.
The first example is introduced in Lesson 13: diànyěngr "movie",
where -ng- and -r represent two overlapping endings.

6.1.2 Sorting finals according to medials. From now on,
words in the "Pronunciation" section of each lesson will be sorted
into four groups depending on four "medial conditions". (1) If
the final has no medial, it is "plain": èr, È-, dà, Dé-, sì. (2)
If it begins with the front of the tongue placed high in the front

88

part of the mouth, near the alveolar ridge, and if at the same time
the lips are relatively unrounded, it is "frontalized": yào, yě,
yī, biǎo, -xiē, qī. (3) If the final begins with strong rounding
of the lips, it is said to be "labialized": Wáng, wǒ, wǔ, huà, guó
lù. (4) If the final begins with a simultaneous combination of
high-front placement of the front of the tongue and rounding of the
lips, it is "frontalized and labialized": yuǎn.

The new words introduced in this lesson are presented below
according to this grouping, with a selection of old words.

Note that sometimes two or more finals are spelled with the
same letters (see e.g. 4.1). Such spelling conventions are possible
to follow without ambiguity, because differences in the initial will
always determine which of two or more same-spelled finals is intended.

Plain: finals beginning with a and e; -i alone after zh-, ch-, sh-,
  r-, and z-, c-, s-; and ou:

a: bā; yìdá "a dozen"; nà.

e: Déguo; kěshi; zhè; Èguo.

i: yìzhī; zhǐ "paper"; yìchǐ "one foot"; shí; Rìběn; sì.

ai: yìbǎi "one hundred"; mǎi; mài "sell"; tài; háizi.

ei: Měiguo; něige?; gěi; shéi?

ao: Máo; yìmáo "ten cents"; gāo; yíhào "number one"; Zhào; Cáo.

ou: dōu; gòu "enough".

an: yíbàn "one half"; nánháizi; kàn; shān; sān.

en: yìfēn "one cent"; yìběn; hěn; zhēn.

ang: máng; yìfānglǐ "one square mile"; gāngbǐ; yìzhāng.

eng: péngyou; Zhèng; zhèng hǎo "just right".

ar: yíbàr "one half"; xiǎohár "(small) child".

er: èr.

<u>Frontalized</u>: other finals beginning with <u>i</u> (except <u>-iong</u>); free-
standing finals beginning with <u>y-</u> (except <u>yong</u>):

<u>ia</u>: Jiānádà.

<u>ie</u>: Xiáojie; yìxiē "a few"; xièxie; yě.

<u>i</u>: bǐ; yìlǐ "one mile"; nǐ; jǐge? "how many?"; qī; yíbàn "half";
    yígòng "altogether".

<u>iao</u>: biǎo; yìtiáo; jiào; yào.

<u>iu</u>: liù; jiǔ; yǒu.

<u>ian</u>: piányi; yìqiān "one thousand"; qián.

<u>in</u>: nín; jìn.

<u>iang</u>: liǎngge; Jiǎng; xiǎng "think".

<u>ing</u>: míngzi; líng "zero"; qǐng; qǐngwèn "may I ask...?"; Yīngwén;
    yì-Yīnglǐ "one English mile".

<u>Labialized</u>: finals beginning with <u>u</u> except after <u>j-</u>, <u>q-</u>, <u>x-</u>, <u>y-</u>; <u>-ong</u>;
    <u>-o</u> alone after <u>b-</u>, <u>p-</u>, <u>m-</u>, <u>f-</u>; free-standing finals beginning with
    <u>w-</u>.

<u>ua</u>: huà.

<u>uo</u>: shíduō "ten plus"; duōshao "how many?"; duó? "to what extent?";
    něiguo?; zhuōzi; wǒ.

<u>u</u>: bù; lù; shū; wǔ.

<u>uai</u>: yíkuài "one dollar".

<u>ui</u>: guì; yíwèi.

<u>uan</u>: yíwàn "ten thousand".

<u>un</u>: yícùn "one inch"; wèn.

<u>uang</u>: Huáng; Wáng.

<u>ong</u>: dǒng; yígòng "altogether"; yìgōnglǐ "one kilometer"; Zhōngwén.

<u>uar</u>: huàr "picture".

<u>uor</u>: (none yet)

uer: (none yet)

ur: (none yet)

Frontalized and labialized: ü; finals beginning with u after j-, q-,
     x-, y-; -iong, yong.

ue: xuéxiào "school"; xuésheng "student".

ü: nǚháizi.

uan: yuǎn.

un: (none yet)

6.1.3. Labialized syllables. Notice that syllables that are
labialized (whether they are at the same time frontalized or not)
begin with the lips rounded. This pre-rounding is different from
the comparable situation in most versions of English: "loot" and
"swan", for example, are usually pronounced with late rounding of
the lips. It is important in Chinese to begin the lip rounding
before the rest of the syllable is actually pronounced.

6.1.4. Frontalized and labialized syllables. Syllables that
are both frontalized and labialized in Chinese usually present a
problem for the English speaker. These syllables begin with a "u-
umlaut" sound, like the u of French tu and lui, or the ü of German
Grüne. It is not found in standard English. To produce it, make
a sound like the oo of English cool, with the lips strongly rounded;
then, keeping the lips rounded, move the tongue to a high front
position, as though to make a sound like the ee of English "Lee".
Because of English speech habits, it is hard to prevent automatic
unrounding of the lips when the tongue is moving to the high front
position.

Dialogs

I

A: ni xǐhuan zhèizhāng huàr ma?   Do you like this painting?

B: wǒ hěn xǐhuan. zhèizhāng   Yes, very much. Is it Chinese or
   huàr, shi 'Zhōngguo huàr,   Japanese?
   shi 'Rìběn huàr?

A: wo xiǎng shi 'Rìběn huàr.   I think it's Japanese. Look at
   ni kàn 'nèizhāng; 'nèizhāng   that one; that one is a Chinese
   shi Zhōngguo huàr.   painting.

B: ta 'mài bumài?   Will he sell it?

A: wo bùzhidào. ni wènwen ta.   I don't know. Ask him.

B: qǐngwèn; zhèizhāng huàr,   Excuse me, is this painting for
   'mài bumài?   sale?

C: mài.   It is.

B: zhèizhāng huàr, mài duōshao   How much does it sell for?
   qián?

C: sìbǎi 'wǔshikuài qián.   Four hundred fifty dollars.

B: 'nèizhāng ne?   What about that one?

C: nèizhāng, liùbǎi.   That one is six hundred.

B: dōu bupiányi.   They're neither of them cheap.

C: 'zhèizhāng piányi; yìbǎi   This one is cheaper: one hundred
   'sānshikuài.   thirty dollars.

B: zhèisānzhāng, yígòng yì-   How about a thousand dollars for
   qiānkuài, 'xíng buxíng?   all three?

C: xíng; wǒ màigei ni.   Fine; I'll sell them to you.

II

A: ni yǒu zhǐ ma?   Do you have any paper?

B: yǒu. ni kàn, 'zhèiyíbàn   Yes. Look, this half is Chinese
   shi 'Zhōngguo zhǐ; 'nèiyíbàn   paper; that half is Japanese.
   shi 'Rìběn zhǐ. ni yào   Which kind do you want?
   'něiguó zhǐ?

A: wo yào 'Rìběn zhǐ.

B: ni yào 'duōshaozhāng?

A: 'duōshao qián yìzhāng?

B: yìmáo qián yìzhāng; liǎng-
   máowǔ, sānzhāng.

A: wo jiù yào 'liǎng-sānzhāng.

B: wo gěi nǐ 'sānzhāng, 'hǎo
   buhǎo?

A: ni gěi wǒ 'liǎngzhāng ba.
   tā xiǎng mǎi xiē 'Zhōngguo
   zhǐ.

B: wǔzhāng 'gòu bugòu?

A: gòu le.

I'd like the Japanese.

How many sheets would you like?

How much per sheet?

Ten cents a sheet; three for twenty-
   five.

I just want two or three sheets.

I'll give you three sheets, all
   right?

You'd better just give me two.
   He would like to buy some Chinese
   paper.

Will five sheets be enough?

Yes.

III

A: Měiguo yǒu duóma dà?

B: Měiguo yǒu èrbǎi-jiǔshiqí-
   wàn qīqiān-yìbǎi-èrshibā-lǐ.

A: shi 'Yīnglǐ, shi 'gōnglǐ?

B: búshi 'Yīnglǐ, yě búshi
   'gōnglǐ; shi 'fānglǐ.

How big is America?

America is two million nine hundred
   seventy-seven thousand one hundred
   twenty-eight (square) miles.

Is that in miles or kilometers?

It's not English miles, nor is it
   kilometers; it's square (English)
   miles.

IV

A: zhèizhāng zhuōzi, gòu
   'cháng bugòu cháng?

B: wǔchǐbàn; búgòu cháng.

A: 'nèizhāng ne?

B: nèizhāng, liùchǐ qícùn;
   zhèng hǎo.

Is this table long enough?

It's five and a half feet; it's
   not long enough.

What about that one?

That one is six feet seven inches:
   just right.

V

A: yìzhī gāngbǐ, yíkuài-líng-   One pen, one dollar and five cents;
   wǔfēn; èrshizhī fěnbǐ, sìmáo   twenty pieces of chalk, forty
   qián; bàndá qiānbǐ,   cents; half a dozen pencils,
   qīmáowǔ.   seventy-five cents.

B: yígòng, 'duōshao qián?   How much altogether?

A: yígòng, liǎngkuài èr.   Altogether, it's two dollars and
                                      twenty cents.

VI

A: nimen xuéxiào yǒu 'duōshao   How many students are there in
   xuésheng?   your school?

B: yǒu yíwànduō xuésheng.   Over ten thousand.

A: 'yǒu meiyǒu 'nǚxuésheng?   Are there any female students?

B: yǒu yíbàn shi 'nǚxuésheng.   Yes, half are.

A: 'nánxiānsheng duō, 'nǚxiān-   Are there more male teachers or
   sheng duō?   female teachers?

B: 'nánxiānsheng duō.   There are more male teachers.

VII

A: méiyou rén zhīdao, ta yào   Doesn't anyone know how many
   'jǐběn ma?   (books) he wants?

B: yǒurén shuō, tā yào 'sān-   Some say he wants three; others
   běn; yǒurén shuō, ta yào   say he wants two.
   'liǎngběn.

A: wǒmen jiù yǒu 'liùběn. yíge   We only have six: two for each of
   rén, 'liǎngběn. Nǐ, liǎng-   us. Two for you, two for him,
   běn; tā, liǎngběn; wǒ,   and two for me.
   liǎngběn.

VIII

A: 'duōshaohào?   What's (your telephone) number?
B: èr-sān-jiǔ, yī-líng-líng-   It's 239-1001.
   yī.

New words

huàr, huà N (M: -zhāng)	painting, picture
zhǐ N (M: -zhāng)	paper
bàn- NU	half
bànběn[1]	half a volume
--- M	one half
yíbàn, yíbàr N	one half
yíbàn cháng; yíbàn bùcháng.	Half are long; half, not.
zhèiyibàn hǎo.[2]	This half is better.
wo buyào nèiyibàn.	I don't want that half.
yíge-bàn[3]	one and a half
wǔzhāng-bàn	five and a half sheets
xuéxiào N	school
xuésheng N	student
nǚxuésheng N	female student
nánxuésheng N	male student
xiānsheng N	gentleman (5); teacher
nǚxiānsheng N	female teacher
nánxiānsheng N	male teacher
duōshao? NU[4]	how much? how many?
duōshaoběn shū?	How many books?
--- N	
duōshao qián?	How much money?
mǎi duōshao?	How much will he buy?
'jǐ NU[4]	how many (up to ten)?
'jǐběn shū?	How many books?
sānshi'jǐběn shū?	How many books (between thirty and thirty-nine)?

'jǐshige?	How many tens (of them)?
shí'jǐge?	How many (of them, between ten and nineteen)?
-duō M[5]	plus a fraction (of the preceding M); and then some
yìběnduō	one (book) plus a fraction of another
sānshiduō	thirty plus (up to thirty-four or -five)
sānshiduōběn	thirty plus (books, up to thirty-four or -five)
-bǎi M [6]	hundred
yìbǎi	one hundred
yìbǎige	a hundred of them
jǐbǎige	a few hundred of them
'jǐbǎige?	How many hundreds of them?
liǎngbǎi [7]	two hundred
èrbǎi [7]	two hundred
sānbǎiyīshí [8]	three hundred ten
sānbǎiyīshíge	three hundred ten of them
sānbǎiyīshiyī	three hundred eleven
sānbǎiyīshiyīzhang	three hundred and eleven sheets
sānbǎiyīshièrzhang	three hundred and twelve sheets
sānbǎi'jǐshige?	Three hundred and how many tens of them?
sānbǎijǐshige	three hundred plus a few tens
-qiān M [6]	thousand
yìqiān	one thousand
yìqiānge	a thousand of them
jǐqiānge	a few thousand of them
'jǐqiānge?	How many thousands of them?
liǎngqiān	two thousand
liǎngqiānyìbǎi	two thousand one hundred

liǎngqiānsānbǎiyīshí	two thousand three hundred and ten
liǎngqiān'jǐbǎi?	Two thousand and how many hundreds?
liǎngqiānjǐbǎi	two thousand and a few hundreds
-wàn M [6, 9]	ten-thousand
yíwàn	ten thousand
yíwànzhāng	ten thousand sheets
jǐwànzhāng	several ten-thousands of sheets
'jǐwànzhāng?	How many ten-thousands of sheets?
liǎngwàn [7]	twenty thousand
liǎngwàn-yì-qiān-yìbǎi- yīshíèrběn	twenty-one thousand one hundred twelve volumes
sìwàn	forty thousand
qīwàn, qíwàn [10]	seventy thousand
báwàn [10]	eighty thousand
shíwàn	one hundred thousand
èrshíwàn [7]	two hundred thousand
yìbǎiwàn	one million
èrbǎiwàn [7]	two million
liǎngbǎiwàn [7]	two million
yìqiānwàn	ten million
liǎngqiānwàn [7]	twenty million
yíwànwàn	one hundred million
liǎngwànwàn	two hundred million
báwànwànduō rén	over eight hundred million people
-fēn M [11]	(divide:) cent
yìfēn qián	one cent
liǎngfēn	two cents
-máo M [11]	dime
yìmáo qián	ten cents
liǎngmáo	twenty cents
liǎngmáo wǔfēn qián	twenty-five cents

-kuài M [11]	dollar
yíkuài qián	one dollar
liǎngkuài qián	two dollars
shíkuài qián	ten dollars
shiyīkuài qián	eleven dollars
shièrkuài qián	twelve dollars
shisānkuài sìmáo wǔfēn qián	thirteen dollars and forty-five cents
yìbǎikuài qián	one hundred dollars
yìbǎiyīshíkuài qián	one hundred ten dollars
liǎngbǎikuài qián	two hundred dollars
èrbǎikuài qián	two hundred dollars
sānbǎièrshikuài qīmáo wǔfēn qián	three hundred twenty dollars and seventy-five cents
yìqiānkuài qián	one thousand dollars
liǎngqiānkuài qián	two thousand dollars
yíwànkuài qián	ten thousand dollars
yíwànwànkuài qián	one hundred million dollars
-xiē M [12]	a few; a small amount of, some
zhèixiē	these
zhèixiē shān	these mountains
--- NU [12]	a few; a small amount of, some
zhèixiēzuò shān	these (few) mountains
zhèixiēzhāng zhǐ	these (few) sheets of paper
mǎi xiē zhǐ[13]	buy some paper
líng NU[14]	zero; and (replacing one or more intermediate zeros in numbers and like phrases)
èr-líng-bā-líng	two-oh-eight-oh (2080)
èr-líng-líng-bā	two-oh-oh-eight (2008)
liǎngqiān-líng-'bāshí	two thousand and eighty
liǎngqiān-líng-bā	two thousand and eight
liǎngkuài-líng-wǔfēn qián	two dollars and five cents

-lǐ M	mile; Chinese mile (about one third of an English mile)
yìlǐ	a mile
èrbǎilǐ	two hundred miles
-Yīnglǐ M	English mile
liǎng-Yīnglǐ	two English miles
liǎngbǎi-Yīnglǐ	two hundred English miles
-gōnglǐ M	kilometer
liǎnggōnglǐ	two kilometers
liǎngqiāngōnglǐ	two thousand kilometers
-fānglǐ M [15]	square English miles
liǎngfānglǐ	two square English miles
-chǐ M	foot (linear measure)
liǎngchǐ	two feet
liǎngwànjiǔqiānduōchǐ	over twenty-nine thousand feet
-cùn M	inch
yícùn	one inch
liǎngcùn	two inches
-dá M [15]	dozen
liǎngdá	two dozen
-hào M	(telephone, house, room) number
'duōshaohào?	What's the number?
xiǎng V	think
wo xiǎng, shi 'Zhōngguo huàr.	I think it's a Chinese painting.
--- AV	have it in mind to, intend to
xiǎng mǎi xiē zhǐ	intend to buy some paper
mài V	sell; be for sale; sell for
ta 'mài bumài?	Will he sell it?
zhèizhāng huàr, 'mài bumài?	Is this picture for sale?
mài 'duōshao qián?	How much does it sell for?
-gei VS [17]	(gěi give:) so that the recipient of the action of the verb (i.e. the direct object) passes into the possession of the beneficiary

	of action of the verb (i.e. the indirect object); to
màigei V[18]	sell to
ni màigei wǒ ma?	Will you sell it to me?
yào V	want (3); require
nèige, yào 'duōshao qián?	How much is that?
yǒu V	have (3); there is
yǒu rén.	Someone is there.
yǒu rén shuō...	Some (people) say...
Zhōngguo yǒu shān ma?	Are there mountains in China?
méiyou, méi V[19]	not have (3); there is not
méiyou rén.	No one's there.
méiren shuō...	No one says...
Zhōngguo méi shān ma?	Aren't there any mountains in China?
gòu SV	sufficient, enough
wǔzhāng 'gòu bugòu?	Will five sheets be enough?
gòu le. IE	(It has become) enough.
--- A[20]	sufficiently, ...enough
wǔchǐ búgòu cháng.	Five feet won't be long enough.
yígòng A[20]	altogether, ...in all
wo yígòng yào mǎi 'sānběn shū.	I want to buy three books in all.
zhèisānzhāng, yígòng, yìqiān-kuài.	Altogether, one thousand dollars for these three (paintings).
duō, duó, duōma, duóma A[21]	to what extent? how?
Měiguo yǒu duó dà?	How large is America?
ba. P	(at the end of a sentence, softens an imperative; see below, 6.9)
gěi wǒ liǎngzhāng ba.	Better give me two (sheets).
duō SV	many, much
rén hěn duō.	There were a lot of people.
zhèng A	exactly, just
zhèng hǎo	exactly right, just right

Notes

[1]bàn- before a measure forms a noun. bànběn is therefore a
noun, for which the measure is -ge: yíge bànběn "one half-volume";
sānge bànběn "three half-volumes". The occasion to use such phrases
(i.e. bàn-M preceded by NU-ge) seldom arises.

[2]The reason why yíbàn can directly follow zhè-, zhèi, etc., is
because its first syllable, yí- is the number yī "one" (cf. 4.8).

[3]The occasion to use phrases like "one and a half volumes",
"three and a half volumes", arises often. The Chinese order is
NU-M-bàn, like the English "one volume and a half", "three volumes
and a half". The following noun is optional.

yìběnbàn (shū)	a book and a half
liǎngzhāngbàn (zhǐ)	two and a half sheets of paper
sānkuàibàn (qián)	three and a half dollars
sìmáobàn (qián)	forty-five cents
wǔfēnbàn (qián)	five and a half cents

[4]duōshao and 'jǐ are both question words that ask "how many?"
duōshao also may ask "how much?", so it applies to non-discrete as
well as to discrete quantities. 'jǐ applies only to discrete quantities. duōshao applies to numbers and amounts of any size, but 'jǐ
applies to discrete quantities numbering up to ten only.

The question word 'jǐ and the indefinite jǐ "several" (see
Lesson 4, "New words," note 3) represent two uses of what is really
only one word. As will be shown in Lesson 14, all question words
occur as indefinites. Context, intonation pattern, and stress
combine to determine whether the question word or the indefinite
is intended. Thus:

wǒ 'jiù yào jǐběn.	I only want a few (books).
nǐ yào 'jǐběn?	How many do you want?

The question word 'jǐ is a number, like its indefinite counter-
part, and can ask about a digit in any place in a number, whether

that number consists of one digit or more. It always occupies the
place of a number, never that of a measure (see below, note 5). Thus:

'jǐběn shū?	How many books?
shí'jǐběn shū?	Ten plus how many books?
èrshi'jǐběn shū?	Twenty plus how many books?
'jǐshiběn shū?	How many tens of books?

Sometimes, Chinese questions with 'jǐ defy smooth English translation, and the "quizmaster" style has to be resorted to (see Lesson
5, "New words", note 5, and 5.8).

[5]-duō is a measure, which, when it occurs at the end of a
numeral after another measure, says "plus a fraction of the preceding
measure". Certain number-like words occur as measures, such as shí
(see Lesson 4, "New words," note 8); just as yìběnduō means "one
volume, plus a fraction of another volume", so sānshiduō means
"three 'tens', plus a fraction of another 'ten'", i.e. plus a number
after ten, up to about four or five.

[6]Bear in mind the difference between the numerals from one to
ten and their compounds which are numbers in the technical sense
used here (see Lesson 4, "New words," note 3) and hence can stand
alone, and -bǎi "hundred", -qiān "thousand", and -wàn "ten thousand",
which are measures and hence must be preceded by a number, or a
measure, or both. shí may stand alone, so it is a number, but it
also follows other numbers, where it functions as a measure.

'yìben shū	'liǎngběn shū	'sānběn shū...
'shíběn shū	.	.
zhèi'shíběn shū	.	.
zhèi'èrshiběn shū	.	.
zhèièrshi'èrběn shū		
yìbǎiběn shū	yìqiānběn shū	yíwànběn shū...
zhèiyìbǎiběn shū	.	.
zhèi'liǎngbǎiběn shū	.	.

[7]The form of "two" before the numeral measures is: either
liǎng- or èr- before -bǎi; liǎng- only, before -qiān and -wàn. The
number-measure shí takes only èr- even in the higher combinations
with -wàn, etc.

[8]After -bǎi, -shí is always preceded by a number, and if this
number is "one", it takes the form yī: sānbǎiyīshí "three hundreds
and one ten, three hundred and ten".

[9]At "ten thousand", the Chinese counting system differs rad-
ically from that used in the West. "Ten thousand" has its own
measure, -wàn, which is in turn counted in tens, hundreds, thousands,
and again ten-thousands to make numbers up to a billion. Thus is
generated a decimal system grouped in fours (rather than threes as
in the West):

yī	1	1
shí	10	10
yìbǎi	100	100
yìqiān	1000	1,000
yíwàn	1,0000	10,000
shíwàn	10,0000	100,000
yìbǎiwàn	100,0000	1,000,000
yìqiānwàn	1000,0000	10,000,000
yíwànwàn	1,0000,0000	100,000,000

[10]Notice that before -wàn, qī optionally changes to qí in slow
speech, but is usually qī in rapid speech. On the other hand, bā
always changes to bá- before -wàn.

[11]Money is measured in -fēn "cents", -máo "dimes", and -kuài
"dollars", instead of just "cents" and "dollars", as in English.
Thus, "fifty cents" is expressed as "five dimes": wǔmáo.

The NU-M combination occurs optionally followed by the noun
qián "money". Also optional, when qián is not present, is the last
in a series of two or more of these money measures. Thus:

shisānkuài sìmáo wǔfēn qián	thirteen dollars and forty-five cents
shisānkuài sìmáo wǔfēn	
shisānkuài sìmáo wǔ	thirteen forty-five
sānbǎikuài qián	three hundred dollars
sānbǎikuài	

[12]-xiē is an indefinite small-number measure applying to both discrete and non-discrete quantities: "a few" and "a small amount of, some". Like a measure, it occurs after a specifier; like a number, it occurs between a specifier and a measure.

[13]A measure sometimes occurs alone, preceded neither by a specifier nor a number. Such a measure always occurs after a verb, either alone as the object of the verb, or before another noun phrase which is the object of the verb. The measure is short for yì-M "one M"; xiē in mǎi xiē zhǐ is therefore short for yìxiē "a small amount of, some".

[14]There are two styles of counting, and in each líng "zero" is used differently. In the first, or "common" style, the numerals are used alone, in counting, or with measures. When they occur with measures, yī, qī, and bā at the end of the numeral are subject to tone change, depending on the original tone of the following measure (see Lesson 4, Vocabulary, notes 4 and 6). In the second, or "telephone" style, the digits are said one by one, omitting all number-measures, such as shí, bǎi, qiān, and wàn; and only èr is used for "two". Measures are not normally used with telephone-style numerals. As the name suggests, this style is used in giving telephone numbers; it is also used for year dates, room numbers, and house numbers.

In the common style líng only occurs in the middle of the number. There, one occurrence of líng replaces one zero, or a string of two or more adjacent zeros. It never occurs replacing a zero or a string of adjacent zeros at the end of a number. But in the telephone style, líng occurs once for each zero, wherever it appears.

liǎngbǎi-líng-yī	èr-líng-yī	201
èrbǎi-yīshí	èr-yī-líng	210
liǎngqiān-yìbǎi-yīshí	èr-yī-yī-líng	2110
yìqiān-líng-yī	yī-líng-líng-yī	1001
yìqiān-líng-yīshí	yī-líng-yī-líng	1010
yíwàn-líng-yìbǎi	yī-líng-yī-líng-líng	10, 100
yíwàn-líng-yìbǎi-líng-yī	yī-líng-yī-líng-yī	10, 101
yíwàn-líng-yìbǎi-yīshí	yī-líng-yī-yī-líng	10, 110
yíwàn-yìqiān	yī-yī-líng-líng-líng	11, 000
yíwàn-líng-yī	yī-líng-líng-líng-yī	10, 001

[15] The fact that there are special words for square measure in both the metric and the native Chinese systems rules out ambiguity here: -fānglǐ corresponds to "square English mile".

[16] -dá is a phonetic borrowing into Chinese of the English word "dozen".

[17] "VS" stands for "verbal suffix", which is a form suffixed to a verb and forming with the verb a co-ordinate compound (see 1.11) in an "and" relationship, often extended to "with the result that, so that". Verbal suffixes are usually derived from verbs; -gei is derived from gěi "give".

[18] màigei is a co-ordinate compound, "sell and give", modified to "sell to". The word for the object sold need not appear in the sentence.

[19] Before a noun, méiyou may be shortened to méi.

[20] When they are used as adverbs, gòu and yígòng are fixed: they always occur in the comment before the main word of the comment and after any topic. Notice that often the corresponding English word or phrase comes after the English verb:

gòu cháng	long enough
búgòu cháng	not long enough
yígòng yào mǎi sānběn	want to buy three (books) in all

[21]The question words <u>duō</u>, <u>duó</u>, <u>duōma</u>, <u>duóma</u> are virtually inter-
changeable, their use depending on the preference of the speaker.
Notice again that these are fixed adverbs and always follow any topic.
In English, sometimes the corresponding expression precedes the topic:

Měiguo duó dà?   How large is America?

More notes on grammar

6.2 <u>Giving prices</u>. The maximum pattern for sentences that give
the price of an item or a group of items is one that has three
elements: (1) the item priced, (2) the price, and (3) the unit or
group that can be bought at that price. The minimum sentence is
just: (2) the price. (2) consists of a money expression, optionally
preceded by a verb; verbs introduced so far that may precede the
money expression here are <u>shi</u> "be", <u>mài</u> "sell for", and <u>yào</u> "(want:)
require". In <u>yíge</u> "apiece", the measure <u>-ge</u> has the fourth tone.

(Topic)	Comment./?	
	Topic	(Comment)./?
(Item priced)	Price	(per unit or group).
(Noun phrase)	(V) Money expression	
1. yǐzi	shi 'duōshao qián	(yìbǎ)?
	shi sānkuài wǔ	(yìbǎ).
2. zhuōzi	mài 'jǐshikuài	(yìzhāng)?
	mài èrshiduō	(yìzhāng).
3. biǎo,	yào 'duōshaokuài qián	(yígè)?
	yào qībǎiduō kuài	(yígè).
4. zhèixiē jiù shū,	'duōshao qián	(yìběn)?
	wǔmáo qián	(sānběn).
5. zhèijǐzhǐ bǐ,	'duōshao qián	(yìzhǐ)?
	wǔmáo qián	(yìdá).

English translations of the above:

1. How much apiece are the chairs?
   They're three fifty apiece.

2. How many tens of dollars each do the tables sell for?
   They sell for twenty dollars each.

3. How much apiece are watches?
   Seven hundred plus dollars apiece.

4. How much are these old books per volume?
   Fifty cents for three.

5. How much are these (few) pencils apiece?
   Fifty cents a dozen.

   6.3 Totals. The fixed adverb yígòng "altogether" appears
before an expression telling the total price, which may be optionally
preceded by a verb.

(Topic)	Comment./?
	Price
(Items)	yígòng (V) Money expression./?
1. zhèisānzhāng zhuōzi,	yígòng shi 'duōshao qián?
	yígòng shi jiŭshiwŭkuàiwŭ.
2. zhèijǐbǎ yǐzi,	yígòng mài 'jǐshikuài qián?
	yígòng mài sìshiduōkuài qián.
3. zhèiliǎngge biǎo,	yígòng yào 'duōshaokuài qián?
	yígòng yào qīqiānwŭ.
4. zhèixiē jiù shū,	yígòng, 'duōshao qián?
	yígòng, yíkuài qián.
5. zhèijǐzhī bǐ,	yígòng, 'duōshao qián?
	yígòng, liǎngmáo wŭ.

   yígòng can be used with other totals. The optional verb is yŏu
"have", for some sentences; for others, it is an optional shì or yŏu.

6. nimen xuéxiào,   yígòng (yǒu) 'duōshao xuésheng?

                             yígòng (yǒu) sānqiānduōge xuésheng.

7. nǐmen,   yígòng (shi/yǒu) 'duōshao rén?

    wǒmen   yígòng (shi/yǒu) 'sìge rén.

English translations of the above:

1. How much is it altogether for these three tables?

    Altogether, it's ninety-five fifty.

2. How many tens of dollars do these (few) chairs sell for altogether?

    They sell for forty-plus dollars, altogether.

3. How much all told for these two watches?

    Seventy-five hundred dollars, all told.

4. How much altogether for these old books?

    One dollar, altogether.

5. How much altogether for these (few) pens?

    Altogether, twenty-five cents.

6. How many students does your school have altogether?

    There are over three thousand students altogether.

7. How many are you, altogether?

    Altogether, we're four.

    6.4 mǎi <u>unit</u> <u>or</u> <u>group</u>. <u>mǎi</u> "buy" may appear before the expres-
sion that tells the unit which can be bought at a price.

'duōshaokuài qián mǎi yìzhāng?   How much money will pay for one?

'duōshaokuài qián yìzhāng?   How much apiece?

shí'yīkuài wǔ mǎi yìzhāng.   Eleven dollars and fifty cents will
                                       pay for one.

shi shí'yīkuài wǔ yìzhāng.   It's eleven dollars and fifty cents
                                       apiece.

    Notice: When <u>mǎi</u> does not occur before the unit or group, <u>shi</u>
(or <u>yào</u>) may appear before the money expression.

6.5 "Apiece", "per person", etc., in other contexts. "Distributional" sentences, telling how many, or what amount, of an item
is distributed (1) upon the outlay of what amount of money, or (2)
to how many people, are characterized by the fact that they optionally
include an appropriate verb. There are two word orders. In the first,
the price comes before the distributed item sānkuài wǔ (mǎi) yìzhāng.
yìzhāng. "Three-fifty apiece." In the second, the person or persons
to whom the items are distributed come before the items distributed:
yíge rén (yǒu) yìzhǐ, but notice that the English order is the oppo-
site of the Chinese: "One (pen) apiece.", "One (pen) per person."
Probably related to these distributional sentences is nǐ, liǎngběn;
tā, liǎngběn; wǒ, liǎngběn. "Two (books) for you, two for him, and
two for me", in Dialog VII, following the second word order. Thus:

bǐ, yíge rén, yìzhǐ.	One pen per person.
bǐ, yíge rén, 'jǐzhǐ?	How many pens per person?
yíge rén yǒu 'sānzhǐ.	Three apiece / per person.
shū, 'duōshao rén (kàn) yìběn?	One book (to be read by) how many people?
'sānge rén, yìběn.	One book for every three people.

Notice that the noun representing the item to be distributed
is lifted from its position after the NU-M expression to the topic
position.

6.6 Grand totals of items bought. The word order is:
first, the item or items bought, then the price for that item, or
for that number of items. The list concludes with the total amount
to be paid, preceded by yígòng. Thus, from Dialog V:

Item(s) bought	Price
yìzhǐ gāngbǐ,	yíkuài-líng-wǔfēn;
èrshizhǐ fěnbǐ,	sìmáo qián;
bàndá qiānbǐ,	qīmáowǔ. yígòng, liǎngkuài èr.

6.7 <u>Measurement</u>. Height, distance, and length are measured
by an expression of measurement, optionally preceded by yǒu and
optionally followed by stative verb. The question word duóma (duó,
duōma, duō), an adverb asking "to what extent?", replaces the NU-M
expression of measurement, and is obligatorily followed by the appropriate stative verb.

(Noun)	(yǒu)	NU-M /<u>duóma</u>	(SV)
1. zhèizuò shān,	(yǒu)	'jǐwànchǐ	(gāo)?
zhèizuò shān,	(yǒu)	liǎngwànduōchǐ	(gāo).
2. nèitiáo lù,	(yǒu)	'duóma	yuǎn?
	jiù yǒu	'bàn-Yīnglǐ	(yuǎn).
3. nèitiáo hé,	(yǒu)	'duóma	cháng?
	(yǒu)	yìqiānduōgōnglǐ	(cháng).
4. zhèige zhuōzi,	(yǒu)	'jǐchǐ	(cháng)?
	(yǒu)	qīchǐ bácùn	(cháng).

Notice that if there is an adverb, yǒu must be present.

English translations of the above:

1. How many tens of thousands of feet high is this mountain?
    This mountain is over twenty thousand feet high.
2. How far away is that road? / How far is it by that road?
    It's just half a mile away.
3. How long is that river?
    It's over a thousand kilometers long.
4. How many feet long is this table?
    It's seven feet eight inches long.

    There are concise forms of these expressions of measurements,
which resemble the corresponding forms of money expressions. Compare:

zhuōzi, shi qíkuài bāmáo qián.   The table is seven dollars and
                                       eighty cents.

zhuōzi, yǒu qīchǐ bácùn cháng.   The table is seven feet and eight
                                       inches long.

zhuōzi,   qíkuài bāmáo.

zhuōzi,   qīchǐ bácùn.

               qíkuài bā.

               qīchǐ bā.

6.8 Indefinite expressions of the type "two or three" occur in
Chinese, and their structure is like that of their English counter-
parts, except that there is no word corresponding to "or", and except
that the Chinese expression must end with a measure: NU_1-NU_2-M,
where NU_1 and NU_2 are different numbers, most often adjacent in the
number series (i.e. NU_2 equals NU_1 plus 1).

yì-liǎngge   one or two

liǎng-sānběn   two or three volumes

sān-sìzhāng   three or four sheets

liù-qībǎi   six or seven hundred

liù-qícùn   six or seven inches

qī-bāqiān   seven or eight thousand

qī-bácùn   seven or eight inches

shiyī-èrge   eleven or twelve

yìbǎiyīshiyī-èrge   one hundred eleven or twelve

     There seems to be no way to say "nine or ten" or "ten or eleven"
(or "one hundred ten or eleven" etc.), using this pattern. Instead,
shíduōge "ten plus" is used, and more likely means "ten plus a few
more" rather than "ten plus a fraction of an eleventh" (see above,
"New words", -duō).

     Chinese also has the variant NU_1-NU_3-M (where NU_3 equals NU_1
plus 2):

sān-wǔge   three or (four, or four or) five

6.9 <u>The imperative sentence</u> expresses a command or request to
the hearer that he do or be something, or that he assent to something that the speaker is planning to do or be. No special word or
intonation pattern is necessary to change a sentence with a first-
or second-person subject into an imperative. The particle <u>ba</u> may
be suffixed to a sentence with the declarative intonation pattern
to make a mild imperative. <u>'hǎo buhǎo?</u> added at the end of a sentence also has the effect of a mild imperative. Finally, <u>qǐng</u> at
the beginning of a second-person imperative sentence has the effect
of a polite imperative.

'wo mǎi shū.	I'm the one that's buying the books./ Let me be the one that buys the books.
'wǒ mǎi shū ba.	Let me be the one that buys the books, if you don't mind.
'wǒ mǎi shū, 'hǎo buhǎo?	How about if I be the one that buys the books?
ni gěi wǒ zhèige.	You'll be giving me this one./ You give me this one.
gěi wǒ zhèige.	(You'll) be giving me this one./ Give me this one.
gěi wǒ zhèige ba.	Give me this one, if you don't mind.
gěi wǒ zhèige, 'hǎo buhǎo?	How about giving me this one?
qǐng nǐ gěi wǒ zhèige.	Please give me this one.
qǐng nǐ gěi wǒ zhèige ba.	Please give me this one, if you don't mind.
qǐng nǐ gěi wǒ zhèige, 'hǎo buhǎo?	Please give me this one, OK?

6.10 <u>Quasi-quotes</u>. In Dialog III, third sentence, there is
the question <u>shi 'Yǐnglǐ, shi 'gōnglǐ?</u> "Is that in miles or kilometers?" and the last sentence consists of the reply: <u>búshi 'Yǐnglǐ,</u>

yě búshi 'gōnglǐ; shi 'fānglǐ. "It's not in English miles, nor is
it kilometers; it's square (English) miles." In these sentences,
measures appear with no preceding specifier or measure, because
they are lifted out of context in a kind of quotation, unmarked by
the presence of a word like "say" or "mean": "Do you mean 'English
miles', or do you mean 'kilometers'?" becomes simply "Is it 'miles'
or 'kilometers'?"

   6.11 xiǎng, "think" is like shuō and zhīdao in that it may
take a whole sentence as its object. See above, 5.7.

ta shuō ta méiyou qián.	He says he has no money.
wo bùzhidào ta yǒu 'qián meiyǒu.	I don't know whether he has any money.
wo xiǎng ta yǒu qián.	I think he has money.
wo xiǎng ta bùzhidào.	I don't think he knows.
wo xiǎng liǎngkuàibàn yìběn búguì.	I don't think two and a half dollars a volume is expensive.
wo xiǎng nèi yíbàn, yě búshi Rìběn zhǐ.	I don't think that half is Japanese paper either.

   Notice the difference in the placement of the negative in the
English.

   xiǎng is also like yào in that it may take another verb plus
any object of that other verb as its own object. See above, Lesson
4, "New words", note 9. Here xiǎng means "have it in mind to, intend
to".

ta yào mǎi shū.	He wants to buy some books.
ta xiǎng mǎi shū.	He intends to buy some books.
ta xiǎng gěi wǒ zhèige.	He intends to give me this one.
ni bùxiǎng kàn shū ma?	Don't you intend to read?
wo bùxiǎng màigei ni.	I don't intend to sell it to you.

   6.12 The pivot after yǒu/méiyou. Like qǐng (3.7) and wèn
(Lesson 5, "New words", note 12), yǒu and méiyou may take an object

which is at the same time the topic of a following embedded sentence.
This pivot (3.6) may be the subject of the following sentence:

yǒu yige xuésheng yǒu qián.   There is a student who has money.

yǒu jiǔwèi xiānsheng, xìng LǏ.   There are nine teachers surnamed
                                     Lee.

yǒu 'duōshao rén, meiyou   How many people are there who have
  míngzi?   no given names?

Or it may be the (transposed) object of the following sentence:

yǒu jǐge rén, ta bùxǐhuan.   There are a few people he doesn't
                                     like.

yǒu yíbàn, tamen bùdǒng.   There is a half that they don't
                                     understand. / They don't under-
                                     stand half of it.

    <u>yǒu</u> <u>rén</u> "there is a person who..." may be translated "some one,
some". <u>méiyou</u> <u>rén</u> (which may be shortened to <u>méiren</u>) "there is no
person who" may be translated "no one, nobody".

yǒu rén shuō, ni búshi hǎo   There is a person who / Someone says
  xuésheng.   you're not a good student.

yǒu rén wèn wǒ, ni dǒng   Someone asked me how much you under-
  duōshao?   stood.

méiren méiyou péngyou.   There is no one who has no friends./
                                     Everyone has friends.

méiyou rén bùdǒng.   Everybody understands.

méiren dǒng ma?   Does no one understand? / Doesn't
                                     anyone understand?

yǒu rén bùdǒng ma?   Is there anyone who does not under-
                                     stand?

méiyou rén zhǐdao, ta yào   Doesn't anyone know how many (books)
  'jǐběn ma?   he wants?

Pyramid drills

búgòu.

sānkuàiwǔ búgòu.

sānkuàiwǔmáo búgòu.

sānkuàiwǔmáo qián búgòu.

zhuōzi, sānkuàiwǔmáo qián búgòu.

zhèixiē zhuōzi, sānkuàiwǔmáo qián búgòu.

zhèixiēzhāng zhuōzi, sānkuàiwǔmáo qián búgòu.

zhèixiēzhāng xīn zhuōzi, sānkuàiwǔmáo qián búgòu.

'jǐcùn cháng?

yícùn cháng.

yǒu yícùn cháng.

'jǐchǐ 'jǐcùn cháng?

yìchǐ yícùn cháng.

yǒu yìchǐ yícùn cháng.

huàr, yǒu yìchǐ yícùn cháng.

huàr, jiù yǒu yìchǐ yícùn cháng.

zhèizhāng huàr, jiù yǒu yìchǐ yícùn cháng.

zhèizhāng Zhōngguo huàr, jiù yǒu yìchǐ yícùn chang.

Exercise

Translate into Chinese:

1. The number is two-oh-two, five-eight-seven, four-oh-oh-eight.

2. I'm thinking of buying a hundred plus pieces of chalk.

3. How many thousand feet high do you think it is?

4. How many thousand feet high do you think that mountain is?

5. Three dozen small tables at three dollars a table comes to only
   a hundred and eight dollars.

6. What's the price per watch? A hundred and fifteen dollars apiece.

7. forty million French people

8.   No one will sell it to me.

9.   two thousand and one

10.   twenty thousand and one hundred

11.   a little over two square miles

12.   this table

13.   these tables

Lesson 7
Eating, drinking, and cooking

Pronunciation

New words introduced in this lesson are grouped according to
medial condition (6.1.2) and listed with selected old words.

Plain:

a: bā; dà; là "peppery", kāfēi "coffee"; chá "tea".

e: Déguo; hē "drink"; hé; zhè; Èguo.

i: zhīdao; chī "eat"; yìchǐ; shì; shìqing "business"; Rìběn; Sītú.

ai: yìbǎi; mǎimai "trade"; tài; háizi; zài "again"; cài "dish of
food"; ài "love".

ei: yìbēi "one cup"; kāfēi "coffee"; něige; gěi; zhèige.

ao: bào; gāo; gàosong "inform"; hǎochī "tasty"; Zhào; zǎo.

ou: dōu; gòu; ròu "meat".

an: yíbàn; fàn "food"; nánháizi; kàn; shān; sān.

en: yìběn; fěnbǐ; hěn; Chén; chénzi "an orange"; rén.

ang: mǎng; tāng "soup"; táng "sugar"; gāngbǐ; cháng.

eng: péngyou; néng "be able to"; Zhèng.

ar: yíbàr; xiǎohár.

er: èr.

aor: yìsháor "one spoonful".

our: (none yet)

Frontalized:

ia: Jiānádà.

ie: yìxiē; yě.

i: bǐ; píjiǔ "beer"; nǐ; qī; qìshuǐ "soda pop"; xǐhuan; yī.

117

iao: biǎo; yìtiáo; jiào; xiǎo; yào.

iu: liù; jiǔ₁; jiǔ₂ "wine"; yǒu.

ian: piányi; yìdiǎn "a little"; tián "sweet"; qián; xiānsheng.

in: nín; jìn; xīn.

iang: liǎngge; Jiāng; xiǎng.

ing: yìpíng "one bottle"; píngguo "apple"; míngzi; líng; qīngcài
      "vegetables"; qǐng; xìng; Yīngguo.

iar: yìdiǎr "a bit".

ier: (none yet)

Labialized:

ua: huà.

uo: duō; guó; shuǐguǒ "fruit"; shuō; yízuò; zuò "make"; búcuò "not
     bad"; wǒ.

u: bù; lù; shū; wǔ.

uai: yíkuài.

ui: duìbuqǐ "excuse me"; guì; huì "know how to"; shuǐ "water";
     shuǐguǒ "fruit"; yíwèi.

uan: suān "sour"; méiyou guānxi "it doesn't matter"; yìwǎn "one
      bowl"; yíwàn.

un: yícùn; wèn.

uang: Huáng; Wáng.

ong: dǒng; Zhōngguo; róngyi "easy".

uar: huàr.

uor: (none yet)

uer: qìshuěr "soda pop"

ur: (none yet)

Frontalized and labialized:

ue: xuéxiào; xuésheng.

ü: nǚháizi; júzi "an orange ".

uan: yuǎn; yuànyi "want to".

un: (none yet)

Dialogs

I

A: nín hē shémma? hē diar jiǔ ba.	What will you have to drink? How about some wine?
B: xièxie; wo jiù xiǎng hē diar shuǐ.	Thanks, but I'll just have some water.
A: nín bùhē kāfēi ma?	Won't you have some coffee?
B: xièxie. gěi wǒ yìbēi shuǐ ba.	Thanks, but just give me a glass of water.
A: nín tàitai ne?	And what about your wife?
B: ta xǐhuan hē chá.	She'd like to have some tea.
A: háizimen ne?	And what about the children?
B: tamen dōu ài hē qìshuǐ.	They're all fond of soda pop.
A: nín neiwei péngyou ne?	How about your friend?
B: ta xǐhuan hē kāfēi.	He likes coffee.
A: yào 'táng buyào?	Does he take sugar?
B: wo bùzhidào; wo wènwen ta, zài gàosong ni. ... ta gàosong wǒ, ta yào 'liǎngsháor.	I'm not sure; I'll ask him and (then) let you know. ... He tells me he wants two spoonsful.
A: hǎo. méiren hē píjiǔ ma? Zhāng Xs, nín yě bùhē píjiǔ ma?	OK. Doesn't anybody want some beer? Mr. Chang, won't you have any beer either?
C: hǎo; wo hē diar píjiǔ.	All right; I'll have some beer.

II

A: ni chī diǎr ròu ba. — Have some meat.

B: wo bùchī ròu, jiù chī qīngcài. — I don't eat meat, just vegetables.

A: ni chī shuǐguǒ ma? — Do you eat fruit?

B: wo chī. — Yes.

A: ni chī 'shémma shuǐguǒ? — What kind of fruit do you eat?

B: wo ài chī píngguo, yě ài chī júzi. — I'm fond of apples, and I'm fond of oranges, too.

A: wǒ yě ài chī júzi. zhèige júzi 'suān busuān? — I love to eat oranges, too. Is this orange sour?

B: wǒ xiǎng, zhèige júzi bùsuān; hěn tián, hěn hǎochī. — I don't think this orange is sour; I think it's sweet and tasty.

III

A: shéi huì zuò Zhōngguo fàn? — Who knows how to cook Chinese food?

B: 'wǒ búhuì; 'tā huì. — I don't but he does.

A: nǐ huì zuò Zhōngguo fàn ma? — Do you know how to cook Chinese food?

C: wo huì zuò yìdiǎr. — Yes, a little.

A: ni huì zuò shémma? — What can you make?

C: wo jiù huì zuò yíge cài. yíge tāng. — All I can make is one dish and one soup.

A: dōu jiào shémma? — What are they called?

C: cài jiào 'tiánsuānròu; tāng jiào 'suānlàtāng. — The dish is called "sweet and sour pork"; the soup is called "hot and sour soup".

A: women dōu xǐhuan chī 'tiánsuānròu, keshi bùxǐhuan hē 'suānlàtāng. suānlàtāng tài là. — We all like to eat sweet and sour pork but not hot and sour soup. Hot and sour soup is too hot.

IV

A: ta néng zuò neige shì ma?   Can he do that job?

B: neige shìqing hěn róngyi.   That job is easy. He can do it.

   ta néng zuò. kěshi wo bùzhidào,   But I don't know whether he wants
   ta 'yuànyi buyuànyi zuò.   to do it.

A: ta shuō ta yuànyi zuò   He says he wants to go into trade.
   mǎimai, 'shi bushì?   Is that so?

B: shì. wǒ xiǎng zuò mǎimai   Yes. I think going into trade is
   yě búcuò. nǐ shuō ne?   pretty good, too. What do you
                                      say?

A: zuò mǎimai hěn búcuò.   It's not bad at all.

V

A: duìbuqǐ; wǒ méiyou gāngbǐ.   I'm sorry; I don't have a pen.

B: méiyou guānxi; 'qiānbǐ yě   It doesn't matter; pencils are OK
   xíng.   too.

New words

yìdiǎr, yìdiǎn, diar, dian N[1]	a little, a bit of; some
dǒng yìdiǎr.	I understand a little.
kàn (yi)diar shū	read a bit
jiǔ N	wine, liquor, alcoholic beverage
píjiǔ N[2]	beer
shuǐ N	water
qìshuǐ, qìshuěr N	(gas water:) carbonated soft drink, soda pop
kāfēi N[3]	coffee
chá N	tea
táng N	sugar; candy
ròu N	meat; pork
qīngcài N	(green vegetable:) vegetable
mǎi diar qīngcài	buy some vegetables

shuǐguǒ N	(water fruit:) fruit
pḯngguo N	apple
júzi N[4]	orange
chénzi N[4]	orange
fàn N	cooked rice; food; meal
cài N	vegetable; dish (of food)
tāng N	soup
háizimen N[5]	children
xiānshengmen N	teachers; gentlemen
xuéshengmen N	students
tàitaimen N	ladies
xiǎojiemen N	young ladies
shì, shìqing N[6]	job
mǎimai N	business, trade
-bēi M[7]	cup, glass
mǎi (yì)bēi jiǔ	buy a glass of wine
jiù xiǎng mǎi yìbēi.	I only intend to buy one cup.
-kuài M	dollar (6); piece
qǐng nǐ gěi wǒ (yi)kuài táng.	Please give me a piece of candy.
wo búyào nèikuài.	I don't want that piece.
ni yào mǎi 'jǐkuài?	How many pieces do you want to buy?
-sháor M[7]	spoonful
liǎngsháor táng, 'gòu bugòu?	Will two spoonsful of sugar be enough?
-wǎn M[7]	bowl
yìwǎn fàn	one bowl of (cooked) rice
liǎngwǎn tāng	two bowls of soup
-pǐng M[7]	bottle
yìbǎiyìshièrpǐng pǐjiǔ.	a hundred and twelve bottles of beer
suān SV	sour
júzi hěn suān.	The oranges are sour.

là SV

  tāng hěn là.

  suānlàtāng N

tián SV

  kāfēi búgòu tián.

  tiánsuānròu N

hǎochī SV

  zhèige cài, hěn hǎochī.

róngyi SV

  kàn Yīngwén shū, hěn róngyi.

búcuò SV

  zhèige cài, hěn búcuò.

xǐhuan AV [8]

ài AV [8, 9]

  ta hěn ài mǎi shū.

huì AV [8, 10]

  wǒ búhuì shuō Zhōngguo huà.

néng AV [8, 10]

  wǒ méiyou qián; wo bùnéng

  gěi nǐ qián.

yuànyi AV [8, 11]

  ta 'néng gěi wǒ qián, keshi

  bú'yuànyi gěi wǒ qián.

zài A [12]

  zài shuō.

  zài shuō yìdiǎr.

  wo wènwen ta, zài gàosong ni.

hē V

  hē jiǔ VO [13]

peppery; hot

  The soup is peppery.

  hot and sour soup

sweet

  The coffee isn't sweet enough.

  sweet and sour pork

(good to eat:) tasty

  This dish is very tasty. / This
    is a very tasty dish.

easy

  It's easy to read books in
    English.

(not wrong:) not bad, pretty good

  This dish is pretty good. / This
    is a pretty good dish.

like to

love to, be fond of

  He's fond of buying books.

know how to, can

  I don't know how to speak Chinese.

be able to, can

  I have no money; I can't give
    you any money.

want to

  He can give me money, but he
    doesn't want to give me money.

again, then (in the future)

  Say it again.

  Say a bit more.

  I'll ask him and then let you
    know.

drink, have (...to drink)

  drink (liquor)

ta hē jiǔ.	He drinks.
zài hē diar kāfēi.	Have some more coffee.
wo xiǎng zài hē yìwǎn tāng.	I think I'll have another bowl of soup.
chī V	eat, have (... to eat)
chī fàn VO [13]	have a meal, eat
chī fàn, chī fàn!	Let's begin eating.
zài chī yikuai ròu, 'hao buhǎo?	How about having another piece of meat?
zuò V	do
zuò fàn VO [13]	cook (a meal); cook rice
ta hěn huì zuò fàn.	He cooks very well.
zuò cài VO [13]	prepare a dish
wo zài zuò ge cài ba.	Let me prepare another dish.
zuò shì VO [13]	work
zuò mǎimai VO [13]	be in business
gàosong, gàosu V [14]	inform, tell
wo búyào gàosong ta.	I don't want to tell him.
ta gàosong wǒ, ta búyuànyi mài neisānběn shū.	He tells me that he doesn't want to sell the three books.
'shì bushì? IE	Is that so?
shì. IE	It is so. / Yes.
duìbuqǐ. IE [15]	Excuse me.
méiyou guānxi. IE [16]	Never mind.

Notes

[1] yìdiǎr (or yìdiǎn) is a NU-M construction: yī "one" and diǎr (or diǎn) "spot, dot". Like other such constructions, it can be reduced to a neutral-tone syllable diar (or dian) between a verb and its object (see Lesson 6, "New words," note 13).

[2] píjiǔ "pí liquor": pí is a sound borrowing from a European language, perhaps German Bier "beer", if not the English word.

[3]kāfēi (also jiāfēi; cf. Jiānádà, and see Lesson 5, "New words,"
note 6) is another sound borrowing, perhaps from French café "coffee".
[4]júzi and chénzi are both loosely used to refer to the fruit
"orange". júzi seems to be the standard form, though many prefer
chénzi, or other terms.
[5]-men is added to certain nouns denoting human beings to
indicate non-specific plurality. When the plural number is pre-
cisely indicated (or asked about) it is not used.

tamen yǒu sānge háizi.	They have three children.
nǐmen yǒu 'jǐge háizi?	How many children do you have?
háizimen dōu ài hē qìshuǐ.	The children all like soda.
ta gěi háizimen yíge rén	He gave the children a dollar
yíkuài qián.	each.

[6]shì occurs in the VO combination zuò shì "work, have a job".
shì and shìqing each take -ge as their measure.
[7]-bēi, -sháor, -wǎn, and -píng are all measures which differ
from -ge, -zhāng, -zhī, etc., in that they add meaning to the noun
phrase in which they occur, namely, they indicate the specific
quantities in which the noun is being measured:

liǎngbēi shuǐ	two cups / glasses of water
liǎngsháor shuǐ	two spoonsful of water
liǎngwǎn shuǐ ·	two bowls of water
liǎngpíng shuǐ	two bottles of water

Unlike the English translations (with "of" phrases modifying
the nouns), the NU-M phrases in Chinese modify the following nouns,
in the usual modifier-modified order.

These measures have free nouns corresponding to them: bēizi
"cup, glass"; sháor "spoon"; wǎn "bowl"; and píngzi "bottle".
[8]AV-V expressions with xǐhuan, ài, huì, néng, and yuànyi may
be preceded by hěn:

wǒ hěn xǐhuan hē kāfēi.   I like coffee (a lot).

ta hěn ài kàn shū.   He likes to read (very much).

ta hěn huì shuō Zhōngguo huà.   He knows how to speak Chinese very
                                       well.

ta hěn yuànyi gěi wǒ qián.   He very much wants to give me money.

ta hěn néng mài shū.   He very much has the capability
                                       to sell books.

[9]ài as an auxiliary verb is more frequently used, and hence
weaker in meaning, than the English "love to".

[10]Both huì and néng may be translated by the English auxiliary
"can", but in this meaning, huì implies knowledge equal to the demands
of the task of performing the action of the verb, whereas néng implies
physical ability equal to such demands.

[11]yuànyi is like yào in that it implies a desire to perform the
action of the verb; but yuànyi is restricted to that meaning. See,
for example, Lesson 6 for another meaning of yào.

[12]The fixed adverb zài is used in commands, suggestions, expressions of intent, and the like, before a verbal expression that denotes
an action that will happen another time in the future ("again") or
that will happen after another action in the future ("then"). It
occurs with simple or reduplicated verbs (reduplication is frequent
here):

zài shuō ba.   Say it again.

zài wènwen ta.   Ask him again.

It also occurs with a verb followed by a noun phrase that includes a
measure, or by a lone measure:

wo xiǎng zài hē yǐwǎn tāng.   I think I'll have another bowl of
                                      soup.

zài chī yíkuài ròu, 'hǎo buhǎo? How about having another piece of
                                      meat?

qǐng nǐ zài gěi wǒ liǎngshǎor táng.	Please give me two more spoonsful of sugar.
zài hē diar kāfēi.	Have some more coffee.
zài hē diar ba.	Have some more (to drink).
wǒ zài zuò ge cài ba.	Let me prepare another dish.

It occurs in the second of two verb phrases, where it introduces subsequent future action:

wo wènwen ta, zài gàosong ni.	I'll ask him and (then) let you know.
women hē diar jiǔ, zài chī fàn ba.	Let's have something to drink and then eat.

[13]Certain Chinese VO expressions are translated in English by a simple verb or verbal expression, with no object expressed. Compare the following:

ta xǐhuan kàn shū.	He likes to read.
ta xǐhuan kàn Zhōngguo shū.	He likes to read Chinese books.
ta xǐhuan shuō huà.	He likes to talk.
ta xǐhuan shuō Zhōngguo huà.	He likes to speak Chinese.
ta xǐhuan zuò fàn.	He likes to cook.
ta xǐhuan zuò Zhōngguo fàn.	He likes to cook Chinese food.
ta xǐhuan hē jiǔ.	He likes to drink.
ta xǐhuan hē Zhōngguo jiǔ.	He likes to drink Chinese wine.
ta xǐhuan zuò shì.	He likes to work.
ta xǐhuan zuò neige shì.	He likes to do that job.
ta xǐhuan zuò mǎimai.	He likes to be in business.
ta xǐhuan zuò neige mǎimai.	He likes to work in that business.
wǒ gěi qián.	I'll pay.
wǒ gěi 'Měiguo qián.	I'll pay in American money.

In such cases, it is important to remember that in Chinese the object

is usually present, even though in English it is absent. There is no
problem when the object is present in the corresponding English
version, as in the following sentences:

ta xǐhuan kàn bào.	He likes (to read) newspapers.
ta xǐhuan chī fàn	He likes (to eat) rice.
ta xǐhuan chī táng.	He likes (to eat) candy.
ta xǐhuan hē tāng.	He likes (to drink) soup.
ta xǐhuan hē chá.	He likes (to drink) tea.
ta xǐhuan hē shuǐ.	He likes (to drink) water.
ta xǐhuan hē qìshuǐ.	He likes (to drink) soda pop.
ta xǐhuan hē píjiǔ.	He likes (to drink) beer.
ta xǐhuan zuò cài.	He likes to prepare dishes.

[14]Like wèn, gàosong (or gàosu) takes two objects, the first
of which is obligatory and the second optional. The first object
names the person to whom the statement is made, and the second
object gives the statement.

wo wèn ta, 'něige hǎo?	I'll ask him which is better.
ta gàosong wo, 'zhèige hǎo.	He tells me this one is better.
ni gàosong ta shémma?	What will you tell him?
wo gàosong ta, wo méiyǒu.	I'm telling him I don't have any.
wo gàosong ta, yǒude dà, yǒude xiǎo.	I'm telling him that some are large and some are small.
ta búgàosong wo, ta yào něige?	He isn't telling me which one he wants.
ta búgàosong wǒ, nǐ shì shéi?	He isn't telling me / He hasn't told me who you are.
qǐng nǐ gàosong wo, zhèige shi shémma?	Please tell me what this is.

[15]duìbuqǐ is literally "(I) can't face up (to you)", which means
something like "I cannot summon up the dignity to face you in my
embarrassment over what I have done,", or, more simply, "Excuse me."
It may be preceded by hěn: hěn duìbuqǐ "I'm very sorry."
[16]méiyou guānxi is literally "It has no (important) implications."
and is a common response to duìbuqǐ.

More notes on grammar

7.1 Review of auxiliary verbs (see Lesson 4, "New words", note 8).
In an AV-V(-O) expression, it is important to remember that the main
word is the AV: it is the auxiliary verb that normally takes the
negative prefix; it is the auxiliary verb that is repeated with bu-
in choice-type questions.

ta néng kàn Déguo shū ma?	Can he read German?
ta néng kàn Déguo 'shū bunéng?	
ta 'néng bunéng kàn Déguo shū?	
ta 'hěn néng kàn Déguo shū.	Yes, he can very well.
Cáo Tt xǐhuan zuò Fàguo cài ma?	Does Mrs. Ts'ao like to cook French food?
Cáo Tt xǐhuan zuò Fàguo 'cài buxǐhuan?	
Cáo Tt 'xǐhuan buxǐhuan zuò Fàguo cài?	
ta hěn xǐhuan.	Yes, very much.
háizimen ài hē Měiguo qìshuǐ ma?	Are the children fond of American soda pop?
háizimen ài hē Měiguo qì'shuǐ buài?	
háizimen 'ài buài hē Měiguo qìshuǐ?	
tamen hěn ài hē.	Yes.

7.2 <u>Review of verbs that take sentences as objects</u>. The main
difference between auxiliary verbs and verbs that take sentences as
objects is that a noun never occurs between an auxiliary verb and
the verb that follows it, whereas a noun regularly occurs as the
first element in the sentence that is the object of a verb. <u>xiǎng</u>
has functions both as an auxiliary verb and as a verb that takes a
sentence as its object, with a slight difference in meaning: as an
auxiliary verb it means "have it in mind to, intend to"; as a verb
with a sentence object it means "think (that)" (6.11).

wǒ xiǎng mài shū.	I intend to sell some books.
wǒ xiǎng ta mài shū.	I think he sells books.

Verbs that take sentences as objects are, so far: <u>qǐng</u> (3.6-7),
<u>shuō</u> and <u>zhīdao</u> (5.7), <u>wèn</u> (Lesson 5, "New words," note 12, and 5.10),
<u>xiǎng</u> (6.11) and <u>gàosong</u> (<u>gàosu</u>). Of these, <u>qǐng</u> and <u>wèn</u> take a
pivot (3.6; the underlined words are the pivots in the sentences
below):

wǒ qǐng <u>ta</u> zuò fàn.	I'm asking him to cook.
wǒ qǐng <u>tā</u> chī fan.	I'm inviting him to a meal.
qǐng <u>nǐ</u> zài shuō yìdiǎr.	Please say a bit more.
wo wèn <u>ta</u> zuò fàn ma?	I'm asking him if he cooks.
wo wèn, <u>ta</u> 'huì buhuì zuò fàn?	I'm asking him if he knows how to cook.
wo wèn, <u>ta</u> qǐng shéi?	I'm asking him whom he's inviting.

<u>shuō</u>, <u>zhīdao</u>, <u>wèn</u> (again), <u>xiǎng</u>, and <u>gàosong</u> may all be fol-
lowed by sentences, the subject of which is not also the object of
<u>shuō</u>, etc., and hence is not a pivot.

ta shuō, ta búhuì hē jiǔ.	He says he doesn't (know how to) drink (liquor).
nǐ shuō, 'něige cài hǎochī?	Which dish would you say is tastiest?

wo bùzhidào, 'nĕige cài hǎochī.	I don't know which dish is tastiest.
wo jiù zhīdao, Zhōngguo cài hĕn hǎochī.	I only know that Chinese food is very tasty.
wo wèn ta, shéi huì zuò Èguo cài?	I'm asking him who can cook Russian dishes.
wǒ xiǎng ta bùxǐhuan hē Zhōngguo jiǔ.	I don't think he likes (to drink) Chinese wine. (Notice the different placement of the English word "not" from that of bù-.)
nǐ xiǎng ta yuànyi qǐng wǒ ma?	Do you think she wants to invite me?
ta gàosong wo, ni bùhĕn xǐhuan hē chá.	He tells me that you don't much like (to drink) tea.
nǐ xiǎng 'nĕige cài hǎochī?	Which dish you think is tastiest?
qǐng nǐ gàosong wo.	Please tell me.
wo gàosong ni, zhèixiē cài, dōu bùhĕn hǎochī.	Let me tell you, none of these dishes are particularly tasty.

Pyramid drills

zuò mǎimai.

yuànyi zuò mǎimai.

yuànyi zuò shì, yuànyi zuò mǎimai?

ni yuànyi zuò shì, yuànyi zuò mǎimai?

ni gàosong wǒ, ni yuànyi zuò shì, yuànyi zuò mǎimai?

zuò shì yě búcuò, kěshi wo yuànyi zuò mǎimai.

hĕn róngyi.

zuò tāng, hĕn róngyi.

zuò tāng, bùhĕn róngyi.

zuò Zhōngguo tāng, bùhĕn róngyi.

zuò suānlàtāng, bùhĕn róngyi.

zuò suānlàtāng, hĕn róngyi ma?

zuò tiánsuānròu, hĕn róngyi ma?

zuò suānlàtāng róngyi, zuò tiánsuānròu róngyi?

zuò tiánsuānròu róngyi.

                                              hěn suān.
                                   píngguo hěn suān.
                        zheige píngguo hěn suān.
                        zheige píngguo hěn suān ma?
                           zheige júzi hěn suān ma?
                 'júzi suān, 'píngguo suān?
                              'júzi suān.

Exercises

    Answer the questions below as follows: first, simply answer the
question; then repeat the answer, adding an auxiliary verb (and a
few other words, as appropriate).

Example:

ni hē kāfēi ma?   wo hē kāfēi. wǒ hěn xǐhuan hē
                                        kāfēi.

ni 'zuò buzuò Zhōngguo cài?
ni chī 'shuǐguǒ buchī?
ni zuò shì ma?
ni mài ni neiběn shū ma?
nèiběn shū, ni màigei wǒ ma?
ni qǐng ta chī fàn ma?
ni mǎi qīngcài ma?
ni 'hē buhē suānlàtāng?
ni hē Měiguo qìshuǐ ma?
ni chī 'něiguo cài?
ni chī 'shémma cài?
ni zuò 'shémma cài?

Make questions to which the following would be appropriate answers:

tiánsuān'ròu hǎochī.

wǒ bùxiǎng gàosong ta.

wǒ xiǎng ta bùhuì.

ta gěi wǒ qī-bǎkuài qián.

bùxíng; wǔkuài qián búgòu mǎi nèikuài ròu.

bùdōu xǐhuan hē; wo jiù xǐhuan hē kāfēi.

hǎo; wo zài hē yìbēi.

hǎo; wo zài gěi nǐ liǎngshǎor.

wo bùzhīdào. wo wènwen ta, zài gàosong ni.

yígòng xiǎng hē sānpíng.

háizimen dōu hěn ài hē.

Translate into Chinese.

1.   I don't think he can cook.
2.   Which are tastier, the apples or the oranges? — The oranges are.
3.   Have another cup of tea. — Fine, please give me another cup.
4.   Do the children all have some money? — Not all of them; some do
     and some don't.
5.   How much is beer per bottle? — It's a dollar five per bottle.
6.   Is the soup too peppery? — No; it's just right.
7.   I'm sorry, I want to buy it but I can't; I haven't any money. —
     Never mind; I'll pay for it.
8.   Do all the ladies want sugar? — Yes, they all do. They all want
     one spoonful of sugar.
9.   Please let me know if you want to read another book.
10. This is a good dish.
11. I don't like tea much.

Modification of nouns; stative verbs as fixed adverbs

Pronunciation

<u>Plain</u>:

a: bǎ; dǎ "hit"; dà; kāfēi; chá.

e: Déguo; gēge "elder brother"; kéyi "can"; hé; zhè; Èguo.

i: shìqing; zì "written character"; sì.

ai: mài; tài; háizi; zài; cài; ài.

ei: méiyou; měi "beautiful"; mèimei "younger sister"; děi "have to"; nèige; gěi; zhèige.

ao: yìmáo; lǎoshī "teacher"; hǎo; Zhào; zǎo.

ou: dōu; gòu; Měizhōu "America"; ròu.

an: bàn; nánháizi; nán "difficult"; lánqiú "basketball"; Hánguo; shān; sān.

en: yìfēn; fěnbǐ; yìfèn "one number (of a newspaper)"; nèmma "in that way"; hěn; zhēn; zhèmma "in this way"; Chén "Ch'en (a surname)" rén; rènshi "be acquainted with"; zěmma? "how?".

ang: bàngqiú "baseball"; máng; táng; gāngbǐ; yìzhāng.

eng: péngyou; néng; zhèng hǎo.

ar: yìbàr; xiǎohár.

er: yìfèr "one number (of a newspaper)"; zèr "written character"; èr.

aor: yìshǎor.

our: (none yet)

<u>Frontalized</u>:

ia: Jiānádà.

ie: jiějie "older sister"; jièshao "introduce"; yìxiē; xiě "write"; xièxie; yě.

i: bǐ; dìdi "younger brother"; nǐ; qī; yī; yìsi "meaning".

iao: biǎo; yìtiáo; jiāo "teach"; jiào; yào.

iu: liù; jiǔ; jiù; qiú "ball"; yǒude.

ian: piányi; tián; qián.

in: nín; xīn.

iang: liǎngge; Jiǎng.

ing: píng; píngguo; Xiǎopíng "(proper name)"; líng; qīngcài; Yīngguo.

iar: yìdiǎr.

ier: (none yet)

iaor: (none yet)

iur: qiúr "ball".

Labialized:

ua: huà.

uo: duōshao; Guóxīn; zhuōzi; zuò; wǒ.

u: bù; mǔqin "mother"; fùqin "father"; lù; shū; wǔ.

uai: yíkuài.

ui: búduì "wrong"; duìbuqǐ; huì; shuǐ; yíwèi; wèishemma "why?"

uan: suān; yìwǎn.

un: yícùn; wèn.

uang: Huáng; Wáng; wǎngqiú "tennis".

ong: tóngxué; yìgōnglǐ; róngyi.

Frontalized and labialized:

ue: xué "study"; xuéxiào.

ü: nǚháizi; júzi.

uan: yuànyi.

un: (none yet)

iong: xiōngdì "brothers".

Dialogs

I

A: Zhāng Xs hǎo?	How are you, Mr. Chang?
B: 'hǎo, hǎo. nimen dōu hǎo ma?	Fine. How are you all?
A: women dōu hěn hǎo. nimen yě dōu hěn hǎo ma?	We're all fine. You're all well, too?
B: women yě dōu hěn hǎo.	Yes, we're all fine.
A: ni fùqin, ta zuò shì ma?	Is your father working?
B: wo fùqin zuò shì. wo mǔqin yě zuò shì. tamen dōu hěn máng.	Yes, my father's working, and so is my mother. They're both very busy.
A: ni xiōngdì jiěmèi-men, tamen dōu hěn hǎo ma?	Your brothers and sisters--they're all fine?
B: tamen dōu hěn hǎo, xièxie.	Yes, thank you.

II

Gāo: ni rènshi neiliǎngge rén ma?	Do you know those two people?
Chén: wo rènshi neige nǚde; bùrènshi neige nánde. neige nǚde shi wǒde tóngxué, Zhāng Měishēng...	I know the woman; I don't know the man. The woman is a fellow student, Mei-sheng Chang...
Chén: Měishēng, nǐ hǎo?	Hello, Mei-sheng.
Zhāng MS: hǎo. nǐ hǎo?	Hello, how are you?
Chén: 'hǎo, hǎo. wo gěi nǐmen liǎngwèi jièshaojieshao. zhèiwei shi Gāo Xs; zhèiwei shi Zhāng Xj.	Fine. Let me introduce you two. This is Mr. Kao; this is Miss Chang.
Zhāng MS: Chén Xj, Gāo Xs, zhè shi wǒ gēge, Zhāng Guóxīn.	Miss Ch'en, Mr. Kao, this is my (older) brother, Kuo-hsin Chang.

Zhāng GX: Chén Xj, ni fùqin   Miss Ch'en, is your father Hsiao-
  'shì bushì Chén Xiǎopíng?   p'ing Ch'en?

Chén: shì.   Yes.

Zhāng GX: Chén Xs shi wǒ   Mr. Ch'en is my teacher. My
  lǎoshī. wo dìdi yě shi Chén   (younger) brother is also a
  Lǎoshī de xuésheng. women   student of Mr. Ch'en's. We both
  dōu hěn xǐhuan Chén Lǎoshī.   like Mr. Ch'en a lot. He really
  ta zhēn huì jiāo shū.   knows how to teach.

III

A: Zhōngguo huà hěn nánxué ma?   Is Chinese hard to learn?

B: Zhōngguo huà hěn róngyi   The language is easy, but it's hard
  xué, kěshi Zhōngguo zì   to write Chinese characters.
  bùróngyi xiě.

A: Zhōngguo zì 'dōu hěn nánxiě   Are all Chinese characters hard to
  ma?   write?

B: búduì. Zhōngguo zì, yǒude   No. Some Chinese characters are hard
  nánxiě, yǒude bùnánxiě.   to write, and some aren't.

A: ni rènshi 'duōshaoge Zhōng-   How many Chinese characters do you
  guo zì?   know?

B: wo 'jiù rènshi jǐge.   I just know a few.

A: ni dōu huì xiě ma?   Can you write them all?

B: wo jiù huì xiě wǒde xìng;   I can only write my surname. I
  bùhuì xiě wǒde míngzi. ni   don't know how to write my
  néng gàosong wǒ, wǒde míngzi   given name. Can you tell me
  zěmma xiě ma?   how to write my given name?

A: nide míngzi shì bushi zhèi-   Aren't these the two characters for
  liǎngge zì? zhèiliǎngge zì   your name? This is how they are
  'zhèmma xiě.   written.

IV

A: zheiliǎngge Zhōngguo zì, shi   What do these two Chinese characters
   shémma yìsi?   mean?

B: ni 'wèishemma yào wèn   Why do you want to ask about these
   zhèiliǎngge zì?   two characters?

A: zheiliǎngge zì shi wo péng-   They are the name of a friend of
   you de míngzi.   mine.

B: zheiliǎngge zì, yíge shi   One of the two characters is měi;
   měi. měi shi hǎo'kàn de yìsi.   měi means "good looking". One is
   yíge shi xīn; xīn shi xīnjiù   xīn; xīn is the xīn of xīn-jiù
   de xīn.   ("new-old").

A: zheige 'měi zì, shi 'Měiguo   This character měi: is it the měi
   de měi ma?   of Měiguo?

B: shi Měiguo de měi. yě shi   Yes. It's the měi of Měizhōu, too.
   Měizhōu de měi.

A: Měizhōu shi shémma yìsi?   What does Měizhōu mean?

B: Měizhōu shi America.   Měizhōu means "America".

A: 'měi zì, wǒ xiǎng wo huì   I think I can write měi; but I
   xiě; kěshi wo bùzhidào 'duì   don't know whether I can do it
   buduì. 'zhèmma xiě, 'xíng   right. Is this how you write
   buxíng?   it?

B: bùxíng; děi nèmma xiě.   No; you have to write it this (other)
                                      way.

V

A: ni xǐhuan dǎ qiú ma?   Do you like to play (basket-)ball?

B: wo bùxǐhuan 'dǎ qiú; keshi   I don't like to play, but I like
   wo xǐhuan 'kàn qiú.   to watch.

A: ni xǐhuan kàn 'shémma qiú?   What ball games do you like to watch?

B: 'lánqiú, 'wǎngqiú, 'bàngqiú,   Basketball, tennis, baseball-- I like
   wo dōu xǐhuan kàn.   to watch them all.

A: dǎ 'wǎngqiú hěn yǒuyìsi.   Tennis is fun. Do you intend to
   ni xiǎng xué ma?   learn it?

B: wo hěn xiǎng xué, keshi méi   I'd like to learn it very much, but
   rén jiāo wo.   there's no one to teach me.

A: ni 'zhēn yuànyi xué ma?   Do you really want to learn?

B: wo 'zhēn yuànyi xué.   Yes, I really do.

A: wo kéyi qǐng Zhēnzhēn de   I'll ask Chen-chen's (older) sister
   jiějie jiāo ni.   to teach you.

                              VI

A: ni xǐhuan zhèi'liǎngzhāng   Do you like these two tables?
   zhuōzi ma?

B: zhèiliǎngzhāng zhuōzi, wo   Yes, I like them both, but they're
   dōu xǐhuan, keshi dōu tài dà.   both too big. Do you have any
   ni you xiǎode meiyou?   small ones?

A: yǒu. keshi xiǎo zhuōzi dōu   Yes, but they're all old ones
   shi jiùde, búshi xīnde.   (they're not new ones).

B: méiyou guānxi; jiùde yě xíng. That's all right; old ones will do.

                              VII

A: ni yào mǎi ge xīnde, mǎi ge   Do you want to buy a new one or an
   jiùde?   old one?

B: xīnde tài guì. wo mǎi ge   New ones are too expensive. Why
   jiùde ba.   don't I buy an old one?

                              VIII

A: nèige yǒuqiánde rén,   What does that rich man like?
   xǐhuan shémma?

B: ta xǐhuan mǎi jiùde   He likes to buy old chairs and tables.
   zhuōzi, jiùde yǐzi.

                              IX

A: ni xǐhuan kàn 'lánqiú, 'duì   You like to watch basketball,
   buduì?   right?

B: búduì.   No.

A: ni xǐhuan kàn 'bàngqiú, 'duì   (Then) you like to watch baseball,
   buduì?   right?

B: duì le.   Right.

X

A: wo xiǎng kàn Měiguo bào.   I think I'll read an American news-
   wo bùzhídào 'něige bào hǎo.   paper. I wonder which one is best.

B: ni kàn 'zhèige bào ba.   Read this one. It's very famous and
   zhèige bào, shi hěn yǒumíng   easy to read, too.
   de bào; yě hěn róngyi kàn.

XI

A: nǐ yào mǎi bào ma?   Do you want to buy a newspaper?
   màitángde, yě mài bào.   That candy vender also sells
                                   papers.

B: 'zhèng hǎo. wo yào mǎi yí-   Perfect. I want to buy a newspaper,
   fèr bào; yě yào mǎi jǐkuài   and I also want to buy some (pieces
   táng.   of) candy.

New words

fùqin N   father

mǔqin N   mother

fùmǔ N   parents

gēge N[1]   older brother

dìdi N[1]   younger brother

xiōngdì N   brothers

jiějie N[1]   older sister

mèimei N[1]   younger sister

jiěmèi N   (fellow) sisters

   wo fùqin   my father

ta mǔqin	his mother
Zhāng Tt de mǔqin	Mrs. Chang's mother
...	(Phrases constructed like these three examples can be made with the other nouns denoting family relationship given above.)
nánde N	man
nǚde N	woman
tóngxué N	fellow student
lǎoshī N	(venerable teacher:) teacher, tutor
Lǎoshī N	Mr., Mrs., Miss (referring to a teacher)
Chén N	Ch'en (a surname)
Xiǎopíng N [2]	Hsiao-p'ing (a given name)
zì, zèr N	(written) character, letter, word
yìsi N	meaning
shi shémma yìsi?	What does it mean?
shi 'nèige yìsi ma?	Is that what it means?
búshi nèige yìsi.	That's not what it means.
Měizhōu N [3]	America
qiú, qiúr N	ball
Měiguo zúqiú N	(American) football
lánqiú N	(basket ball:) basketball
wǎngqiú N	(net ball:) tennis
bàngqiú N	(bat ball:) baseball
-fèr, -fèn M	issue, number, copy (of a newspaper or magazine)
yìfèr bào	a (copy of a) newspaper
liǎngfèr bào	two newspapers
qìfèr bào	seven newspapers
báfèr bào	eight newspapers
děi AV	must, have to, ought to
wo děi kàn diar shū.	I have to do some reading.

wǒ děi gěi ta yige.   I must give him one.

nǐ děi wènwen ta.   You ought to ask him.

kéyi AV   be permitted to, may, can, will

wǒ kéyi mǎi ma?   May I buy it?

ni bùkéyi mǎi.   No, you may not.

wo kéyi qǐng ta màigei ni.   I can ask him to sell it to you.

wo kéyi wènwen ta, zài   I'll ask him, and then let you

   gàosong ni.   know.

měi SV   beautiful

nèizhāng huàr hěn měi.   That is a beautiful painting.

shān, hé, dōu hěn měi.   The mountains and the rivers are

                                                all beautiful.

yǒuyìsi SV^4 (have interest:) interesting, fun

méiyìsi SV^4 (not-have interest:) uninteresting,

                                                no fun

ni xiǎng, dǎ bàngqiú yǒuyìsi   Do you think baseball is fun?

   meiyou?

wo xiǎng, dǎ bàngqiú méiyìsi.   I don't think baseball is fun.

yǒuqián SV^4 (have money:) rich, wealthy

méiqián SV^4 (not have money:) poor, impecunious

yǒumíng SV^4 (have name / fame:) famous, well-

                                                known

nán SV   difficult, hard

dǎ bàngqiú bùnán, hěn róngyi.   Baseball isn't hard; it's easy.

--- A   be difficult to, be hard to

dǎ bàngqiú nán'xué bunánxué?   Is baseball hard to learn?

dǎ bàngqiú bùhěn nánxué.   Not very.

róngyi A   be easy to

dǎ bàngqiú hěn róngyi xué.   Baseball is easy to learn.

rènshi V   be acquainted with, recognize, know

wo burènshi ni péngyou.   I don't know your friend.

ni rènshi zheige zì ma?   Do you recognize this character?

xué V

  ni xué shémma?

  wo xué Zhōngguo huà.

--- AV

  ni xué shuō Zhōngguo huà ma?

wèn V

  wo yao wèn neixie zì.

shì V

  Měizhōu shi shémma?

  Měizhōu shi America.

jiāo V

  ta jiāo shémma? — ta jiāo
  Yīngwén.

  jiāo shū VO

    ta zuò shemma shì? — ta
    jiāo shū.

xiě V

  'měi zì, hěn nánxiě ma?

  bùnán; hěn róngyi xiě.

  xiě zì VO

    háizimen dōu huì xiě zì
    ma?

    xiě Zhōngguo zì hěn nán.

dǎ qiú VO[5]

dǎ Měiguo zúqiú VO

dǎ lánqiú VO

dǎ wǎngqiú VO

study, learn

  What are you studying?

  I'm studying Chinese.

study how to, learn how to

  Are you studying how to speak
  Chinese?

ask (5); ask about

  I want to ask about those characters.

be (5); mean

  What does Měizhōu mean?

  Měizhōu means "America".

teach

  What does he teach? — English.

teach

  What does he do (for a living)? —
  He teaches.

write

  Is the character měi hard to write?

  No; it's easy to write.

write

  Do the children all know how to
  write?

  It's hard to write Chinese.

(hit a ball:) play a sport (in which
  a ball is struck with the hand, or
  with something held in the hand, or
  thrown); play (basket/base)ball

play (American) football

play basketball

play tennis

dǎ bàngqiú VO   play baseball

  ni dǎ shémma qiú?   What (ball-)sport do you play?

  wo jiù huì dǎ lánqiú.   Just basketball.

kàn qiú VO[5]   (look at a ball:) watch a sport;

                               watch basketball / baseball

  ni xǐhuan kàn shémma qiú?   What (ball-)sport do you like to
                                 watch?

  wo xǐhuan kàn 'lánqiú, yě   I like to watch basketball, and
    xǐhuan kàn 'bàngqiú.   baseball, too.

zěmma? A   in what way? how?

  zhèige zì 'zěmma xiě?   How is this character written?

bùzěmma A   not so, not all that

  nèizhāng huàr, bùzěmma hǎo-   That painting isn't so pretty.
    kàn.

zhèmma A   in this way, so

  shi 'zhèmma xiě ma?   Is this how you write it?

nèmma A   in that way, so

  shi 'nèmma xiě.   That's how you write it.

wèishemma? MA   for what reason? why?

  ni wèishemma yào xué Fàguo   Why do you want to learn French?
    huà?

  wèishemma ta bùxǐhuan zuò fàn? Why doesn't he like to cook?

  tamen wèishemma buhuì xiě zì?   Why don't they know how to write?

  wo bùzhidào wèishemma tamen   I don't know why they don't know
    búhuì xiě zì.   how to write.

de P   (follows the modifier in a modifier-
                                 modified construction, where the
                                 modified element is a noun)

  wǒde xiānsheng   my teacher

  wǒde xìng   my surname

  wǒde shū   my book

  Měiguo de měi   the měi of Měiguo

--- P   (follows the modifier, as above, and
                                 replaces the modified noun)

wǒde	mine
shi wǒde.	It's mine.
wo yào neizhang jiùde.	I want that old (table).
jièshao V	introduce (for the time being, use only in the following IE:)
wo gěi nǐmen liǎngwèi jièshao-jieshao. IE	Let me introduce you two.
duì le. IE	That's right. / Yes.
búduì. IE	(not correct:) Wrong. / No.

Notes

[1] The primary words for "brother" and "sister" in Chinese distinguish between whether the person referred to is older or younger than another person, who is his sibling.

nǐ yǒu xiōngdì jiěmèi ma?	Do you have brothers and sisters?
wo jiù you yige dìdi.	I only have a younger brother.
wǒ yǒu yige gēge, liǎngge dìdi.	I have one older brother and two younger brothers.
wo méiyou xiōngdì; jiù you yige jiějie.	I have no brothers; just an older sister.
wǒ yǒu sānge jiějie, wǔge mèimei.	I have three older sisters, five younger sisters.
wǒ yǒu báge jiěmèi, sānge jiějie, wǔge mèimei.	I have eight sisters: three older and five younger.
ta jiějie mèimei dōu huì shuō Yīngwén ma?	Do his sisters all know how to speak English?

[2] Xiǎopíng is literally "small tranquillity", identifiable as a man's name by píng "peace, tranquillity".

[3] Měizhōu is literally "American continent", and refers to the two continents, North and South America, combined.

[4]yǒuyìsi and méiyìsi, yǒuqián and méiqián, and yǒumíng are VO
expressions that behave like stative verbs; for example, they may
be preceded by hěn, zhēn, and similar adverbs.

nà hěn yǒuyìsi.   That's very interesting.

In choice-type questions, the yǒu is repeated, preceded by méi:

dǎ bàngqiú yǒu'yìsi meiyǒu?   Is baseball fun?

[5]dǎ qiú and kàn qiú are VO expressions where the kind of ball
game that is being played or watched is unspecified. In Chinese,
if the context provides no clue as to what kind of game is intended,
it is somewhat likely that "basketball" will be the interpretation
of qiú. Compare "play ball" in American English, in a similar unmarked context, where it is likely to be interpreted as either "play
baseball" or "play basketball".

More notes on grammar

8.1 Modification of nouns. A noun may be modified by another
noun or by a stative verb. The modifying noun or stative verb always
precedes the modified noun. Sometimes the particle de comes between
the two elements.

8.1.1 $N_1 N_2$. Certain nouns modify other nouns without the
addition of de. Names of countries typically follow this pattern:

Zhōngguo xiānsheng	teachers who are Chinese
Èguo huà	Russian (language)
Rìběn huàr	Japanese paintings
Déguo shū	German books
Fàguo cài	French dishes
Hánguo xuéxiào	Korean schools
Jiānádà qìshuǐ	Canadian soda pop

Pronouns also follow this pattern, when a close relationship exists between the person represented by the pronoun and the person represented by the following noun.

wǒ xiānsheng	my husband
wǒ gēge	my (elder) brother
wǒ háizi(men)	my children
nín tàitai	your wife
wǒ lǎoshī	my teacher

8.1.2 N_1 SP-(NU-)M N_2. When an SP-(NU-)M phrase intervenes, there is usually no <u>de</u> after the first noun or pronoun.

wǒ neige biǎo	that watch of mine
nǐ neiliǎngge háizi	those two children of yours

8.1.3 N_1 de N_2. Other nouns, and pronouns where there is no close personal relationship between the person represented by the pronoun and the person represented by the following noun, are usually followed by <u>de</u>.

xiānshengde shū	the teacher's / -s' books
háizimende fùmǔ	the children's parents
wǒ gēgede háizi	my (elder) brother's child(ren)
wǒde xiānsheng	my teacher
wǒde lǎoshī	my teacher
wǒde biǎo	my watch
shéide gāngbǐ?	Whose pen?

8.1.4 N_1 de. The second noun may be omitted, in which case N_1 de is a noun phrase substituting for the original N_1 de N_2, with <u>de</u> acting as a substitute, or "dummy", for de N_2.

shū shi xiānshengde.	The books are the teacher's / -s'.
wǒ gēgede	ones belonging to my (elder) brother

nèige háizi, shi wǒ gēgede.   The child is my brother's. / That's

                                   my 'brother's child. (with extra

                                   stress on brother)

wǒde   mine

nà shi wǒde.   That's mine.

shéide?   Whose?

zhèizhǐ qiānbǐ shi shéide?   Whose is this pencil? / To whom does

                                   this pencil belong?

8.1.5 Money expressions as N_1 in the pattern N_1 de (N_2). This
pattern means "N_1 worth of N_2". qián is always present as part of
the money expression, and de always follows qián.

sānkuài qián de qiānbǐ   three dollars' worth of pencils

wo xiǎng mǎi sānkuài qián de.   I intend to buy three dollars'

                                   worth of them.

yìmáo qián de táng   a dime's worth of candy

wo xiǎng mǎi yìmáo qián de.   I intend to buy a dime's worth.

                                   (Cf. yìmáo qián yíkuài de táng "candy

                                   costing a dime apiece"; wo xiǎng mǎi

                                   yìmáo qián yíkuài de. "I intend to

                                   buy candy costing a dime apiece.")

ni xiǎng mǎi 'jǐkuài qián de   How many dollars' worth of paper do

    zhǐ?   you intend to buy?

wo jiù xiǎng mǎi 'liǎngkuài qián   Just two dollars' worth.

    de.

sānkuài qián yìzhǐ de bǐ   pens costing three dollars apiece

wo xiǎng mǎi sānkuài qián yìzhǐ   I intend to buy (pens) costing three

    de.   dollars apiece.

8.1.6 SV N. A simple stative verb (e.g. one that is not analyz-
able as a VO, as yǒuyìsi is) unmodified by an adverb, precedes the
noun it modifies, and usually no de intervenes.

hǎo rén	a good man
hǎo de rén	
xīn shū	new books
piányi zhǐ	inexpensive paper
gāo shān	high mountains
yuǎn hé	distant rivers
chǎng lù	long roads
tián júzi	sweet oranges
suān píngguo	sour apples

8.1.7 <u>SV</u> de <u>N</u>. Compound stative verbs, or stative verbs modified by adverbs, take <u>de</u> before the noun they modify.

yǒuyìside shū	interesting books
méiyìside shū	uninteresting books
méiqiánde rén	poor people
yǒumíngde lǎoshī	famous teachers
hěn dà de mǎimai	a big business
bútài guì de biǎo	a watch that is not overly expensive
hěn là de tāng	a peppery soup
hěn tián de táng	sweet candy
bújìnde hé	rivers that are not near
bùsuānde júzi	oranges that are not sour
hǎokànde nǚháizi	goodlooking girls
hěn hǎokàn de huàr	a pretty picture

8.1.8 <u>SV</u> de. The modified noun may be omitted, in which case the <u>-de</u> is always present, and SV-<u>de</u> is a noun phrase substituting for the original SV-<u>de</u> N expression.

yǒuyìside	interesting ones
shū, wo yuànyi kàn yǒuyìside,	I want to read interesting books,
búyuànyi kàn méiyìside.	not uninteresting ones.

jiùde   old ones
xīn zhuōzi piányi; jiùde guì.   New tables are cheaper; old ones
                                         are more expensive.

dàde   big ones
ni yào mǎi dàde, yào mǎi   Do you want to buy the big one or
   xiǎode?   the small one?

piányide   inexpensive ones
wo búyào neige piányide; wo yào   I don't want that cheap one; I want
   neige guìde.   the expensive one.

hǎochīde   something tasty
wo xiǎng mǎi diar hǎochīde.   I intend to buy something tasty.

8.2   VO-de expressions as noun phrases denoting occupation or
trade.

màibàode   newspaper seller
màibàode yě mài táng.   The newspaper vender also sells candy.

màishūde   bookseller
màishūde bùdōu mài bào.   Not all booksellers sell newspapers.

zuòfànde   cook
women méiyou zuòfànde.   We don't have a cook.

zuòmǎimaide   tradesman
zuòmǎimaide, yǒude yǒuqián   Some tradesmen are rich, some are
   yǒude méiqián.   poor.

yàofànde   beggar
Zhōngguo méiyou yàofànde.   There are no beggars in China.

8.3   More on "bound" forms.   In Lesson 2, "New words", note 5,
the term "bound form" was defined as a form that always occurs in
construction with another form, and which never stands alone as a

sentence. In opposition to bound forms are "free forms", which are not so limited in their occurrence. For example, a free form may occur alone as a complete sentence. yǒu "have" occurs in construction with méi- in méiyou "not have", but because it also occurs alone as a sentence, yǒu "(1) have.", it is a free form.

Some examples of bound forms are:

8.3.1 One-syllable surnames. Zhāng, etc., never occur alone. See Lesson 5, "New words," note 1. They always occur followed by a title (Zhāng Xiansheng) or a given name (Zhāng Měishēng), or preceded by xìng "be surnamed" (xìng Zhāng) or by an affectionate prefix such as Xiǎo "little" (Xiǎo Zhāng). Surnames of more than one syllable are free: Sītú "Seeto", Lánmuxī "Ramsey".

8.3.2 Measures. -zhī, -zhāng, -ge, etc., never occur alone. A measure is always preceded by a specifier, or a number, or by a specifier-number expression: zhèizhī, liǎngzhāng, zhèiliǎngzhāng. It also occurs alone between a verb and its object, where it substitutes for yì-M: wǒ xiǎng mǎi zhī bǐ. "I intend to buy a pen."

8.3.3 Other bound forms. fù, mǔ, qin (qīn: "relative"), gē, dì, xiōng, jiě, mèi are all bound forms.

8.3.4 nán- and nǚ-: attributives. nán- and nǚ- are bound forms of a special variety. They are prefixed to nouns, and to -de, which serves as a dummy noun (see above, 8.1.4), substituting for an unspecific N_2 in an original N_1 de N_2 expression. Such bound forms are called "attributives". See Lesson 5, "New words", note 3.

nánpéngyou	male friend
nǚpéngyou	female friend
nánren	male person, man
nǚren	female person, woman
nánháizi	boy
nǚháizi	girl
nánxiānsheng	male teacher

nǚxiānsheng	female teacher
nánxuésheng	male student
nǚxuésheng	female student
nántóngxué	male fellow student
nǚtóngxué	female fellow student
nánlǎoshī	male teacher
nǚlǎoshī	female teacher
nánde	one who is male, man
nǚde	one who is female, woman

8.4 <u>SV</u> as <u>A</u>. Certain stative verbs occur before another verb and modify it. Stative verbs introduced so far that are used in this adverbial function are <u>hǎo</u>, <u>róngyi</u>, <u>nán</u>, and <u>gòu</u> (p. 105, note 20).

zheiběn shū hěn hǎo.	This is a very good book.
zheige cài hěn hǎochī.	This dish is very good-to-eat / tasty. This is a very tasty dish.
ta háizimen dōu hěn hǎokàn.	His children are all good-to-look-at / good-looking. / He has very good-looking children.
neige shì hěn róngyi.	That job is easy.
neige shì hěn róngyi zuò.	That job is easy to do.
zheige cài róngyi 'zuò buróngyi zuò?	Is this dish easy to prepare?
Zhōngguo huà hěn róngyi xué.	Chinese is easy to learn.
Zhōngguo zì bùróngyi xiě.	Chinese characters are not easy to write.
neige shì hěn nán.	That job is hard.
neige shì hěn nánzuò.	That job is hard to do.
zheige cài nán'zuò bunánzuò?	Is this dish hard to prepare?
Zhōngguo huà hěn nánxué.	Chinese is hard to learn.
yǒude Zhōngguo zì, bùnánxiě.	Some Chinese characters are not so hard to write.

8.5 <u>xué</u> occurs both as a functive verb and as an auxiliary verb.

As a V, it means "study, learn":

ni xué shémma?	What are you studying?
wo xué Yīngwén.	I'm studying English.

As an AV, it means "study how to, learn how to":

ni xué dǎ shémma qiú?	What ball are you learning how to hit? / What sport are you learning?
wo xué dǎ 'wǎngqiú.	I'm learning tennis.
wo xiǎng xué xiě Zhōngguo zì.	I intend to study how to write Chinese characters.
ta yuànyi xué zuò Zhōngguo cài.	He wants to study Chinese cooking.

Pyramid drills

shémma yìsi?

shi shémma yìsi?

zhè shi shémma yìsi?

zhèige zì, shi shémma yìsi?

zheige 'xiān zì, shi shémma yìsi?

zheige 'xiān zì, shi 'xiānsheng de xiān ma?

shì.

kàn bào.

kàn yìfèr bào.

xiǎng kàn yìfèr bào.

xiǎng kàn yì-liǎngfèr bào.

děi kàn yì-liǎngfèr bào.

kéyi kàn yì-liǎngfèr bào ma?

kéyi.

                                            'zěmma xiě?

                                    shi 'zěmma xiě?

                            zhèige zì shi 'zěmma xiě?

                    zheiliǎngge zì shi 'zěmma xiě?

                    zheiliǎngge zì shi 'zhèmma xiě ma?

            zheiliǎngge zì, 'shì bushi 'zhèmma xiě?

            zheiliǎngge zì, búshi 'zhèmma xiě.

                                    shi 'nèmma xiě.

                            wèishemma?

                            'wèishemma zhèmma zuò?

                    búzhèmma zuò, 'zěmma zuò?*

                            bùzhidào zěmma zuò.

                    wo bùzhidào zěmma zuò.

            nǐ 'wèishemma bùzhidào zěmma zuò?

    wǒ bùzhidào 'wèishemma bùzhidào zěmma zuò.

    * "Not this-way do, how do? / If we don't do it this way, how
shall we do it?"

                        Exercises

Answer the following questions, to make a continuous dialog:

nín guìxìng?

Huáng Xs hǎo?

nín rènshi neiwei tàitai ma?

shi Cáo Lǎoshī ma? ta jiāo shémma?

ta 'Yīngwén, 'Zhōngwén, dōu huì shuō ma?

ta xiǎng 'zài xué yìdiǎr Zhōngguo huà ma?

wo yǒu yíge péngyou, tade Yīngwen, Zhōngwen, dōu hen hǎo. Ta hen
    xǐhuan jiāo shū. ta keyi jiāo Cáo Lǎoshi.

wo xiǎng ta hen yuànyi jiāo Cáo Lǎoshī.

Make questions, to which the following would be appropriate answers:

'dǎ qiú, kàn qiú, wo dōu xǐhuan.

wǒ bùzhidào; wo kéyi wènwen ta, zài gàosong ni.

shi 'zhèmma xiě, búshi nèmma xiě.

wo bùzhidào "Coca-Cola", Zhōngguo huà zěmma shuō.

'Zhōngguo shān měi.

liǎngmáo yífèr.

wǎngqiú, lánqiú, wo dōu huì dǎ yìdiǎr; Měiguó zúqiú, bàngqiú, wo dōu
    búhuì.

búshi píngguo de píng; yě búshi yìpíng jiǔ de píng.

búshi wǒde.

búduì. búshi tāde shū.

'Zhāng Tt zhīdao nèiběn shū shi shéide.

hǎokànde shi wǒ gēgede; bùhǎokànde shi wǒde.

wǒ xiǎng mǎi 'wǔmáo qián yìzhī de bǐ.

shi wo jiějiede háizi.

hěn 'dà de shū guì.

budōu buguì; yǒude xiǎo shū yě hěn guì.

màibàode yǒu.

Lesson 9
Clauses modifying nouns, and change of status le

Pronunciation

__Plain:__

__a:__ bā; yìbǎ; bàba "dad"; māma "mom"; mǎ "horse"; dǎ; kāfēi; chá.

__e:__ Déguo; gēge; zhè; chē "vehicle"; yánsè "color"; Èguo.

__i:__ yìzhī$_1$; yìzhī$_2$ "one (animal)"; zì; zìjǐ "oneself"; sì.

__ai:__ báide "white"; yìbǎi; tài; hái "still"; háizi; zài; cài; ài.

__ei:__ yìbēi; děi; gěi; hēide "black"; zhèige.

__ao:__ bào; lǎoshī; hǎo; yíhào; Zhào; Cáo.

__ou:__ dōu; yìtóu "one (cow)"; gāo; Měizhōu.

__an:__ fàn; lánde "blue"; lánqiú; Hánguo; shān; sān.

__en:__ yìběn; nèmma; hěn; zhèmma; rènshi; zěmma.

__ang:__ bàngqiú; tāng; táng; gāngbǐ; cháng$_1$; cháng$_2$ "often"; nóngchǎng "farm".

__eng:__ péngyou; néng; Zhèng; zhèngzai "just in the process of".

__ar:__ yíbàr.

__er:__ yífèr; érzi "son"; èr.

__Frontalized:__

__ia:__ Jiānádà.

__ie:__ xiě; yě.

__i:__ píjiǔ; yìpǐ "one (horse)"; dìdi; xiūlǐ "repair"; jǐge; zìjǐ "oneself"; qìshuǐ; qìchē "automobile"; yī; yīshang "clothing".

__iao:__ biǎo; yìtiáo; jiāo; yào.

__iu:__ niú "cow"; liù; qiú; xiūlǐ "repair"; yǒu.

156

<u>ian:</u> xiàngpiān "photograph"; piányi; tián; yijiàn; "one (article of
   clothing)"; qián; xiānsheng; xiànzài "now"; yánsè "color".

<u>in:</u> nín; xīn.

<u>iang:</u> liǎngge; yíliàng "one (vehicle)"; xiǎng; xiàngpiān "photograph".

<u>ing:</u> míngzi; yídìng "definitely"; líng; xìng; Yīnglǐ.

<u>iar:</u> xiàngpiār "photograph"; yìdiǎr.

<u>ier:</u> (none yet)

<u>Labialized:</u>

<u>ua:</u> Huá Shān: huà$_1$; huà$_2$ "paint".

<u>uo:</u> duō "many"; duōshao?; yìduǒ "one (flower)"; shuǐguǒ; shuō; zuò;
   búcuò; wǒ.

<u>u:</u> bù; lù; Zhū Jiāng; zhū "pig"; shū; wǔ.

<u>uai:</u> kuài; huài le "be broken"; wàiguo "foreign".

<u>ui:</u> búduì; huì; shuǐ; zuì "most"; wèishemma?.

<u>uan:</u> chuān "wear"; suān; yìwǎn; yíwàn.

<u>un:</u> yícùn; wèn.

<u>uang:</u> Huáng; huángde "yellow/brown"; Wáng.

<u>ong:</u> tóngxué; nóngchǎng "farm"; yígòng; hóngde "red"; Zhōngguo;
   zhòng "grow"; cōngming "intelligent".

<u>uar:</u> huār "flower"; huàr.

<u>uor:</u> yìduǒr "one (flower)".

<u>uer:</u> (none yet)

<u>ur:</u> (none yet)

<u>Frontalized and labialized:</u>

<u>ue:</u> xué.

<u>ü:</u> nǚde; nǚer "daughter"; lùde "green"; júzi.

Dialogs, etc.

I

A: nǐ huì huà huàr ma?   Do you know how to paint?

B: wo huì yìdiǎr.   Yes, a little.

A: zhèizhāng huàr, shi nǐ   Did you paint this picture?
   huà de ma?

B: búshì; shi wo mǔqin huà de.   No, my mother did.

A: ta cháng huà huàr ma?   Does she paint often?

B: ta cháng huà huàr. ta   Yes. Right now she's in the process
   xiànzài 'zhèngzai xué huà   of learning how to paint Chinese
   Zhōngguo huàr.   paintings.

A: shéi jiāo ta?   Who's teaching her?

B: jiāo wǒmen Zhōngguo huàr de   The Mr. Chang who's teaching us
   neiwei 'Zhāng Xs jiāo ta.   Chinese painting is teaching her.

A: nèizhāng huàr hěn měi; shi   That painting is beautiful; who
   shéi huà de? yě shi ni   painted it? Is it also by your
   mǔqin huà de ma?   mother?

B: búshì. shi 'Zhāng Xs huàde.   No, it's by Mr. Chang.

A: wo yě xiǎng xué huà huàr.   I also intend to study painting.
   wo kéyi qǐng Zhāng Xs jiāo   Could I ask[1] Mr. Chang to teach
   wo ma?   me?

B: wèishemma bùkéyi? ni kéyi   Why not? You could ask[2] him.
   wènwen ta.

II

A: Gāo Xs you 'jǐge nǚer?   How many daughters has Mr. Kao?

B: ta you sānge nǚer, liǎngge   He has three daughters and two sons.
   érzi.

A: Měizhēn, shì bushi zuì dà?   Is Mei-chen the oldest?

B: shì. Měizhēnde liǎngge   She is. Mei-chen's two brothers
   dìdi, shi Guóxīnde tóngxué.   are fellow students of Kuo-hsin's.

Guóxīn cháng shuō, Měizhēnde
xiōngdìjiěmèi-men, dōu hěn
cōngming.

A: tamen 'shéi zuì cōngming?

B: wǒ kàn, Měizhēn zuì cōngming.

Kuo-hsin often says that Mei-
chen's brothers and sisters are
all smart.

Who is the smartest among them?

Mei-chen is, in my opinion.

III

A: wǒde chē huài le. neige
xiūlǐ qì'chē de rén gàosong
wǒ, zhèiliàng chē hěn nán-
xiūlǐ.

B: wèishemma nèmma nán xiūlǐ
ne?

A: tā shuō, wàiguo chē, dōu
bùróngyi xiūlǐ.

B: wo yǒu yige péngyou, hěn
huì xiūlǐ qìchē.

A: ta yě huì xiūlǐ wàiguo
qìchē ma?

B: ta gàosong wo, ta huì; wo
xiǎng ta yídìng huì.

My car is broken. The car repair
man tells me that this car is
hard to fix.

Why is it so hard to repair?

He says foreign cars are all hard
to repair.

I have a friend who really knows
how to repair automobiles.

Does he know how to repair foreign
automobiles, too?

He tells me he does; I think he
certainly knows how to.

IV

A: ta fùqin neige nóngchǎng,
zhēn dà.

B: yǒu 'duóma dà ya?

A: ni yíkàn zhèizhāng xiàngpiār, jiu zhīdao le. yǒu
nèmma duō de niú; nèmma duō
de mǎ; hái yǒu nèmma duō de
zhū.

B: nèixiē cài, dōu shi tā
zhòng de ma?

That farm of his father's is really
big.

How big?

As soon as you look at this photograph, you'll know. There are so
many cattle, so many horses, and
so many pigs.

Did he grow all those vegetables?

A: nèixiē cài, dōu shi tā   Yes.
   zhòng de.

B: nèixiē huār ne?   And the flowers?

A: nèixiē huār, dōu shi ta   His mother planted the flowers.
   'mǔqin zhòng de. zhēn hǎokàn.   They're really pretty.

B: kě bushì ma?   Isn't that a fact!

                              V

A: zhèijiàn yīshang shi nǐ   Did you make this garment/dress?
   zuò de ma?

B: búshi; shi wo mǔqin mǎi de.   No, my mother bought it.

A: ni xǐhuan zheige yánsè ma?   Do you like the color?

B: wo hěn xǐhuan zheige yánsè.   Yes, very much.

A: hóngde, lǜde, zheiliǎngge   Which do you like better, red or
   yánsè, ni xǐhuan něige?   green?

B: wo xǐhuan hóngde. keshi   Red. But I like green, too.
   wo yě xǐhuan lǜde.

A: ni cháng chuān de nèijiàn   Did your mother also buy the green
   lǜde, yě shi ni mǔqin mǎi   one that you often wear?
   de ma?

B: búshi. nà shi wo zìjǐ   No, I bought that one myself.
   mǎi de.

                              VI

ta jiějie huì zuò fàn; ta   His (older) sister can cook; so can
   gēge yě huì zuò fàn; keshi   his (older) brother. But he
   tāmen zuò de fàn, ta dōu   doesn't like the cooking of either
   búài chī; ta jiù ài chī, ta   of them; he only likes his mother's
   māma zuò de fàn. ta shuō ta   cooking. He says he wants to learn
   yào xué māma zěmma zuò fàn.   how his mother cooks. He asked his
   ta qǐng māma jiāo ta; māma   mother to teach him and she said:
   shuō; wǒ bùjiāo ni. ni   "I won't teach you. Why don't you

'wèishemma bùqǐng ni bàba   ask your father?"
jiāo ni ne?

New words

érzi N   son
nǚér N   daughter
  dà érzi   oldest son
  èr nǚér   second oldest daughter
chē N (M: -liàng)   vehicle; car
qìchē N (M: -liàng)   (gas vehicle:) automobile
wàiguo N   (outside nation:) foreign; non-
                                    Chinese

  wàiguo shū   foreign books; books in a language
                                      other than Chinese

  wàiguo rén   foreigners; non-Chinese people
nóngchǎng N   (farm field:) farm
xiàngpiār, -piān N (M: -zhāng)   (picture card:) photograph
niú N (M: -tóu)   cow, ox, cattle
mǎ N (M: -pǐ)   horse
zhū N (M: -zhī)   pig
huār N (M: -duǒ, -duǒr)   flower
yīshang N (M: -jiàn)   article of clothing; dress
yánsè N   color
hóngyánsède N[3]   something colored red, red
hóngde N[3]   something red, red
huángde N[3]   something yellow/brown, yellow/brown
lánde N[3]   something blue, blue
báide N[3]   something white, white
hēide N[3]   something black, black
lǜde N[3]   something green, green
zìjǐ N[4]   oneself
māma N[5]   mom; mother
bàba N[5]   pop; father

-liàng M	(vehicles)
-tóu M	(lit. "head": certain domestic animals and vegetables)
-pǐ M	(horses)
-zhǐ M	(lit. "one of a pair": certain domestic animals)
-duǒ, -duǒr M	(flowers)
-jiàn M	(lit. "item": articles of clothing)
xiànzài TW[6]	the present, now
xiànzàide yīshang, hěn guì.	Clothing of the present time is expensive./Clothing is expensive nowadays.

ta xiànzài xué huà huàr.	She's learning how to paint now.
xiànzài ta xué huà huàr.	
cháng A[7]	often
ta cháng kàn shū.	He reads often.
ta cháng hē jiǔ.	Often, he drinks.
ta bùcháng zuò fàn.	He doesn't often cook.
chángcháng A[7]	often
ta chángcháng kàn shū.	He reads often.
ta chángcháng hěn máng.	She's busy often.
wo bùchángcháng hěn máng.	I'm not busy very often.
zuì A	the most, the more (of two)
tā liǎngge háizi, dà érzi zuì hǎokàn.	Of his two children, the older son is the better looking.
zhèisānběn shū, nèiběn zuì guì.	That one is the most expensive of the three books.
wǒ bùxiǎng mǎi zuì 'guì de shū.	I don't intend to buy the most expensive book(s).
ta xǐhuan zuì piányi de.	He likes to buy the cheapest one(s).
zhèng, zhèngzai A	just (now), exactly, be right in the process of ...-ing
wǒ dà érzi zhèngzai xué xiě zì.	My oldest son is just learning how to write.

yídìng A   definitely, certainly
  wo yídìng mǎi.   I'll certainly buy it.
  yídìng yāo A AV   must, have to
bùyídìng A   not necessarily
  wo bùyídìng mǎi.   I'm not sure I'll buy it.
hái A   still, furthermore
  hái yǒu nèmma duō zhū.   And (furthermore) there are so
                                   many pigs.
  wo hái xiǎng mǎi yìběn shū.   I still want to buy a(nother) book.
  wo hái xiǎng zài mǎi yìběn shū.   I still want to buy yet another book.
zhèmma A   in this way (8); to this degree,
                                 so, such
  zhèmma hǎokàn de háizi   such good-looking children
nèmma A   in that way (8); to that degree,
                                 so, such
  nèmma duō de mǎ   so many horses
dà SV   big (5); old (in comparing ages of
                                 people)
  nǐmen liǎngge rén, shéi dà?   Which is the older of you two?
  wǒ dà yidiar.   I'm a bit older.
cōngming SV   intelligent, bright
  cōngming rén   intelligent people
  cōngming xuésheng   bright students
  ta dà nǚer, zuì cōngming.   His oldest daughter is the brightest.
duō SV[8]   many, much (6)
  ta xiǎng kàn hěn duō shū.   He intends to read many books.
  nǐ yě xiǎng kàn hěn duō de   Do you also intend to read a lot
    shū ma?   of books?
  tāde shū hěn duō.   He has a lot of books.
  wǒde shū bùduō.   I don't have a lot of books.
  rén bùduō.   There aren't many people.
  rén hěn duō.   There are a lot of people.

huà V   draw, paint
  huà huàr VO   draw, paint
    zhèizhāng huàr shi wǒ huà de.   I painted this painting.
    ni huì huà huàr ma?   Do you know how to paint?
    Zhōngguo huàr hěn nánhuà.   It's hard to paint Chinese
                           paintings.

xiūlǐ V   repair, fix
  wo búhuì xiūlǐ qìchē.   I don't know how to repair cars.
kàn V   read (2); look at
  wo hen xǐhuan kàn xiàngpiār.   I like to look at photographs.
  nǐ kàn; yǒu nèmma duō de niú.   (You) look how many cows there are.
  wǒ kàn, ... IE   (as I look at it:) in my opinion
    wǒ kàn, nèiběn shū, tài guì.   That book is too expensive,
                           in my opinion.

zhòng V   plant, grow
  huār, cài, women dōu zhòng.   We grow both flowers and vegetables
chuān V   (pass through, thread:) wear (a
                           jacket, shirt, pair of trousers)
  ni zuì xǐhuan chuān 'něijiàn   Which article of clothing do you
    yīshang?   like to wear most?
  wo zuì xǐhuan chuān zhèijiàn   I like to wear this green one
    lǜde.   best.
ne? P   (following a noun:) And what about
                           (the noun)? (5); (at the end of
                           a content question:) And...
  tā shi shéi ne?   And who is she?
  tā xiǎng huà shémma huàr ne?   And what's he going to paint a
                           picture of?
  nǐ xiǎng mǎi shémma ne?   And what do you intend to buy?
  tā 'zěmma zhīdao ne?   And how does he know?
  nǐ 'wèishemma búmài hóngde ne? And why don't you sell red ones?
a?, ya?[9]   (at the end of a question, softens
                           the question)

'něige hǎo a?	Which one is better?
Měiguo duóma dà ya?	How big is America?
yí-, yì- P[10]	(lit. "one, once":) as soon as, once
le P[10,11]	(sentence particle - i.e. occurring
	at the end of a sentence, -
	indicating changed status)
jiù, jiu A[10]	only (4); then, afterwards
nǐ yíkàn, jiu zhīdao le.	As soon as you look at it you'll
	know.
ta yìshuō huà, wo jiu zhīdao	As soon as he speaks, I'll know
ta shi shéi le.	who he is.
huài le IE[10,11]	broken, out of order, spoiled
wode qìchē huài le.	My automobile is out of order.
wode xīn gāngbǐ huài le.	My new pen is broken.
zhèige júzi huài le.	This orange is spoiled.
kě bushì ma? IE	(Is it not, indeed, so?:) How true!
	And how! I'll say!
Zhōngguo huàr hěn nán huà -	It's hard to paint Chinese paint-
kě bushì ma?	ings. -- I'll say!

Notes

[1]This "ask" occurs in the English pattern "ask X to V" and means "request, invite"; it corresponds to the Chinese qǐng.

[2]This "ask" occurs in the English pattern "ask X (whether S)" and means "inquire of"; it corresponds to the Chinese wèn (or wènwen, especially if there is no embedded question).

[3]Corresponding to these nouns denoting colors are stative verbs: hóng "red", huáng "yellow/brown", lán "blue", bái "white", hēi "black". and lǜ "green". In rattling off the names of the colors, a five-syllable word results (lǜ is left out): hóng-huáng-lán-bái-hēi.

Sentences using these stative verbs as the main word in a comment are perfectly grammatical, but semantically somewhat unlikely:

'něiběn shū hóng?   Which book is redder?

'zhèiběn hóng. zhèiběn 'zhēn   This one is. This one is very red
hóng.   indeed.

    Far more frequent are nouns consisting of any of these stative
verbs plus either -yánsède or -de alone. (For this use of the noun-
making suffix -de, see 8.1.8.) Notice that -yánsède may be added to
the other stative verbs, not only to hóng, as in the vocabulary:
huángyánsède, etc.

    Such nouns behave like other nouns. They modify other nouns;
they do not ordinarily stand alone as comments; they do not take
intensifying adverbs like hěn, zhēn, and tài.

Huáng Hé de shuǐ, shi huángde   Is the water of the Yellow River
  ma?   yellow/brown?

wo xiǎng mǎi yíjiàn hěn guì   I intend to buy an expensive dress.
  de yīshang.

wo xiǎng mǎi yíjiàn lányánsède   I intend to buy a blue dress.
  yīshang.

nèijiàn yīshang hěn guì.   That dress is expensive.

nèijiàn yīshang shi hēiyánsède.   That dress is black.

nèijiàn yīshang de yánsè, shi   Is the color of that dress red or
  'hóngde, shi lǜde?   green?

shi hóngde.   It's red.

    [4]zìjǐ is a noun which usually occurs in apposition to (4.11) a
preceding noun (or pronoun).

wo zìjǐ zuò fàn.   I, myself, cook. / I do my own
                                 cooking.

ta zìjǐ chuān yīshang.   She dresses herself.

ta yào kàn ta zìjǐ de shū.   He wants to read his own books.

nèizhī gāngbǐ, shi wǒ zìjǐ   I bought that pen myself.
  mǎi de.

[5] māma and bàba are more frequently used in Chinese than the corresponding English words "mom" and "dad", and hence they are not so likely to be considered childish or over-familiar.

[6] "TW" stands for "time word", which is a noun telling the "time when" the action or condition described in the sentence takes place. Time words behave like movable adverbs, in that they typically precede the verb, and may either precede or follow any topic.

[7] Before stative verbs, cháng alone is avoided; instead use chángchang, chángchang hěn, or cháng hěn.

[8] duō is a stative verb with the peculiarity that when used to modify a noun, it must be preceded by an adverb. Usually this adverb is hěn; between hěn duō and the following noun, de is optional.

ta yǒu hěn duō xīn yīshang.   He has a lot of new clothes.
ta yǒu hěn duō de xīn yīshang.

[9] The question particle a has two main forms, depending on how the preceding syllable ends. If the preceding syllable ends in a sound other than -a, -e, or nuclear -o, the particle a develops an initial like the sound in which the preceding syllable ends. Thus, 'něige hǎo wa?' "Which one is better?", dúoma nán na? "How difficult is it?". These changes are not registered in the transcription, and we write simply hǎo a?, nán a? After -a, -e, or nuclear (i.e. non-ending) -o, the particle a develops a y initial: yǒu duó dà ya? "How big is it?" For this form of the particle, we write ya.

[10] The verbal prefix yí- / yì- is derived from yī "one" and, like yī, its tone depends on the tone of the following syllable. It occurs in a pattern with jiù (regularly weakened to a neutral-tone form: jiu):

wǒ yízuò fàn, jiu xiǎng chī   As soon as I (begin to) cook, I
   fàn.   (begin to) think of eating.
wǒ yìxiǎng, jiu zuò.   As soon as I think (of doing some-
                                      thing), I do it.

wǒ yíkàn yizhang huàr, jiu yào   As soon as I look at a painting, I
mǎi.   want to buy it.

The sentence particle le may be added at the end of the last
clause, and one effect of adding le is to emphasize that the action
or state mentioned in the second clause has changed from a previous
action or state. This is the so-called "changed status" meaning of le.

nǐ yíkàn zheizhang huàr, ni   As soon as you look at the painting,
  jiu yào mǎi le.   you'll (change your mind and) want
                                      to buy it.

ni yíkàn, jiu zhīdao le.   You'll know as soon as you look at
                                      it.

ta yìshuō huà, wo jiu zhīdao   As soon as he speaks, I'll know who
  ta shi shéi le.   he is (whereas now I don't.)

nèige píngguo huài le ma?   Is that apple spoiled?
wo bùzhidào; wo yìchī, jiu   I don't know; as soon as I begin to
  zhīdao le.   eat it, I'll know.

[11]The le that occurs at the end of certain idiomatic expressions
is probably the same as the "changed status" le; in these cases that
meaning has by now eroded or disappeared entirely:

huài le   (from huài "bad": "has become bad":)
                                     broken, out of order, spoiled
gòu le   (from gòu "enough, sufficient":
                                     "has become enough":) enough
duì le   (from duì "correct, right": has
                                     become correct":) correct

     This le often follows a tài SV construction:
nà tài guì le.   That's too expensive.

More notes on grammar

9.1 Adjective and noun clauses with de. A clause may be formed from one or more verbs and one or more nouns, suffixed by de; a clause thus formed may then modify yet another noun. The words in the clause and the noun that the clause modifies may be usefully related to an ideal sentence that underlies the clause-noun expression, as follows.

9.1.1 S V de O. From an underlying sentence of the form Subject Verb Object, the Object may be made the Modified term in a Modifier-Modified construction, where the Modifier is the Subject and the Verb of the sentence, followed by de.

Clause		Noun	
S	V	de O	
[wǒ	chī	fàn.	I eat.]
wǒ	chī	de fàn	the food that I eat
[tāmen	xiě	zì.	They write.]
tāmen	xiě	de zì	the characters that they write
[nǐmen	mǎi	gāngbǐ.	You buy pens.]
nǐmen	mǎi	de gāngbǐ	the pens that you buy
[ta	qǐng	péngyou.	He's inviting some friends.]
ta	qǐng	de péngyou	the friends that he invites
[wǒ	gěi	qián.	I'll pay.]
wǒ	gěi	de qián	the money that I give
[tā	huà	huàr.	He paints.]
tā	huà	de huàr	the paintings that he paints
[tā	yào mài	mǎ.	He wants to sell horses.]
ta	yào mài de mǎ		the horses that he wants to sell
[tāmen	xiǎng mǎi	zhū.	They intend to buy pigs.]
tāmen	xiǎng mǎi de zhū		the pigs they intend to buy
[nǐ	mǎigei wǒ	gāngbǐ.	You'll sell me some pens.]
nǐ	mǎigei wǒ de gāngbǐ		the pens you sell me

9.1.2 <u>V O</u> de <u>S</u>. From an underlying sentence of the same structure, <u>Subject Verb Object</u>, the <u>Subject</u> may be made the <u>Modified term</u>; and the <u>Verb</u> and the <u>Object</u> may become the <u>Modifier</u>, followed by <u>de</u>.

	Clause		Noun
	V	O	de S
1.			[rén shuō huà.]
	shuō	huà	de rén
2.			[Měiguo rén shuō Zhōngguo huà.]
	shuō	Zhōngguo huà	de Měiguo rén
3.			[Zhōngguo rén hěn ài hē tāng.]
	ài hē	tāng	de Zhōngguo rén
4.			[háizi zuì ài chī táng.]
	zuì ài chī	táng	de háizi
5.			[rén huì xiūlǐ qìchē.]
	huì xiūlǐ	qìchē	de rén
6.			[xuésheng búhuì xiě Zhōngguo zì.]
	búhuì xiě	Zhōngguo zì	de xuésheng

Translations of the above sentences:

1. People are talking.
   people who are talking
2. (Some) Americans speak Chinese.
   Americans who speak Chinese
3. The Chinese love soup.
   the Chinese who love soup
4. Children like candy best.
   children who like candy best
5. (Some) people know how to repair automobiles.
   people who know how to repair automobiles
6. The students don't know how to write Chinese characters.
   the students who don't know how to write Chinese characters

9.1.3 <u>Clause</u> de <u>SP-NU-M N</u>. The modified noun may be specified.

Clause				Noun
(S)	V	(O)	de SP-NU-M	N
1. ta	cháng chuān		de	yīshang
ta	cháng chuān		de nèijiàn	yīshang
2. tamen	xiǎng mǎi		de	mǎ
tamen	xiǎng mǎi		de zhèiwǔpǐ	mǎ
3. wo	zuì xǐhuan		de	huār
wo	zuì xǐhuan		de nèiduǒ	huār
4. wo	mǎigei ta		de	píjiǔ
wo	mǎigei ta		de nèiqīpíng	píjiǔ
5. ta	kàn		de	xiàngpiār
ta	kàn		de nèizhāng	xiàngpiār
6.	jiāo wǒmen	Zhōngguo huà	de	lǎoshī
	jiāo wǒmen	Zhōngguo huà	de nèiwǔwèi	lǎoshī
7.	huì xiūlǐ	qìchē	de	rén
	huì xiūlǐ	qìchē	de neige	rén
8.	xǐhuan zhòng huār		de	Yīngguo tàitai
	xǐhuan zhòng huār		de nèiwèi	Yīngguo tàitai
9.	huì zuò	Zhōngguo cài	de	wàiguo rén
	huì zuò	Zhōngguo cài	de nèixiē	wàiguo rén
10.	xiǎng mǎi	nóngchǎng	de	rén
	xiǎng·mǎi	nóngchǎng	de neige	rén

English translations (notice that the first, unspecified member of these pairs of sentences usually implies that the modified noun is plural):

1. clothes that he often wears
    the article of clothing that he often wears
2. horses that they intend to buy
    these five horses that they intend to buy

3. flowers that I like best
     the flower   that I like best
4. beer that I sold him
     the seven bottles of beer that I sold him
5. photographs that he looked at
     the photograph that he looked at
6. teachers that teach us Chinese
     the five teachers that teach us Chinese
7. people who know how to repair automobiles
     the person who knows how to repair automobiles
8. English ladies who like to grow flowers
     the English lady who likes to grow flowers
9. foreigners who know how to cook Chinese dishes
     the foreigners who know how to cook Chinese dishes
10. people who want to buy farms
     the person who wants to buy a farm / some farms.

9.1.4 <u>Clause</u> de. The modified noun (and any attendant SP-NU-M expression) may be omitted, in which case the <u>Clause de</u> expression substitutes for the noun that it modifies.

ta cháng chuān de	(the) one(s) he often wears
tamen xiǎng mǎi de	(the) one(s) they intend to buy
wo zuì xǐhuan de	(the) one(s) I like best
wo mǎigei ta de	(the) one(s) I sold him
ta kàn de	(the) one(s) he looked at
jiāo wǒmen Zhōngguo huà de	(the) one(s) who teach(es) us Chinese
huì xiūlǐ qìchē de	(the) one(s) who know(s) how to repair automobiles
xǐhuan zhòng huār de	(the) one(s) who like(s) to grow flowers
huì zuò Zhōngguo cài de	(the) one(s) who know(s) how to cook Chinese dishes

xiǎng mǎi nóngchǎng de   (the) one(s) who intend(s) to buy
                                       a farm / some farms

9.1.5 Clauses in sentences. These clauses, with or without the
nouns that they modify, are noun expressions, and as such they occur
in sentences wherever a noun may occur.

1. wǒ hěn xǐhuan ta cháng chuān de.
    wǒ hěn xǐhuan ta cháng chuān de yīshang.
    wǒ hěn xǐhuan ta cháng chuān de nèijiàn yīshang.
    ta cháng chuān de, hěn guì.
    ta cháng chuān de yīshang, hěn guì.
    ta cháng chuān de nèijiàn yīshang, hěn guì.
2. wǒ búrènshi huì xiūlǐ qìchē de.
    wǒ búrènshi huì xiūlǐ qìchē de rén.
    wǒ búrènshi huì xiūlǐ qìchē de neige rén.
    huì xiūlǐ qìchē de, yě huì zuò cài ma?
    huì xiūlǐ qìche de rén, yě huì zuò cài ma?
    huì xiūlǐ qìchē de neige rén, yě huì zuò cài ma?

English translations of the above:

1. I like the one she often wears.
    I like the clothes that she often wears.
    I like the article of clothing / dress that she often wears.
    What she often wears is expensive.
    The clothes that she often wears are expensive.
    The article of clothing / dress that she often wears is expensive.
2. I don't know anyone who knows how to repair automobiles.
    I don't know any people / person who know(s) how to repair
      automobiles.
    I don't know the person who knows how to repair automobiles.
    Do those who know how to repair automobiles also know how to cook?
    Do people / Does a person who know(s) how to repair automobiles
      also know how to cook?

Does the person who knows how to repair automobiles also know
how to cook?

9.1.6 <u>Clauses in sentences where the original noun modified by</u>
<u>the clause occurs elsewhere in the sentence</u>. A common pattern is
(SP-NU-M) N shi S V de, where N is the noun originally modified by
the S V de clause.

1. nèijiàn yīshang shi ta cháng chuān de.
2. zhèiwǔpǐ mǎ, shi tamen xiǎng mǎi de.
3. nèiduǒ huār, shi wǒ zuì xǐhuan de.
4. nèiwǔwèi lǎoshī, shi jiāo wǒmen Zhōngguo huà de.
5. nèige rén, shi huì xiūlǐ qìchē de.
6. nèiwèi Yīngguo tàitai, shi xǐhuan zhòng huār de.
7. nèixiē wàiguo rén, shi huì zuò Zhōngguo cài de.
8. nèige rén, shi xiǎng mǎi nóngchǎng de.

English translations of the above:

1. The dress is the one she often wears.
2. These five horses are the ones they intend to buy.
3. That flower is the one I like best.
4. Those five teachers are the ones that teach us Chinese.
5. That person is one who knows how to repair automobiles.
6. That English lady is one who likes to grow flowers.
7. Those foreigners are ones who know how to cook Chinese dishes.
8. That person is someone who wants to buy a farm / some farms.

9.1.7 <u>(SP-NU-M) N shi S V de with punctual verbs</u>. Certain verbs
and verbal expressions are "non-punctual". This means that they denote
non-punctual acts or conditions, such as habitual actions (<u>cháng chuān</u>
"often wears"), and continuing states (<u>xiǎng mǎi</u> "intend to buy", <u>zuì</u>
<u>xǐhuan</u> "like best"). Other verbs are "punctual", which means that they
denote single actions, viewed as having short and definite duration.
Punctual verbs and verbal expressions include <u>kàn</u> "(take a) look at",

<u>màigei</u> "sell to", and <u>mǎi</u> "shop for, buy".

When a punctual verb occurs as V in the pattern <u>(SP-NU-M) N shi</u> <u>S V de</u>, it is viewed as having already occurred, and the English translation will be in a past tense form. Often the S has special emphasis.

nèiqīpíng píjiǔ, shi 'shéi
  màigei ta de?
	Who sold him the seven bottles of
	  beer?

shi 'wǒ màigei ta de.	I did.
nèizhāng xiàngpiār, shi 'shéi gěi nǐ de?	Who gave you that photograph?
shi 'tā gěi wǒ de.	He did.
zhèijiàn yīshang, shi nǐ 'zìjǐ zuò de ma?	Did you make that dress yourself?
búshi. shi wǒ māma mǎi de.	No. My mother bought it.

9.2 <u>xiànzài...le</u>. The particle <u>le</u> which indicates change of status often occurs with <u>xiànzài</u> "now".

shū hěn guì.	Books are expensive.
shū guì le.	Books have gotten more expensive.
xiànzài, shū guì le.	Books have gotten more expensive now.
shū, xiànzài guì le.	
wo zhīdao.	I know.
wo zhīdao le.	(Now) I know.
wo xiànzài zhīdao le.	Now I know.
ta zhòng cài.	He grows vegetables.
ta zhòng cài le.	He has started to grow vegetables.
xiànzài, ta zhòng cài le.	Now he's growing vegetables.

Exercises

Answer the following questions:

nèiwèi Zhōngguo xiānsheng, shi shéi?

nèiběn Rìběn shū, yǒuyìsi ma?

ni bàba huì xiūlǐ chē ma?

ni māma xǐhuan zhòng huār ma?

nǐ neige Měiguo péngyou xué huà huàr ma?

tā nèiwei Zhōngguo lǎoshī hěn yǒumíng ma?

zhè shi hǎo zhǐ ma?

nǐ xǐhuan chī guì cài ma?

nèige nánháizi xǐhuan chī wàiguo cài ma?

nèige xuéxiào you duōshao nǚxuésheng?

Make questions to which the following would be appropriate answers:

nà shi wǒ lǎoshī de shū.

búshi ta bàba de nóngchǎng.

shi 'wǒde biǎo.

shi Zhōngguo xiānsheng de.

wǒ yào mǎi wǔmáo qián de zhǐ.

ta xiǎng mài tā nèisānpǐ, sānqiānkuài qián yǐpǐ de
    mǎ.

yǒuyìside shū, yǒude guì, yǒude búguì.

hěn tián de júzi, bùróngyi mǎi.

wo yào neige hǎokànde.

wo xiǎng, yàofànde, bùyídìng dōu méiqián.

Translate into Chinese:

1. What color clothes does she like to wear? - Red.
2. You like the food of what country best? - France.
3. The books I like to read are all expensive.

4. Who are those people speaking Russian? - They are our Russian
   teachers.

5. Is this a dish she prepares often? - Not very often.

6. Who planted these flowers? - My mother did.

7. And what do you think you'll draw? - I think I'll draw one or
   two horses; how about you? - I think I'll draw two or three
   flowers.

8. I don't like those red flowers she's planted.

9. Mrs. Ts'ao's oldest daughter can write for herself now.

10. This apple is spoiled; please give me another one.

11. As soon as I see the character he wrote, I'll know who he is.

12. As soon as I have money, I want to spend it on books.

13. She's planted a lot of vegetables.

<u>Review of modification of nouns</u>

After having done the exercises, and after having re-read 8.1-8.3
and 9.1-9.1.7, and other relevant material on the modification of
nouns, take the following informal test.

In the following sentences, fill in the blanks with "de" if <u>de</u>
is required, "(de)" if <u>de</u> is optional, and "0" if no <u>de</u> is permitted.

nǐmen xiǎng mǎi _____nóngchǎng, mài duōshao qián?

ta xiě_____zì, zhēn hǎokàn.

nèizhǐ zhū, shi wǒ péngyou mǎi_____.

nǐ_____nèiliǎnge nán_____háizi, cháng huà huàr ma?

nǐ kàn, yǒu nèmma duō_____qīngcài.

wǒ_____lǎoshǐ yǒu hěn duō_____Zhōngguo_____shū.

piányi_____zhǐ, bùyídìng hǎokàn_____.

nèige màibào_____yě mài shū ma?

nǐ_____biǎo hěn guì ma?

hěn guì_____biǎo, bùyídìng hěn hǎo.

tā zìjǐ zhòng_____cài, hǎo'chǐ buhǎochǐ?

Lesson 10
Location and existence, and continuative ne

Pronunciation

<u>Plain</u>:

<u>a</u>:   Fàguo; náli"where?"; nà; nàli "there"; là; kāfēi; chá.

<u>e</u>:   Déguo; hé; zhè; zhèli "here"; chē; yánsè; Èguo.

<u>i</u>:   shì; sì.

<u>ai</u>: yìbǎi; Táiběi "Taipei"; tài; kāi "drive"; hái; Shànghǎi "Shanghai"
       cài; zài$_1$; zài$_2$ "at"; ài.

<u>ei</u>: yìbēi; Běijīng "Peking"; měi; děi; gěi; shéi.

<u>ao</u>: yìmáo; lǎoshī; hǎo; zhǎo "look for"; Zhào; duōshao; shǎo "few";
       zǎo.

<u>ou</u>: yìtóu; tóuyíge "the first"; lóu "building"; gòu; hòutou "back
       part"; Méizhōu; Guǎngzhōu "Canton"; zǒu "travel".

<u>an</u>: fàn; nánde; Nánjīng "Nanking"; Hánguo; shān; sān.

<u>en</u>: yìběn; mén "door"; nèmma; hěn; zěmma.

<u>ang</u>: bàngqiú; pángbiār "side"; yìfānglǐ; fángzi "building"; táng;
       gāng "just now"; gāngbǐ; Xiānggǎng "Hong Kong"; Xīngǎng "New Haven";
       cháng; shàngtou "top".

<u>eng</u>: péngyou; néng; zhèngzai; chéng "city".

<u>ar</u>: yíbàr; nǎr? "where"; xiǎohár.

<u>er</u>: fèr; nèr "there"; zhèr; èr.

<u>Frontalized</u>:

<u>ia</u>: jiā "family"; Jiānádà; xiàtou "below".

<u>ie</u>: bié "do not...!"; xiě; yě.

<u>i</u>: dǐxia "underneath"; dìyíge "the first"; dìdi; Lǐ; yìlǐ; lǐtou
       "inside"; xǐhuan; yǐzi.

178

<u>iao</u>: biǎo; yìtiáo; xiǎo; yào.

<u>iu</u>: niú; Niǔyuē "New York"; qiú; yǒu.

<u>ian</u>: biān "side", pángbiān "side"; xiàngpiān; piányi; diǎnxin "snack";
shūdiàn "bookstore"; yìtiān "one day"; tián; niàn "study"; jiàn;
yìjiān "one (room)"; qián; qiántou "front"; yánsè.

<u>in</u>: nín; xīn; diǎnxīn "snack".

<u>iang</u>: yíliàng; Xiānggǎng "Hong Kong"; xiàngpiān.

<u>ing</u>: píngguo; Běipíng "Peiping"; míngzi; yídìng; tīng shuō "hear it
said that"; Běijīng "Peking"; Nánjīng "Nanking"; qīngcài; Yīngguo.

<u>iar</u>: pángbiār "side"; xiàngpiār; yìdiǎr; yìjiār "(M: shops)".

<u>ier</u>: (none yet)

Labialized:

<u>ua</u>: huà.

<u>uo</u>: duō; guó; shuō; zuò; yízuò; zuòzai "sit at"; yìsuǒ "one (build-
ing)"; wǒ.

<u>u</u>: bù; pùzi "a shop"; shūpù "bookstore"; lù; zhū; zúqiú; wǔ; wūzi
"room".

<u>uai</u>: huài le; wàitou "outside".

<u>ui</u>: búduì; huì; shuǐ; zuì; yíwèi.

<u>uan</u>: chuān; suān; fànguǎnzi "restaurant" yìwǎn.

<u>un</u>: yícùn; wèn.

<u>uang</u>: Guǎngzhōu "Canton"; huángde; Wáng.

<u>ong</u>: dōngxi "thing"; dǒng; hóngde; róngyi; cōngming.

<u>uar</u>: fànguǎr "restaurant"; huār; huàr.

<u>uor</u>: yìduǒr; yìsuǒr "one (building)".

<u>uer</u>: (none yet)

<u>ur</u>: (none yet)

Frontalized and labialized:

ue: xué; Niǔyuē "New York".
ü: lǜde; júzi.

Dialogs, etc.

I

Zhāng Guóxīn, gāng huì kāi
chē. ta mèimei zhèngzai
xué ne.

yǒu yìtiān, Guóxīn kāi chē;
ta fùmǔ yě zuòzai chēshang;
mèimei zuòzai Guóxīn pángbiār, fùmǔ zuòzai Guóxīn
hòutou. tāmen dōu bùshuō
huà.
māma shuō: 'zěmma nǐmen dōu
bùshuō huà ya?
bàba shuō: Guóxīn; ni 'wèishemma bùzǒu 'nèitiáo lù a?
mèimei shuō: nèitiáo lù yuǎn;
zhèitiáo lù jìn. 'wèishemma
yào zǒu 'nèitiáo lù ne?

bàba shuō: Guóxīn; wǒ gàosong
ni; nèitiáo zuì hǎozǒu. nǐ
'zěmma bùzǒu 'nèitiáo lù ne?
Guóxīn gāng yào shuō huà; māma
shuō: Guóxīn; nǐ bié shuō
huà. ni kāi chē ba.

Kuo-hsin Chang had just learned how
to drive. His (younger) sister
was just in the process of learning.
One day, Kuo-hsin was driving, and
his parents were also sitting in
the car; his sister was sitting
next to him, and his parents were
sitting behind him. No one said
anything.
His mother said, "How come none of
you are saying anything?"
His father said, "Kuo-hsin, why
don't you take that road?"
His sister said, "That way is
longer; the way we're going is
shorter. So, why do you want to
go that way?"
His father said, "I'm telling you,
Kuo-hsin, that way is easier.
Why don't you go that way?"
Just as Kuo-hsin was about to speak,
his mother said, "Kuo-hsin, don't
talk; just drive."

II

xiǎoháizi shuō huà, zhēn
   yǒuyìsi. yǒu yìtiān, yǒu
   sānge háizi shuō tāmende chē.

yíge shuō: wǒmende chē, yǒu
   sìge mén.

yíge shuō: wǒmende chē, yǒu
   'liǎngge mén.

yíge shuō: wǒmende chē, yǒu
   'sānge mén.

tóuliǎngge háizi, wèn dì'sānge
   háizi: 'zěmma nǐmende chē,
   néng yǒu sānge mén ne?

dì'sāngge háizi shuō: wǒmende chē, yìbiār you yíge mén;
   hòutou yě yǒu yíge mén. nà
   búshi sānge mén ma?

nèiliǎngge háizi shuō: 'nèige
   ya! 'nèige búshi mén!

What children say is really cute.
   One day, there were three children
   talking about their cars.

One said, "Our car has four doors."

One said, "Our car has two doors."

And one said, "Our car has three
   doors."

The first two children asked the
   third, "How come your car can
   have three doors?"

The third child said, "Our car has
   one door on each side; and there's
   a door in the back, too. Isn't
   that three doors?"

The two other children said, "That!
   That isn't a door."

III

A: ni dìdi zài 'nǎr niàn
   shū?

B: ta zài chéng 'wàitou
   yìsuǒ xuéxiào, niàn shū.

A: shi zài 'shānshang de
   nèiyisuǒ ma?

B: búshi. shi zài hé 'pángbiār de nèiyisuǒ.

A: nèisuǒ xuéxiào, fángzi
   'duō buduō?

Where does your (younger) brother
   go to school?

He goes to a school outside the
   city.

Is it the one on the mountain?

No, it's the one by the river.

About that school: are its buildings
   many or not? / Does that school
   have a lot of buildings?

B: nèisuǒ xuéxiào de fángzi,
    zhēn bùshǎo. you liù-qízuǒ
    dà lóu; èrshi-duōsuǒ fángzi.

The buildings of that school are
truly un-few. / Yes, quite a few
indeed. There are six or seven
big (storied) buildings; over
twenty (smaller) buildings.

A: nǐ dìdi zài 'nǎr chī fàn ne?

And where does your brother eat?

B: ta chángchang zài xuéxiào
    wàitou de yíge fànguǎr chī fàn.

He often eats at a restaurant
outside the school.

A: shi nèijiā 'Zhōngguo fànguǎr
    ma?

Is it that Chinese restaurant?

B: búshi. shi nèijiā Zhōngguo
    fànguǎr pángbiār de yíge xiǎo
    wàiguo fànguǎr.

No, it's a small foreign restaurant
next to the Chinese restaurant.

A: wo tīng shuō, ta zài yige
    'pùzili zuò shì. shì ma?

I hear he has a job in a shop. Is
that so?

B: shì. ta zài yíge shūpùli
    zuò shì.

Yes. He works in a bookstore.

A: nèijiā shūpù 'yuǎn buyuǎn?

Is that bookstore far away?

B: bùyuǎn. nèijiā shūpù,
    jiù zai ta chī fàn de
    neijia fànguǎr lóushàng.

No. It's just upstairs from the
restaurant where he eats.

IV

A: wo yào mǎi diar 'chī de
    dōngxi. zhèr yǒu mài
    diǎnxin de 'pùzi méiyǒu?

I want to buy a little something to
eat. Is there a place around
here that sells snacks?

B: 'zhèr méiyǒu. hé neibiar
    you liǎngjiā. yìjiā mài
    'Měiguo diǎnxin; yìjiā mài
    'Fàguo diǎnxin. liǎngjiā
    de diǎnxin dōu hěn hǎo.

Not around here. Over by the river
there are two. One sells American
snacks, one sells French ones.
Both are good.

A: nèr yě yǒu mài yīshang de
    pùzi ma?

Are there any shops that sell
clothing around there, too?

B: nèr yǒu 'hǎojǐjiā mǎi   Yes, quite a few. I often go
   yīshang de pùzi. wo cháng   there to buy clothes.
   zài nèr mǎi yīshang.

A: nǎyijiā de yīshang zuì hǎo?   Which is the best?

B: nèijiā jiào Zhōng-Měi de,   The one called "China-America" is
   zuì hǎo. dōngxi hǎo; yě   best. The things (they sell) are
   piányi.   good, and cheap, too.

V

A: zhuōzi shàngtou de nèiběn   Whose is the book on the table?
   shū shi shéide?

B: búshi wǒde. wo xiǎng shi   It's not mine. I think it's Chen-
   Zhēnzhēnde.   chen's.

A: Zhēnzhēn; nèiběn shū shi   Chen-chen, is that book yours?
   nǐde ma?

C: búshi. wǒ nèiběn shū...   No. My book... Hey! Where's my
   you? wǒ nèiběn shū zài nǎr   book?
   ne!

A: yǐzi dǐxia yǒu yìběn shū.   There's a book under the chair.
   nǐ kànkan shi nǐde bushi?   Take a look and see if it's yours.

C: nà búshi wǒde shū.   That's not my book; there's no
   shūshang méiyou míngzi.   name on it.

A: nǐ kànkan, shū'lǐtou yǒu   Take a look and see if there's a
   meiyou míngzi?   name inside the book.

C: nèixiē zì shi Zhōngguo zì,   Those characters are Chinese, and
   wo búrènshi.   (so) I don't know (them).

A: 'shéi jiào Zhāng Měishēng?   Whose name is Chang Mei-sheng?

B: o. nà shi 'wǒde shū.   Oh. That's my book.

VI

A: Guóxīn zài jiā ma?   Is Kuo-hsin at home?

B: ta búzài jiā.   No.

A: Guóxiān ne?   How about Kuo-hsien?

B: Guǒxiān yě búzài jiā.   He's not home, either. They're
    tamen dōu zài xuéxiào ne.   both at school.

A: tamen dōu zài xuéxiào zuò   And what are they (both) doing at
    shémma ne?   school?

B: tamen dōu zài dǎ wǎngqiú ne.   They're playing tennis.

A: Měishēng yě búzài jiā ma?   Isn't Mei-sheng home either?

B: Měishēng zài wūzili niàn   Mei-sheng is in her room studying.
    shū ne. Měishēng! nǐ yǒu   Mei-sheng! You have a friend
    yíge péngyou zhǎo nǐ.   looking for you.

New words

shàngtou PW[1]	surface, top, above
xiàtou PW	bottom, below
lǐtou PW	inside
wàitou PW	outside
qiántou PW	front
hòutou PW	back
dǐxia PW	area underneath
pángbiār, pángbiān PW	area nearby, next to
shàngtou yǒu shū.	There are some books on top.
xiàtou, hái yǒu yige zì.	There is one more character below (the last one).
lǐtou yǒu míngzi ma?	Is there a name inside?
wàitou yǒu hěn duō rén.	There are a lot of people outside.
qiántou yǒu yìtiáo dà lù.	There's a big road in front.
hòutou yǒu yízuò xiǎo shān.	There's a little mountain in back.
dǐxia méiyou shuǐ.	There's no water underneath.
pángbiār yǒu xuéxiào.	There's a school nearby.
-shang L[2]	surface, top, above
-li L[2]	inside
zhǐ shàngtou / zhǐshang	the surface of the paper

shān shàngtou / shānshang	the surface of the mountain
zhuōzi shàngtou / zhuōzishang	the top of the table
shū shàngtou / shūshang	the surface of the book; the surface (of a page) of the book
shū shàngtou de míngzi	the name on the book
shūshang shuō	it says (on:) in the book
bào shàngtou / bàoshang	the surface of the newspaper; the surface (of a page) of the newspaper
bào shàngtou de huàr	the drawing in the newspaper
bàoshang shuō	it says (on:) in the newspaper
huàr lǐtou / huàrli	the inside of the drawing
shān lǐtou / shānli	the inside of the mountains
shuǐ lǐtou / shuǐli	the inside of the water
yǐzi xiàtou	the bottom of the chair
xuéxiào wàitou	the area outside of the school
xuéxiào qiántou	the area in front of the school
xuéxiào hòutou	the area in back of the school
zhuōzi dǐxia	the area underneath the table
xuéxiào pángbiār	the area next to / near the school
zài V	be located at
zài shàngtou.	It's on the top.
zài xiàtou.	It's on the bottom.
zài lǐtou.	It's inside.
zài wàitou.	It's outside.
zài qiántou.	It's in front.
zài hòutou.	It's in back.
zài pángbiār.	It's next to it. / It's nearby.
shū zài shàngtou.	The books are on the top.
zì zài xiàtou.	The characters are further down.
míngzi zài lǐtou.	The name is inside.
rén dōu zài wàitou.	The people are all outside.
dà lù zài qiántou.	The big / main street is in front.

nèizuǒ xiǎo shān zài hòutou.	The little mountain is in back.
shuǐ zài dǐxia.	The water is underneath.
xuéxiào zài pángbiār.	The school is next to it.
--- CV³	(located) at
zài xuéxiào kàn bào	read a newspaper in a school
zài fànguǎrli chī fàn	eat in a restaurant
zài pùzili mǎi táng	buy candy in a store
zài lóushang huà huàr	paint paintings upstairs
zài lóuxia zuò fàn	cook downstairs (in the area)
zài chéng wàitou kāi chē	drive outside the city
zài shūli xiě míngzi	write a name in the book
--- A	(be at:) be in the process of
nǎr?, náli? PW	where?
zhèr, zhèli PW⁴	here
nèr, nàli PW⁴	there
'nǎr yǒu xuéxiào?	Where is there a school?
'zhèr méiyou xuéxiào.	There's no school (around) here.
'nèr yǒu xuéxiào.	There's a school over there.
zhèr mài wàiguo bào ma?	Do they sell foreign newspapers here?
zhèr búmài wàiguo bào.	No, they don't.
nǐ shi 'nǎrde rén?	Where are you from?
wǒ shi 'zhèrde rén.	I'm from around here.
dìdi zài nǎr?	Where is your (younger) brother?
tā zài zhèr ma?	Is he here?
tā zài nèr.	He's over there.
chéng N (M: -zuò)	city
chéng lǐtou / chéngli	the area inside of the city; downtown
chéng wàitou	the area outside of the city
Běijīng PW	(northern capital:) Peking
Běipíng PW	(northern plain:) Peiping
Nánjīng PW	(southern capital:) Nanking

Táiběi PW	(Tai[wan]'s north:) Taipei
Shànghǎi PW	(going up to the sea:) Shanghai
Xiānggǎng PW	(fragrant harbor:) Hong Kong
Guǎngzhōu PW	(Kwang[tung Province]'s administrative region / provincial capital:) Canton
Niǔyuē PW	(Cantonese Nīuyēuk:) New York
Xīngǎng PW	(new harbor:) New Haven
Xīngǎng chéngli, hǎo xuéxiào, bùhěn duō.	There aren't many good schools in New Haven.
mén N	door; gate
mén wàitou PW	outdoors (near the house)
fángzi N (M: -suǒ)	building
lóu N (M: -zuò)	building of two or more stories
fànguǎr, fànguǎnzi, fàndiàn N (M: -jiā)	restaurant
pùzi N (M: -jiā)	shop
shāngdiàn N (M: -jiā)	(goods shop:) store
shūpù, shūdiàn N (M: -jiā)	bookstore
jiǔpù, jiǔdiàn N (M: -jiā)	liquor store
zhǐpù, zhǐdiàn N (M: -jiā)	stationery store
hǎo fànguǎr	a good restaurant
dà mén	a big door; main gate
dà lóu	a big (storied) building
xiǎo pùzi	a small shop
zuì dà de shūpù	the biggest bookstore
fànguǎr lǐtou / fànguárli	the inside of the restaurant
fángzi wàitou	the area outside of the building
dà lóu qiántou	the area in front of the big (storied) building
jiǔpù hòutou	the area behind the liquor store
zhǐdiàn pángbiār	the area next to / near the stationery store

lóushàng PW	upstairs
lóuxià PW	downstairs
lóu dǐxià PW	downstairs
yīlóu PW	first floor
èrlóu PW	second floor

èrlóu yǒu liǎngge shūpù.   There are two bookstores on the second floor.

lóuxiàde fànguǎr tài guì.   The restaurant downstairs is too expensive.

jiā PW, N[5]   home; family

zhè shi shéide jiā?   Whose home is this?

zhè shi 'shémma rén de jiā?

zhè shi Wángjia.   This is the Wang's.

ni jiāli yǒu 'jǐge rén?   How many people are there in your family?

wo jiāli yígòng yǒu bāge rén.   Altogether, there are eight.

ni jiāli yǒu 'shémma rén?   Who are there in your family?

ni jiāli de rén, dōu shi shéi?

ni jiāliren, dōu shi shéi?

ni jiāde rén, dōu shi shéi?

wo jiāli yǒu wo bàba, māma,   There are my father and mother,
    yíge gēge, sānge jiějie,   one older brother, three older
    yíge mèimei, hái you wǒ.   sisters and one younger sister,
                                and me.

zài jiā   be at home

nǐ fùmǔ 'zài buzài jiā?   Are your parents home?

tamen dōu búzài jiā.   No, they're both out.

dōngxi N (M: jiàn)   thing, object

zài pùzili mǎi dōngxi   buy things in a store

tamen mài de dōngxi, hěn hǎo.   The things they sell are good. /
                                 They sell good products.

'chī de dōngxi   something to eat

wūzi N (M: -jiān)   room

diǎnxin, diǎnxīn N

   'nǎr yǒu mài hǎo diǎnxin
      de pùzi?
   wǒmen chī shémma diǎnxin?

Zhōng-Měi AT
   Zhōng-Měi Shūdiàn
tóu- SP[6]

   tóuyíge rén
   tóuliǎngge háizi
   tóusān-sìge zì
dì- SP[6]

   dìyíge rén
   dìshíèrsuǒ fángzi
   dìèrge háizi
   dìyī... IE
hǎojǐ- NU
   hǎojǐjiā fànguǎr
   hǎojǐge péngyou
-suǒ, -suǒr M
-jiā, -jiār M
-biān, -biār M
biān, biār N
   chē yǒu liǎngge biār.
   yìbiār you yíge mén.

   'něibiār yǒu shūpù?

   'zhèibiār yǒu ma?

-jiān M

(dot a "heart" [character]:)
snack; light refreshment; dessert
   Where is there a shop which sells
      good snacks?
   What shall we have as an appetizer
      / for dessert?
(Zhōng[guo]-Měi[guo]): China-America
   China-America Bookstore
(head:) the first...
   the first person
   the first two children
   the first three or four characters
(ordinalizing prefix, makes an
   ordinal number out of a cardinal
   number) the...-st, the...-th, etc.
   the first person
   the twelfth building
   the second child
   first of all...
(a good few:) quite a few
   quite a few restaurants
   quite a few friends
(buildings)
(lit. "family"; shops, restaurants)
(side)
side
   A car has two sides.
   One side has a door. / Each side
      has a door.
   On which side / Where is there a
      bookshop?
   Is there one on this side /
      (around) here?
(rooms)

'zhèibiār méiyou. 'nèibiār yǒu.	Not around here; there's one over there.
sìbiār PW	(all) four sides; all around
sìbiār dōu shi shuǐ.	It was / There was water all around.
!7	(exclamatory intonation pattern: indicates surprise, irritation, emphasis)
'zěmma! MA	How come...?!
'nǐ 'zěmma kāi chē le!	How come you're driving?!
'zěmma nǐ kāi chē!	
yào AV	want to (4); be about to, be going to
wo búyào kàn shū.	I don't want to read. / I am not about to read.
ta yào mǎi dōngxi.	He wants to buy some things. / He's going to buy some things.
gāng A	just (recently, in the past), was about to.
wo gāng yào mǎi.	I was just going to buy it.
wo gāng màigei ta.	I just sold it to him.
wo gāng yào màigei ta.	I was just going to sell it to him
wo gāng shuō...	Just as I said...
wo gāng yào shuō...	Just as I was about to say...
ta gāng yào shuō huà.	He was just about to speak.
bié AV	(negative imperative auxiliary verb) Don't...!
bié shuō huà.	Don't talk!
nǐ bié zài kàn le. -- hǎo; wo búzai kàn le.	Don't look again. -- OK; I won't.
wǒmen bié zài xiǎng nèijiàn shì ba.	Let's not think of that matter again.
bié zài chī táng le.	Don't take any more candy.

búyào AV

not want to (4); be not going to; (negative second person auxiliary verb)

búyào gàosong ta.

Don't tell her!

búyào shuō huà.

Don't talk!

huì AV

know how to, can (7); learn how to

ta gāng huì kāi chē.

He has just learned how to drive.

ta gāng huì xiě zì.

He has just learned how to write.

ta gāng huì shuō huà.

He has just learned how to talk.

yǒuyìsi SV

interesting, fun (8); cute, appealing (activities of children, small animals, etc.)

xiǎoháizi zhēn yǒuyìsi.

(What) children (do) is really cute.

xiǎoháizi shuō huà, zhēn yǒuyìsi.

Children say things that are very cute.

shǎo SV[8]

few, little (in amount)

ta huà de huàr, hěn bùshǎo.

He painted quite a few paintings.

ta xiě de shū zhēn bùshǎo.

He wrote quite a few books.

tāde shū bùshǎo.

He has quite a few books.

wǒde shū hěn shǎo.

I have very few books.

rén hěn shǎo.

There are very few people.

rén bùshǎo.

There are quite a few people.

kāi V

(open [the throttle of a car]): drive; open

kāi chē VO

drive (an automobile)

wo búyuànyi kāi chē.

I don't want to drive.

kāi mén VO

open the door / gate

-zai VS

(zài: be at:) so that the actor is located at the place denoted by the place-word object of the verb; at; in; beside zuòzai V

sit, so that one is at:) sit at /
in / beside...

zuòzai yǐzishang

sit on a chair

zuòzai zhuōzi pángbiār

sit next to the table

zuòzai Zhēnzhēn pángbiār

sit next to Chen-chen

zǒu V

(travel:) take (a route / road)

women zǒu 'nèitiáo lù?

Which road shall we take?

women zǒu 'nèitiáo; 'hǎo
  buhǎo?

Let's take that one, OK?

hǎozǒu SV[9]

easy to travel

nèitiáo lù, bùhǎozǒu.

That road isn't easy to travel. /
That way / route is harder.

zhèitiáo lù hǎozǒu.

This way / route is easier.

shuō V

speak (4); say (5); talk about

tamen shuō tamende chē.

They're talking about their cars.

tamen shuō tamende mǎimai.

They're talking about their
business.

niàn V

read, study

niàn shū   VO

read, study, go to school

ni niàn shémma shū?

What book are you reading /
studying?

ni niàn shémma?

What are you studying?

zài xuéxiào niàn shū

study in a school

nǐ zài nǎr niàn shū?

Where do you go to school?

wo xiànzài niàn Fǎwén; wo
  zhèngzai yào niàn Yīngwén.

I'm studying French now; I'm
just about to study English.

tīng shuō V

(hear say:) (I) hear that...

wo tīng shuō, ni māma hěn
  huì zuò mǎimai.

I hear that your mother's a
very good businesswoman.

wo tīng shuō, nèijiā fànguǎr de
  cài, bùhěn hǎochī.

I hear that the dishes at that
restaurant aren't too good.

ne P   (following a noun:) And what about
                                        (the noun)? (5.12); at the end
                                        of a content question:) And...?
                                        (9); (at the end of a statement:
                                        emphasizes the fact that the
                                        state, location, or action is
                                        continuing at the time of the
                                        statement)

ta zhèngzai chī fàn ne.   She's right in the process of
                                            eating.

ta zhèng chī fàn ne.

ta zài chī fàn ne.   She's in the process of eating.

tamen zài dǎ bàngqiú ne.   They're playing baseball at the
                                            moment.

kànkan V[10]   take a look and see

  ni kànkan, you 'duōshao   Take a look and see how many
    rén?   people there are.

  ni kànkan, lǐtou 'yǒu   Take a look and see if there's
    meiyǒu shuǐ.   any water inside.

yǒu yitiān IE   (there was a day:) One day...

  yǒu yitiān, tamen dǎ   One day, they played basketball;
    lánqiu; yǒu yitiān, tamen   one day they played baseball.
    dǎ bàngqiu.

you? I[11]   Hey!

o. I[11, 12]   Oh.

Notes

[1]"PW" stands for "place word", which is a noun that has certain
characteristic privileges of occurrence. One of the places in which
a place word may occur but in which other nouns may not, is after the
verb zài "be located at". Place words include many, but not all,
nouns denoting places. Names of cities and countries are place words,
but names of rivers, mountains, and other geographical entities are

not. Thus, it is possible to say zài Zhōngguo "in China" and zài
Shànghǎi "in Shanghai", but not *zai Tài Shān or *zai Huáng Hé.
xuéxiào is a place word but fángzi "building" is not.

Like other nouns, a place word may be modified by another noun,
and the resulting expression functions in a sentence like a place word:
it has the same privileges of occurrence as the PW, such as the position after zài:

zài Zhōngguo	in China
zài Shànghǎi	in Shanghai
zài xuéxiào	in school
zài Tài Shān shàngtou	on top of Mt. T'ai
zài Huáng Hé lǐtou	in the Yellow River
zài fángzi lǐtou	inside the building

Notice that the place words introduced in this lesson do not
usually take a preceding de when modified by another noun.

[2]"L" stands for "localizer", which is a bound noun used in
combination with other nouns to form place words. shàng, xià, lǐ,
wài, qián, and hòu are all localizers. Combined with the nominal
suffix -tou, they all make the place words mentioned above, note 1.
shàngtou and lǐtou are different from the other place words in that
they may be shortened to just the localizer, with the neutral
tone, and suffixed to a noun, to make a place word. Thus shàngtou
becomes shang and is added directly to a preceding noun: zhuōzishang
"the top of the table"; similarly, lǐtou becomes li: shuǐli "the
inside of the water".

[3]"CV" stands for "co-verb", a functive verb or verbal expression,
which with its direct object precedes another verb and modifies it.
The CV-O expression forms a verbal expression with the verb that it
modifies, such that a negative adverb, like bù, normally precedes the
coverb, not the verb.

ni zài Niǔyuē niàn shū ma?   Do you study in New York?

wo búzài Niǔyuē niàn shū.   No, I don't study in New York.

[4]The demonstrative place words zhèr (zhèli) "here" and nèr (nàli) "there" occur with the neutral tone suffixed to nouns to form place words:

nǐner yǒu táng ma?   Is there any sugar over there by
                                       you?

wǒzher méiyou táng. tāner   No, not over here; there's some
   you. táng zài tāner.   over there where she is; the
                                       sugar is over there by her.

ménner yǒu huār.   There are some flowers over there
                                       by the gate / door.

[5]jiā is both a place word, in that it occurs alone after zài: zài jiā "is at home"; and a noun, in that it occurs with the localizer -li to form a new place word: jiāli "the inside of the family: the family". jiāli de rén "people in (one's) family" may be abbreviated to jiāliren, with the neutral tone on -ren.

jia, the toneless form of jiā, occurs suffixed to surnames to form new place words: Wángjia "the Wang's (residence)".

[6]The prefixes tóu- and dì- are specifiers, because they occupy the SP slot in SP-NU-M expressions, replacing zhèi-, nèi-, and něi-there.

dì- ordinalizes a cardinal number, that is, it turns "one" into "the first", "ten" into "the tenth", and so on. It occurs only before numbers, i.e., the words from yī to shí and their compounds. It does not occur directly before -bǎi, -qiān, and -wàn and their compounds, because, grammatically speaking, these are not numbers, but measures: so instead of *dìbǎige, one says dìyìbǎige "the hundredth". (See Lesson 6, "New Words," note 6.)

tóu- ordinalizes the cardinal number that it precedes and

specifies that it is "the first" such a number. That is, it turns
"one" into "the first (one)", "ten" into "the first ten", and so on.
Like dì-, it only occurs before numbers; unlike dì-, it occurs before
indefinite expressions of the type "two or three": tóuliǎng-sānge
"the first two or three."

[7] : stands for the "exclamatory" intonation pattern. It resembles
the declarative intonation pattern (.) in that it ends with a lower
range of pitches than when it starts. It differs from the declarative
pattern in that the high pitches are higher and the low pitches are
lower. (See 1.1.)

[8] Like duō, shǎo must be preceded by an adverb when it modifies
a noun. Usually this adverb is bù: bùshǎo means "un-few, quite a
few, quite a lot of". Again like duō, the adverb-verb expression
formed with shǎo, viz. bùshǎo, is optionally followed by de when it
modifies a following noun. (See Lesson 9, "New Words," note 8.)

[9] hǎo "good" combines with functive verbs to form hǎo-V compounds
that are stative verbs. There are two meanings of hǎo in these compounds. One is "good to", as in hǎokàn "good to look at, good-looking"
and hǎochī "good to eat, tasty". The other is "easy to", as in hǎozǒu
"easy to travel". Other compounds with hǎo in the latter meaning are
exemplified below.

Zhōngguo biǎo, hěn bùhǎomǎi.	Chinese watches are hard to buy.
huār hěn hǎozhòng.	Flowers are easy to grow.
zhèiliàng chē, hǎo'kāi buhǎokāi?	Is this car easy to drive (cars)?
-- bùhǎokāi.	-- No.
wàiguo chē, bùhǎoxiūlǐ.	It's not easy to repair foreign cars.
Zhōngguo huàr, bùhǎohuà.	It's hard to paint Chinese paintings.
Měiguo zúqiú, bùhǎodǎ.	It's hard to play American football.
yǒude Zhōngguo zì, hěn hǎoxiě.	It's easy to write certain Chinese characters.
wo xiǎng, tā zuòde shì, hěn hǎozuò.	I think it's easy to do his job.

Zhōngguo táng, bùhǎomài.   It's hard to sell Chinese candy.

zhèige dōngxi, hěn hǎomài.   It's easy to sell this thing.

zhèitiáo lù, hěn hǎozǒu.   It's easy to go on this road.

[10]Cf. wènwen, Lesson 5, note 13.

[11]"I" stands for "Interjection". Interjections are exclamatory
words which stand alone as sentences. Some Chinese interjections
carry no tone of their own, but instead carry an intonation. you?
and o. are such interjections. you? starts relatively high, and
stays high.

[12]o. has the vowel of wǒ "I". It starts at about the middle of
the pitch range, and drops.

More notes on grammar

10.1 Location. When the location of an object or person occupies
the focus of attention in a sentence, the expression denoting the location occurs in the comment (see 1.5) as the place word object of zài
"(be) located at", which may be a verb or a co-verb; the expression
denoting the object or person occurs in the topic.

Notice that three semantic elements expressed in Chinese are
often translated by a single preposition in English. For example,
zài zhuōzi shàngtou is literally "at table's top". The "at", is
expressed by zài; the "-'s" is expressed by the modifier-modified
relationship (see 1.6) that obtains between the noun zhuōzi and the
place noun shàngtou; the "top" is expressed by shàngtou. In English,
the "at", plus the "-'s", plus the "top" collapse into the single
preposition "on".

10.1.1 zài as V.

```
(Topic)  Comment.
(S)      (A)   V    O.
(N)      (bú)zài (N)   PW.
```

	zài		nǎr?	Where is it?
gāngbǐ	zài		nǎr?	Where is the pen?
gāngbǐ	zài	zhuōzi	shàngtou.	The pen's on the table.
	bú-zài	yǐzi	-shang ma?	It's not on the chair?
	zài	zhuōzi	-shang.	It's on the table.
	zài		shàngtou.	It's on top.
nǐde chē,	zai		nǎr ne?	Where's your car at the moment?
wǒde chē,	zai	xuéxiào	qiántou ne.	It's in front of the school.

ni gāng mǎi de dōngxi, zài
nǎr ne?

Where are the things you just
bought?

wo gāng mǎi de dōngxi, dōu
hái zài pùzili ne.

They're all still at the store.

diǎnxin dōu zài nǎr ne?

And where are the snacks, at the
moment?

diǎnxin dōu zài lóu dǐxia ne.

They're downstairs.

jiǔpù zài zhǐpù pángbiār.

The liquor store is next to the
stationery store.

māma zài wàiguo ne.

Mother's out of the country, at
the moment.

wo xiānsheng zài fángzi hòutou
ne.

My husband is behind the building,
at the moment.

háizimen dōu zài Cáojia.

The children are all at the Ts'ao's.

tamen zài dà lóuner.

They're over by the big (storied)
building.

10.1.2 zài <u>as CV.</u>

```
    (Topic)        Comment.
    (S)            (A) CV  O                      V   O.
    (N)            (bú)zài (N)            PW       V   N.
```

1.		zài		'năr	zuò shì ne?
2.	ni xiānsheng	zài		'năr	zuò shì ne?
3.	ta	bú-zài	neijia pùzi -li		zuò shì ma?
4.	ta	bú-zài		nèr	zuò shì.
5.	ta	zài chéng		wàitou	zuò măimai.

English translations of the above:

1. And where is (he) working, at the moment?
2. And where is your husband working at the moment?
3. Isn't he working at that shop?
4. No, he's not working there.
5. He has a business outside the city.

ta zài pùzili măi dōngxi ne.	At the moment, he's buying things at the store.
ta zài lóuxià niàn shū.	He studies downstairs.
ta zài lóuxià niàn shū ne.	He's studying downstairs, at the moment.
ta búzài lóuxià niàn shū.	He doesn't study downstairs. / He isn't studying downstairs.
nǐmen bié zài shūli xiě míngzi.	Don't write your names in your books.
wŏmen zài hòutou chī fàn ba.	Let's eat in back.
ta zài fángzi pángbiār xiūlǐ chē ne.	At the moment, he's at the side of the house, fixing a car.
ta zài 'jiāli kàn shū ne ma?	Is he reading at home, at the moment?
ta zài jiā kàn shū ne.	Yes, he is.
ta zài Zhōngguo xué Zhōngguo huà ne.	At the moment, he's in China, learning Chinese.
ta zài Niŭyuē jiāo Yīngwén.	He teaches English in New York.

ta zài ménshang xiě dà zì ne.   He's writing big characters on the
                                       door, at the moment.

    Notice that the continuative particle <u>ne</u> is not used with <u>bu-</u>
in sentences of this pattern.

    10.2 <u>Existence</u>. When the object or person that exists at a
certain location occupies the focus of attention in a sentence, the
expression denoting the location occurs in the topic, and the expression denoting the object or person occurs in the comment as the object
of the verb <u>(méi)yǒu</u> "(not) have, there is (not)".

    The fact that the place word is in topic position before <u>(méi)yǒu</u>
implies an "at". So when we analyze the sentence <u>zhuōzi shàngtou yǒu</u>
<u>gāngbǐ</u>, which is literally "The table's top has pens. / (At) the
table's top, there are pens.", the "at" is expressed by the fact that
the place word occupies the topic position; the "-'s" is expressed by
the modifier-modified relationship that obtains between the noun
<u>zhuōzi</u> and the place word <u>shàngtou</u>; the "top" is expressed by <u>shàngtou</u>
Once again, the "at", plus the "-'s", plus the "top" collaspe in Engli
into the single preposition "on". Notice further that whereas in
English the "there is/are (not)" often occurs at the beginning of the
sentence, the corresponding word in Chinese, <u>(méi)yǒu</u>, always occupies
the position after any place word and before its direct object.

(Topic)   Comment.
(S)   (A) V
((N)   PW)   (méi)yǒu

zhuōzi-shang   yǒu shémma dōngxi? What objects are there on
                                            the table?

                      yǒu gāngbǐ ma?   Are there pens?
zhuōzi shàngtou   yǒu gāngbǐ ma?   Are there pens on the table?
                      yǒu.   Yes, there are.
      'shàngtou   yǒu,   There are some on top,
      'dǐxia   méi-yǒu.   but not underneath.
      dǐxia   méi-you gāngbǐ.   There are no pens underneath.

Èguo you hěn cháng de hé.	There are some long rivers in Russia.
Táiběi you hěn hǎo de fànguǎr.	There are some good restaurants in Taipei.
wǒzher you píjiǔ.	There's some beer over here by me.
nóngchǎng, yǒu 'hǎojǐpǐ mǎ.	There are quite a few horses on the farm.
xuéxiào you jǐbǎige xuésheng.	There are a few hundred students at the school.
zhuōziner you liǎngbǎ yǐzi.	There are two chairs over there by the table.
ta jiā you hěn duō qián.	There is a lot of money in his family. / His family has a lot of money.
jiāli you hěn duō qián.	There's a lot of money in the house.
zhuōzishang you hǎo jiǔ.	There's some good wine on the table.
mén pángbiār, you jǐzhǐ zhū.	There are a few pigs next to the door / gate.
shūshang you 'huàr meiyǒu? -- méiyǒu.	Are there any pictures in the book? -- No.
cài lǐtou you diǎr táng.	There's a little sugar in the dish.
dà lóu hòutou, yǒu yige xiǎo pùzi.	There's a little shop behind the big (storied) building.

10.3 <u>The location and existence patterns compared.</u> In the comment expressing location, <u>zài (N) PW (VO)</u>, the focus is usually on the <u>(N) PW</u> expression, but the noun is usually definite and hence takes "the" in English: <u>zài zhuōzi shàngtou</u> is nearly the same as <u>zài neige zhuōzi shàngtou</u> "on the table", (not "on a table, on some table or other", which would be <u>zài yige zhuōzi shàngtou</u>, a sentence which might occur as a hint given in a guessing game).

In the comment expressing existence, <u>yǒu O</u>, the focus is on the object which is usually indefinite, and hence takes "a" or "some" in

English: you gāngbǐ is nearly the same as yǒu xie gāngbǐ "there are
some pens" or yǒu zhi gāngbǐ "there is a pen".

   Nominal expressions in the topic position are usually definite,
requiring "the" in English, whether the comment expresses location
or existence.

zhǐ zài yǐzi dǐxia.	The paper is under the chair.
yǐzi dǐxia you zhǐ.	There's some paper under the chair.
yǐzi zài zhuōziner.	The chair is there by the table.
zhuōziner you yǐzi.	There's a chair there by the table.
zhuōzi zai lóushàng.	The tables are upstairs.
lóushàng you zhuōzi.	There are some tables upstairs.

   But when a comment expressing existence has a question word as
its topic, the focus shifts to the question word, even though it is
in topic position, because question words are by their nature centers
of focus, whatever their position in the sentence. The object of yǒu
is still indefinite.

'nǎr yǒu shūpù?	Where is there a bookstore?
zhèr méiyou shūpù.	There are no bookstores here.
Cf.: shūpù zài nǎr?	Where is the bookstore?
shūpù zài chéngli.	The bookstore is downtown.

   10.4 Modification by place expressions.

   10.4.1 PW-de N. From a sentence N zài PW "N is at PW" is derive
PW-de N "N which is at PW". Notice the absence of zài in the modifier

fángzi hòutoude dōngxi	things behind the house
lóushàngde fànguǎr	the restaurant upstairs
kāfēilide táng	the sugar in the coffee
huàrshangde fángzi	the building (on:) in the painting
xiàngpiārshangde niú	the cattle (on:) in the photograph

   When the N is specified, the de in the modifier remains (cf.

wǒde shū, but wǒ nèibĕn shū -- see 8.1.2):

xuéxiào qiántou de neige pùzi	The shop in front of the school
zhuōzishangde zheiben shū	the book on the table
chálide neige táng	the sugar in the tea
zhǐpù pángbiār de neixie rén	the people next to the stationery store
dà lóuner de nèisānliàng qìchē	the three automobiles over by the big building
Zhāngjiade neixie háizimen	those children of the Chang's

10.4.2 zài <u>PW V O</u> de <u>N</u>. From a sentence <u>N zài PW VO</u> "N V O at PW" is derived <u>zài PW V O de N</u> "N which VO at PW". Notice the presence of <u>zài</u> in the modifying clause.

zài zhèr chǐ fàn de rén	the people who eat here
zài Zhōngguo xué Zhōngwén de xuésheng	the students who study Chinese in China
zài chéng wàitou zuò mǎimai de nèijǐge rén	the few people who do business outside the city
zài xuéxiào qiántou mài bào de xiǎoháizimen	the children selling newspapers in front of the school
zài fànguárli zuò shì de neiwei xiáojie	the young lady working in the restaurant

10.5 <u>Constructions ending in</u> de (SP-NU-M). Modifier-modified constructions ending in <u>de SP-NU-M N</u> may be shortened to ones ending in <u>de SP-NU-M</u> (in addition to the further shortening to just <u>de</u>-- see 8.1.8 and 9.1.4).

ta chuān de neijian yīshang	the dress she wears
ta chuān de nèijiàn	that one that she wears
ta chuān de	what she wears

hé pángbiār de nèiyisuǒ xuéxiào   the school next to the river
hé pángbiār de nèiyisuǒ   the one next to the river
hé pángbiār de   what is next to the river

10.6   Review: constructions with de in sentences.

nèiliàng qìchē shi shéide?   Whose is that car?

shi nǐ dìdi de ma?   Does it belong to your (younger)
   brother?

búshi wǒ dìdi de.   It's not my brother's.

wo dìdi de qìchē, shi fángzi   My brother's car is the one in
   qiántou de nèiliàng.   front of the building.

zhuōzishangde gāngbǐ, dōu   All the pens on the table are mine.
   shi wǒde.

shūpù hòutou de neige pùzili,   There's nothing (to be bought:) for
   méiyou kéyi mǎi de dōngxi.   sale in the shop behind the book-
   shop.

zheige xuéxiàolide xuésheng,   Half of the students in this school
   yíbàn shi nánde.   are male.

cháng zài nèr chī fàn de rén,   The people who eat there often are
   dōu shi hǎo péngyou.   all good friends.

zài zhǐpù pángbiār kàn bào de   The person reading a newspaper next
   nèiwèi, shi wǒde lǎoshī.   to the stationery store is my
   teacher.

zài mén qiántou hē shuǐ de   The one in front of the door / gate
   neige, shi wo èrnǚér.   drinking water is my second
   daughter.

zài chéng wàitou zhòng qīngcài   None of the people who grow
   de rén, dōu búhuì shuō   vegetables outside the city
   Yīngwén.   know how to speak English.

10.7   Uses of ne.

10.7.1   ne? after a noun (5.12).

dà yǐziner de neixie dōngxi,   Are the things over there by the
   shi nǐ gāng mǎi de ma?   big chair the things that you
                                  just bought?

búshi.   No.

neige zhuōzishang de ne?   And what about the ones on the table?

shì. zhuōzishangde neixiē,   Yes, the ones on the table are what
   shi wǒ gāng mǎi de.   I just bought.

10.7.2 ne? after a content question (Lesson 9, "New words").

xiàtoude nèijiàn, bùhǎokàn;   The one below isn't good-looking,
  ni 'wèishemma yào mǎi   so why do you want to buy it?
  'nèijiàn ne?

Měiguo rén búài shuō huà;   If Americans don't like to talk,
  'nǎrde rén ài shuō huà ne?   people from where do?

10.7.3 ne indicating continuing state, location, or action.

Guóxiān! ni zài nǎr ne?   Kuo-hsien! Where are you?

wo zài lóushàng zhǎo shū ne. I'm upstairs looking for some
                              books / a book, at the moment.

ta zài zuò fàn ne.   He's in the process of cooking.

wǒ zhèngzai xué dǎ wǎngqiú ne. I'm just in the process of learning
                              how to play tennis.

Notice how this ne is associated with the adverbs zài "be in the
process of" and zhèngzai "be right in the process of". Notice also
the effect of contrasting a sentence that ends in ne with one that
does not.

ta zuò shémma?   ta zuò shémma ne?
      What does he do?   What is he doing, at the
                                 moment?

ta jiāo shū.   ta jiāo shū ne.
      He teaches.   He's teaching, at the
                               moment.

Context will usually determine whether a <u>ne</u> at the end of a content question is the continuative particle or the particle that is translated "And...?"

Exercises

Answer the following questions, using complete sentences for your answers.

dà mén zài nǎr?

zhèr yǒu shūpù ma?

fángzi you 'jǐbiār?

zhǐpù pángbiār de xiǎo fángzi, shi shémma pùzi?

chéng wàitou de neixie nóngchǎng, dōu yǒu shémma?

zài lóuxià zuò fàn de rén shi shéi?

nǐner you shémma dōngxi?

zài Wángjia dǎ qiú de rén, dōu shi shéi?

Make questions to which the following would be appropriate answers.

chéngli 'méiyou nóngchǎng.

shi wǒ 'dìdi gāng mǎi de.

ta zài niàn shū ne.

ta cháng zài lóu dǐxia kàn shū.

ta zhèngzai chī fàn ne.

wǒ tīng shuō, zhèitiáo lù bùhǎozǒu.

hǎo, wǒ kànkan...lǐtou méiyou míngzi, kěshi wo xiǎng yídìng shi wǒde.

Combine the pairs of sentences given below into one sentence, in which the material given in the first sentence is contained in a clause that modifies the underlined noun in the second sentence. Then translate the new sentence into English.

Example: zài hòutou. wǒ xiǎng mǎi nèibén <u>shū</u>. wǒ xiǎng mǎi hòutoude nèibén shū.

I intend to buy the book that is in back.

Exercises

zài pángbiār.   wo búhuì xiūlǐ nèiliàng wàiguo <u>qìchē</u>.

zài xiàngpiārshang.   nèisuǒ <u>fángzi</u> shi wo bàbade.

zài lóushàng chī fàn.   neige <u>rén</u> shi wǒde xiānsheng.

zài chéng wàitou.   <u>lù</u> dōu bùhǎozǒu.

zài pùzi hòutou de nèisuǒ xiǎo fángzi, zuò mǎimai.   nèixiē <u>rén</u> dōu
   shi wǒ xiōngdì.

zài neige nóngchǎng zuò shì.   wǒ búrènshi neige <u>rén</u>.

zài 'měi zì xiàtou.   qǐng nǐ gàosong wǒ, nèige <u>zì</u> shi shémma yìsi?

Lesson 11

Going and coming, purpose clauses,

and future change of status (with and without le)

Pronunciation

Plain:

a: bā; Bālí "Paris"; mǎ; mǎchē "horse-drawn carriage"; dǎ; dǎsuan "plan to"; kāfēi; chá.

e: Déguo; tèbié "uncommon"; Zhījiāgē "Chicago"; gēge; chē; yánsè; Èguo.

i: yìzhī; Zhījiāgē "Chicago"; zì; yícì "once"; sì.

ai: mǎi; Táiběi; lái "come"; hái;. Shànghǎi; xiànzài; cài; ài.

ei: Měizhōu; fēi "fly"; Fēizhōu "Africa"; děi; hēide; shéi.

ao: bào; dào "arrive"; lǎoshī; gāo; gāoxìng "happy"; zhǎo; zǎo; Àozhōu "Australia".

ou: dōu; hòutou; Měizhōu; Fēizhōu "Africa"; Àozhōu "Australia"; Ōuzhōu "Europe"; Yàzhōu "Asia"; Guǎngzhōu; zǒu.

an: yíbàn; màn "slow"; Nánjīng; Hánguo; huǒchēzhàn; sān.

en: yìběn; běnlái "originally"; nèmma; gēn "and"; hěn; zhèmma; zěmma.

ang: yìfānglǐ; fāngbiàn; "convenient"; tāng; Xiānggǎng; fēijīchǎng "airfield"; nóngchǎng; shàngtou; shàngyícì "the time before"; shàngwǔ "morning".

eng: péngyou; néng; chéng.

Frontalized:

ia: jiā; Zhījiāgē "Chicago"; guójiā "nation"; yíjià "one (machine)"; xiàtou; xiàyícì "next time"; xiàwǔ "afternoon"; Yàzhōu "Asia".

ie: bié; tèbié "uncommon"; jiē "street"; jiē "meet"; jiějie; jièshao; yě.

i̲: dìfang "place"; dìdi; Bālí "Paris"; yǐyǐnglǐ; fēijǐ "airplane";
    tóngjǐ "same plane"; hǎojíle "extremely good"; jǐge; yǐshang.

i̲a̲o̲: biǎo; yìtiáo; jiāo; jiāotōng "communication"; Jiàoshòu; yào.

i̲u̲: niú; xiūlǐ; xiūxi "rest"; yǒu.

i̲a̲n̲: pángbiān; fāngbiàn "convenient"; yìtiān; tiānqi "weather"; tián;
    yìjiān; jiàn; xiān "first"; xiānsheng; xiànzài;
    yánsè.

in: nín; jīntian "today"; jìn; jìnbù "progress".

i̲a̲n̲g̲: liǎngge; yíliàng; Xiānggǎng; xiǎng; xiàngpiān.

i̲n̲g̲: Běipíng; líng; lìngwài "another"; qǐngcài; qǐng; xíng; xìng;
    gāoxìng "happy"; Yīngwén.

Labialized:

u̲a̲: huà.

u̲o̲: duō; yìduǒ; guójiā "nation"; Guóxiān; shuǐguǒ; huǒchē "train";
    zhuōzi; zuò₁; zuò₂ "ride"; wǒ.

u̲: bù; jìnbù "progress"; zhū; zhūròu "pork"; zhù "reside"; wūzi
    wǔ; shàngwǔ "morning"; xiàwǔ "afternoon"; zhōngwǔ "noon".

u̲a̲i̲: kuài "quick"; wàitou.

u̲i̲: duì "correct"; huí lai "return here"; huǐ; shuǐ; zuǐ; wèishemma.

u̲a̲n̲: fànguǎnzi; lǚguǎn "hotel"; huàn "change"; chuān; chuán "ship";
    yìwǎn; yíwàn.

u̲n̲: yícùn; wèn; qǐngwèn "May I ask...?".

u̲a̲n̲g̲: Guǎngzhōu; wǎngqiú.

o̲n̲g̲: dōngxi; jiāotōng "communication"; Tóngzhì; tóngjǐ "same plane";
    gōnglǐ; gōnggòngqìchē "bus"; yígòng; Zhōngguo; zhōngwǔ "noon";
    cōngming; cóng "from".

u̲a̲r̲: fànguǎr.

u̲o̲r̲: yìduǒr; yìsuǒr.

u̲e̲r̲: qìshuěr "soda pop".

u̲r̲: (none yet)

Frontalized and labialized:

<u>ue</u>: juéde "feel that"; tóngxué; Niǔyuē.

<u>ü</u>: lǚguǎn "hotel"; lǜde; júzi; qù "go".

<u>uan</u>: yuànyi.

<u>un</u>: (none yet)

<u>iong</u>: xiōngdì.

Dialogs, etc.

I

wǒmen xiànzài cháng shuō,
   jiāotōng hěn yǒu jìnbù;
   cóng yíge dìfang, dào
   lìng'wài yíge dìfang qu,
   hěn róngyi. zhèige búduì.
   cóng yige dà chéng, dào
   lìng'wài yige dà chéng qu,
   hěn róngyi, nà hěn duì;
   kěshi cóng yíge dìfang dào
   lìng'wài yige dìfang qu,
   bùyídìng hěn róngyi.
yǒuyícì, wo zài Fēizhōu yige
   guójiā, zuò fēijī, cóng yige
   dà chéng, dào lìng'wài yige
   dà chéng qu. zài fēijīshang,
   wo gāoxìngjíle. wo juéde,
   hěn 'kuài jiu kéyi dào wo
   yào 'qù de neige dìfang le.
wǒ běnlai dǎsuan cóng zhèige
   dà chéng, huàn fēijī, fēidao
   wo yào qù de neige dà chéng
   qu. kěshi nèitiān xiàwǔ,

We often say, now, that communications have made great progress,
and that it's very easy to get
from one place to another. This
isn't so. It's true that it's
easy to go from one large city to
another. But it's not necessarily
easy to get from (just any) place
to another.

Once, I was in an African country,
and was going by plane from one
big city to another. On the plane,
I was extremely happy. I thought
that I could get to the place I
wanted to go to very quickly.

I had originally planned to change
planes and fly from this big city
to the other big city that I wanted
to go to. But that afternoon,

tiānqi bùhǎo; fēiji bùnéng
zài fēi; women yídìng děi
dào 'chénglǐtou yige lǚguǎn
qu xiūxi.

cóng fēijīchǎng, dào lǚguǎn qu,
méiyou qìchē; women zuòde shi
'māchē. tóng'jī de yige rén
shuō; jīntiān búcuò; women
kéyi zuò 'māchē; shàngyícì,
zai zhèige dìfang, wo zuòde
shi 'niúchē.

women 'zhù de neige lǚguǎn,
shi yǐsuǒ 'jiù fángzi.
lǐtou 'jiù yǒu èrshiduō-
jiān wūzi. women chī de
fàn, hen tèbié. jiù yǒu
'niúròu, méiyou zhūrou.
women yào hē qìshuǐ, méiyou.
women yào hē kāfēi; yě
méiyǒu. jiù yǒu chá gēn
jiǔ. tamen mài de nèixiē
jiǔ, guìjíle.

dìèrtiān, tiānqi hǎo le. women
zuò māchē dào fēijīchǎng qu.
zài fēijīshang, wo shuō; hǎo;
wo xiànzài zhīdao le; cóng
yíge dìfang, dào lìng'wài
yige dìfang qu, bùyídìng hěn
róngyi.

the weather was bad, the plane
couldn't fly on, and we (definitely) had to go to a hotel in the
city to rest.
There were no cars from the airport
to the hotel, so we went by horse
and carriage. A person on the
same plane (as I) said: "It's
not (so) bad today; the last time
when I was at this place, I went
by oxcart."
The hotel we stayed at was an old
building, with only twenty-odd
rooms. The food we ate was quite
strange: there was only beef, no
pork. We wanted a soft drink, but
there wasn't any. We wanted some
coffee, but there wasn't any of
that, either. All they had was
tea and liquor. And the (various)
liquors that they sold were
extremely expensive.
The next day, the weather was better.
We went to the airport by horse
and carriage. On the plane, I
said, "Fine; now I know; it's not
necessarily easy to get from one
place to another.

II

A: wǒ yào dào Zhījiāgē qu, kàn   I'm going to go to Chicago to see a
    yige péngyou.   a friend.

B: ni zěmma qù ne?   How are you going?

A: wo dǎsuan zuò huǒchē qu.   I plan to go by train.

B: wèishemma búzuò fēijī ne?   And why don't you go by plane?

A: háizimen dōu shuō yào zuò   The children all said that they
    huǒchē. wǒ shuō, hǎo ba.   wanted to go by train. So I said,
    women zhèicì zuò huǒchē.   "All right; we'll go by train this
    tamen gāoxìngjíle.   time." They were extremely happy.

                                III

A: nín zài nǎr zhù a?   Where do you live?

B: wo zhùzai chéng wàitou.   I live outside the city.

A: dào chéng lǐtou qu fāng-   Is it convenient to get into the
    biàn ma?   city?

B: hěn fāngbiàn. wǒmen   Yes, it is. There's a bus on our
    nèitiáo jiē, yǒu gōnggòng-   street.
    qìchē.

A: cóng nín nèr, dào gōnggòng-   Is it far from your place to the
    qìchēzhàn, 'yuǎn buyuǎn?   bus stop / station?

B: bùyuǎn. cóng wǒmen nèr   No, it's not. From where we are to
    dào chēzhàn, jiù yǒu bànlǐ   the stop / station is just half
    lù. huǒchēzhàn, fēijīchǎng,   a mile. The railway station and
    yě dōu bùyuǎn. fāngbiànjíle.   the airport are not so far away,
                                        either. It's extremely convenient.

                                IV

A: wo dào fēijīchǎng, qu jiē   I'm going to the airport to meet a
    yige péngyou qu. ni 'qù   friend. Are you (going:) coming
    buqù?   along?

B: jiē shéi a?   Whom are you meeting?

A: Zhēnzhēn. ta gāng cóng   Chen-chen. She's just come back
    Ōuzhōu huí lai.   from Europe.

B: ta búshi shuō, ta yào zuò   Didn't she say that she was going
    'chuán huí lai ma?   to come back by ship?

A: shì; kěshi wo xiǎng, ta   Yes, but I think she wants to come
    yào 'kuài yidiar huí lai.   back a little faster. By ship
    chuán tài màn.   would be too slow.

V

A: qǐng nǐ kuài yidiar.   Please hurry. The train is leaving
    huǒchē jiù yào kāi le.   right away.

B: wo xiān wènwen ni. zhèige   First, let me ask: is this train
    huǒchē, shi dào Niǔyuē qù   the one that goes to New York?
    de neige ma?

A: shì de.   It is.

VI

A: cóng Niǔyuē, kéyi zuò   Can you go by plane from New York
    fēijī, dào Běijīng qù ma?   to Peking?

B: xiànzài bùkéyi. ni kéyi   You can't, at present. (But) you
    xiān zuò fēijī dào Bālí qu;   can first go by plane to Paris,
    zài Bālí huàn fēijī, zài   change planes in Paris, and then
    dào Běijīng qu.   go on to Peking.

New words

jiāotōng N   (mutually pass through, go back and
                     forth freely:) communication(s),
                     transportation

jìnbù N   (go a step forward:) progress,
                     improvement

   jiāotōng you hěn dà de   In communications, progress has
    jìnbù.   been great. / There has been great
                     progress in communications.

yǒu jìnbù SV	improved
xiànzài, jiāotōng hěn	Now, communications are greatly
yǒu jìnbù le.	improved.
dìfang PW	place
chī 'fàn de dìfang	place to eat at
niàn 'shū de dìfang	place to study at
Fēizhōu PW	Africa
Ōuzhōu PW	Europe
Yàzhōu, Yàzhōu PW	Asia
Àozhōu PW	Australia
zài Fēizhōu niàn shū	study in Africa
Ōuzhōu yǒu bùshǎo dà chéng.	There are quite a few big cities
	in Europe.
Yàzhōu, rén hěn duō.	There are a lot of people in Asia.
Àozhōu, rén hěn shǎo.	There aren't many people in
	Australia.
guójiā PW	(nation-family:) nation, country
wǒ xiǎng zài Měi'zhōu yige	I intend to study in one of the
guójiā niàn shū.	American nations.
fēijī N (M: -jià)	(flying machine:) airplane
nèijià fēijīshang, yǒu	There are over three hundred
sānbǎi'duōge rén.	people on that airplane.
tóngjī N[1]	(same machine:) same airplane
tóngjīde ren	people / a person on the same plane
huǒchē N	(fire vehicle:) train
zài huǒchēshang kàn bào.	read a newspaper on the train
gōnggòngqìchē N (M: -liàng)	(public sharing automobile:) bus
kāi gōnggòngqìchē de	someone who drives a bus
fēijīchǎng PW	(airplane field:) airport
zài fēijīchǎng mài bào	sell papers in an airport
zhàn N	station (for buses, trains, etc.)
hái you yige zhàn ma?	Is there one more station?

-zhàn M   (station, stop)

  cóng Xīngǎng, dào Niǔyuē,   How many stops are there between

    you duōshaozhàn?   New Haven and New York?

  tóuliǎngzhàn, dou hái zai   The first two stops are both

    Niǔyuē.   still in New York.

huǒchēzhàn PW   railway station

  zài huǒchēzhàn hē chá   have some tea at the railroad

                                station

(gōnggòng-)qìchēzhàn PW   bus stop; bus station

  qìchēzhànner, rén hěn duō.   There are a lot of people at the

                                bus stop.

  qìchēzhànli, yǒu màibàode.   There's a newspaper-seller in

                                the bus station.

  zài qìchēzhàn, kàn bào.   read a paper at the bus stop /

                                station

jiē (M: -tiáo)   street

  jiēshang PW   on the street; shopping district

  zài jiēshang mǎi dōngxi   buy something in the shopping

                                district

mǎchē N (M: -liàng)^2 horse and carriage

niúchē N (M: -liàng)^2 oxcart

chuán N (M: -tiáo)   ship

zhūròu N^2 (pig meat:) pork

niúròu N^2 (cattle meat:) beef

lǚguǎn PW (M:-suǒ)   (travel house:) hotel

  zài lǚguǎn, hē píjiǔ   have some beer at the hotel

Zhījiāgē PW   Chicago

Bālí PW   Paris

  zài Bālí, niàn shū   study in Paris

-tiān M	day
liǎngtiān	two days
zhèiliǎng-sāntiān, wo bùxiǎng niàn shū.	I don't intend to study for the next two or three days.
tiānqi N	(sky emanation:) weather
Xīngǎngde tiānqi, hěn hǎo.	The weather in New Haven is good.
jīntian TW	today
jīntian, tiānqi búcuò.	The weather today hasn't been bad.
nèi(yi)tiān TW	that day (in the past)
nèiyitiān, ta xiǎng niàn diar Yīngwén.	That day, he thought he'd study a little English.
dìèrtiān TW	(the second day:) the next day
dìèrtiān, ta xiǎng xué dǎ wǎngqiú.	The next day, he thought he'd learn how to play tennis.
běnlái TW	original time, time at the very beginning
běnláide nèijià fēijī	the original plane
ta běnlái zuòzai nèr.	She originally sat there.
běnlái wo xiǎng zhòng cài; xiànzài bùxiǎng zhòng cài le.	I originally intended to grow vegetables, but now I don't any more.
běnlái wo bùzhidào, ta zài nǎr; xiànzài wo zhīdao le.	Originally, I didn't know where she was; now I do.
shàngwu TW	forenoon, morning
zhōngwu TW	noon
xiàwu TW	afternoon
nèitiān xiàwu, tiānqi hǎo le.	In the afternoon of that day / That afternoon, the weather got better.
-cì M	occasion, time
zhèi(yi)cì TW	this time
nèi(yi)cì TW	that time
shàngyicì TW	the last time

xiàyicì TW	the next time
xiàyicì, wǒmen bié qǐng ta zuò fàn le.	Let's not ask her to cook, next time.
yǒuyícì TW	(there was a time:) at a certain time, once
yǒuyícì, wǒ gen Lù Xj dǎ wǎngqiú.	Once, Miss Lu and I were playing tennis.
-jiān M	(rooms)
wǔjiān wūzi de fángzi	a house with five rooms
-jià M	(machines)
nèijià fēijī búgòu dà.	That plane isn't big enough.
lìngwài SP[3]	another, other, different
lìngwàiliǎngjià fēijī	two other airplanes
duì SV	correct, right
nà hěn duì.	That's quite correct.
ta shuōde, dōu búduì.	All of what he says is wrong.
kuài SV	fast, quick
qìchē kuài, huǒchē kuài?	Which are faster, cars or trains? / Which would be quicker, by car or by train?
huǒchē bùhěn kuài.	Trains are not very fast. / By train wouldn't be very fast.
qǐng nǐ kuài yidiar.	Please be a little faster. / Please hurry up.
--- A[4]	quickly, soon
kuài yidiar shuō.	Speak faster! / Hurry up and say it!
kuài yidiar xiě ba.	Write faster! / Hurry up and write!
nǐ kuài gàosong wǒ.	Tell me right away!
chē kuài kāi le.	The bus is just about to leave.
chē kuài yào kāi le.	
chá kuài méiyou le.	(We'll) soon be out of tea.
hěn kuài MA	(very fast:) very soon
hěn kuài, qìshuǐ jiu méiyǒu le.	In a minute, there won't be any soda pop.

màn SV   slow

  chuán tài màn.   Ships are too slow. / It would be
                                            too slow to go by ship.

  qǐng nǐ màn yidiar.   Please be a little slower. /
                                            Please slow down.

--- A⁴   slowly

  màn yidiar shuō.   Speak slower!

  màn yidiar xiě ba.   Write slower!

gāoxìng SV   (highly happy:) happy

  ta chángchang hěn gāoxìng.   She's often happy.

tèbié SV   (special and separate:) odd;
                                            uncommon; unique

  ta huà de huàr, hěn tèbié.   The paintings he paints are odd.

fāngbiàn SV   convenient

  zài jiāli niàn shū, hěn   It's convenient to study at home.
    fāngbiàn.

jiù A   only (4); then, afterwards (9);
                                            (right after I say this:) right
                                            away

  women jiù yào chī fàn le;   We're just about to eat, and
    ni hái hē qìshuǐ ne?   you're still drinking pop?

  chē, jiù yào kāi.   The bus/train is leaving right away.

xiān A   first, beforehand, earlier

  shéi xiān shuō?   Who'll speak first?

  women xiān hē tāng.   We have soup first.

  ta (shi) xiān dào de.   He arrived first.

dǎsuan AV   plan to

  wo dǎsuan mǎi wǔběn.   I plan to buy five (books).

  wo dǎsuan jīntian mǎi.   I plan to buy them today.

lái V   come

qù V   go, go to

  ta dǎsuan jīntian shàngwu lái.   He plans to come here this morning.

wo dǎsuan jīntian'xiàwu qù.	I plan to go there this afternoon.
ni 'lái bulái?	Are you coming (to this place)?
ni 'qù buqù?	Are you going (to that place)? /
	Are you coming (along with me
	to that place)?
ta kuài lái le.	He'll be here in a minute.
wo yào 'qù de dìfang[5]	the place(s) I want to go to
cóng CV	from
dào CV	to
cóng zhèr, dào nèr qu, hěn	It's hard to go from here to
nán.	there.
cóng nèr, dào zhèr lai, hěn	It's hard to come here from there.
nán.	
--- V	arrive
wǒmen kuài dào le.	We'll get there in a minute.
hěn kuài, wǒmen jiu dào le.	In a minute, (and then) we'll
	arrive.
zuò CV	by (a means of conveyance)
ta dǎsuan zuò 'chuán lái.	He plans to come by boat.
ni xiǎng zuò 'shémma lái?	What do you intend to come by?
wǒ xiǎng zuò huǒ'chē lái.	I plan to come by train.
--- V	sit; use... as a means of conveyance
qǐng zuò.	Please be seated.
zuò chuán, tài màn.	It's too slow to go by ship.
juéde V[6]	feel that, be of the opinion that
wo juéde, bùhěn nán.	I don't feel that it's very
	difficult.
wo bùjuéde hěn nán.	
ni juéde 'xíng buxíng?	Do you feel that it'll be OK?
huàn V	replace by another; change
wǒmen děi zài Niǔyuē, huàn	We have to change trains/buses
chē.	in New York.

fēi V

    fēijī bùnéng zài fēi le.

-dao, dào VS

fēidao V

    fēidao Bālí

    cóng zhèr, fēidao nǎr?

xiūxi V

    women xiān děi xiūxi, zài qù.

kàn V

    kàn péngyou

zhù[7]

    ni zài 'nǎr zhù?

    wo zài péngyou jiā zhù.

    wo zhùde lǚguǎn[5]

zhùzai V[7]

    ni zhùzai nǎr?

    wo zhùzai péngyou jiā.

jiē V

    wo dǎsuan dào fēijīchǎng
      qu jiē ta.

    wo děi jiē yige péngyou.

lai P

qu P

huí V

    wo xiān qu jiē yige péngyou,
      zài huí lai.

to fly

    The plane can't fly on.

so that the actor arrives at the

    place-word object of the verb; to

fly to

    fly to Paris

    Where do (we) fly to from here?

rest

    First, we must rest, and then go.

read (2); look at (9); have the

    opinion that (9); see, visit

    (a friend)

    see a friend / some friends

reside, live; live at

    Where do you live?

    I live at a friend's.

    the hotel I'm living in

live at

    Where do you live?

    I live at a friend's.

meet (someone at e.g. a railroad

    station)

    I plan to go to the airport to

      meet her.

    I have to meet a friend.

(lái "come":)(sentence particle,

    indicates motion toward the

    speaker) to here

(qù "go":)(sentence particle,

    indicates motion away from the

    speaker) to there

return (with lai and qu)

    First I'll go meet my friend and

    then come back.

ta jīntian huí qu.	He's going back today.
ta cóng Bāli huí qu.	He's going back from Paris.
ta zuò chuán huí lai.	He's coming back by ship.
shì V	be (5); mean (8); be true that
ta 'shì bushì jīntian lái?	Is it true that he's coming today?
shì.	Yes.
shì de. IE	Yes.
kāi V	drive (train, bus, etc.) (10)
	leave, start away
gōnggòngqìchē kuài yào	The bus is leaving soon.
kāi le.	
gēn, gen C[8]	and
jiù yǒu chá gen jiǔ.	There was only tea and liquor.
wo xiǎng mǎi yífèr bào gen	I intend to buy a newspaper and
jǐběn shū.	some books.
-jíle BF[9]	(suffix added to stative verbs)
	extremely
xué Èguo huà, nánjíle.	It's extremely difficult to learn
	Russian.
Zhèng Xs mángjíle.	Mr. Cheng is extremely busy.
zhèixie xīn shū, piányijíle.	These new books are extremely cheap.
zhèige tāng, làjíle.	This soup is extremely peppery.
ta huà de huàr, měijíle.	The paintings he paints are
	extremely beautiful.
zhèijià fēijī, kuàijíle.	This plane is extremely fast.

Notes

[1]tóng "same" is a rare stative verb that often occurs in combination with nouns to form compounds meaning "the same N". Sometimes the noun assumes a simpler form when it appears after tóng. The tóng-N compound may occur after such expressions as wǒmen shi..., and wǒmen shi tóng-N means "we share the same N". tóng-N de rén means "persons who share the same N". Sometimes tóng-N alone stands for tóng-N de rén.

tóngxué	fellow student (5) (xué stands for xuéxiào, and tóngxué stands for tóngxué de rén.)
tóngxìng	sharing the same surname
tóngmíng	sharing the same proper name
tóngshì	colleague (lit. "sharing the same job")
tóngfù	sharing the same father (as half-brothers, etc.)
tóngmǔ	sharing the same mother
tóngchē	being in the same bus/train/car
tóngchuán	being in the same boat
tóngfēijī	being in the same airplane
tóngjī	(an abbreviation of the above; this word has a literary flavor)
tónglǚguǎn	being in the same hotel
tóngwū	roommate (lit. "sharing the same room")
tóngzhì	Comrade (5) (lit. "sharing the same aim")

Other combinations with tóng are understood but not much used, and should be avoided: e.g. tónglóu "being in the same (storied) building", tóngdìfang "coming from the same place", etc.

[2]The meanings of mǎchē, niúchē, zhūròu, and niúròu all happen to be obvious, once the meanings of mǎ, niú, zhū, chē, and ròu are learned. But it is unsafe to make new words by combining old ones. It might seem logical to combine mǎ with fángzi to arrive at a word for "stable", but the combination, while it may be logical, is not Chinese: one word for "stable" is mǎjuàn; neither *mǎfángzi nor *mǎfáng occur. Similarly, if a Chinese person learning English learns that zhūjuàn is "pigpen", he might reasonably assume mǎjuàn is "*horsepen", which, of course, it is not, English being no more logical than Chinese.

[3]lìngwài is a specifier (like nèi-) because it occupies the SP position in SP-NU-M constructions. Compare lìngwàiliǎngjià with nèiliǎngjià.

[4]Notice that both <u>kuài</u> and <u>màn</u>, optionally followed by <u>yidiar</u>
"a bit", occur as fixed adverbs in commands. In such sentences,
<u>kuài yìdiǎr</u> V has two meanings, either "do the action of the verb
faster" or "begin the action of the verb sooner"; <u>kuài</u> V means only
"begin the action of the verb sooner". <u>màn</u> V means only "do the
action of the verb slower".

<u>kuài</u> (but not <u>màn</u>) also occurs as a fixed adverb in declarative
sentences, with change-of-status <u>le</u> (Lesson 9, "New words", notes 10
and 11, and 9.2), meaning "(up to now the action of the verb was not
about to happen, but now) the action of the verb will happen soon".

[5]<u>qù</u> "go" and <u>zhù</u> "reside" occur in clauses that modify nouns
denoting the place someone is going to, and the place someone is
residing at, respectively. Notice the absence of <u>dào</u> and <u>zài</u> in
these clauses.

wo yao dào yige dà chéng qu.   I want to go to a big city.
wo yao qù de neige dà chéng   the big city that I want to go to

wo zài yige lǔguǎn zhù.   I live in a hotel.
wo zhù de neige lǔguǎn   the hotel that I live in

[6]Notice that whereas "I don't think it's very difficult." is <u>wǒ</u>
<u>xiǎng, bùhěn nán.</u>, with negation possible only in the clause, the
sentence "I don't feel that it's very difficult." is either <u>wǒ juéde,</u>
<u>bùhěn nán.</u> or <u>wǒ bùjuéde hěn nán.</u>, with little difference in meaning.

[7]<u>zài PW zhù</u> means about the same as <u>zhùzai</u> PW. All other factors
being equal, a word attracts more of the focus of attention the closer
it is to the end of the sentence, so the PW in <u>zhùzai</u> PW is likely to
be more "interesting" than the one in <u>zài</u> PW <u>zhù</u>.

[8]"C" stands for "conjunction", which is a word that connects two
other words that are in a co-ordinate relationship (1.11).

[9]-<u>jíle</u> is only suffixed to stative verbs that are not negated,
and the SV-<u>jíle</u> expression only functions as a comment. Thus it is
impossible to say *<u>búcuòjíle</u> or *<u>hǎokànjílede háizi</u>.

More notes on grammar

11.1 The co-verbs zuò, cóng, and dào with the verbs lái and qù.
lái "come", and qù "go" often occur with preceding CV-O phrases expressing means of conveyance, place from which the subject is coming
or going, and place to which the subject is coming or going. zuò
(from the verb meaning "sit") is the co-verb that introduces the
means of conveyance and is usually translated "by". cóng introduces
the place from which the subject is coming or going, and is usually
translated "from". If zuò O and cóng O both occur in the sentence,
either one may precede the other. dào (from the verb meaning
"arrive") is the co-verb that introduces the place to which the
subject is coming or going, and is usually translated "to". The
dào O phrase always immediately precedes the lái or qù. Thus there
are two ways that all three CV-O phrases occur before lái or qù:
zuò O cóng O dào O lai/qu, and cóng O zuò O dào O lai/qu. The tones
on lái and qù are sometimes weakened. huí lai "come back" and huí qu
"go back" may be used instead of lái and qù.

11.1.1 zuò O "by O".

ni dǎsuan 'zěmma qù?	How do you plan to go?
ni dǎsuan zuò shémma chē qu?	What (means of conveyance) do you plan to go by?
wo xiǎng zuò huǒchē qu.	I intend to go by train.
ni búzuò gōnggòngqìchē huí lai ma?	Aren't you coming back by bus?
zhèiyicì, wo zuò fēijī huí lai.	This time I'm coming back by plane.

11.1.2 cóng O "from O".

ni cóng 'nǎr lái?	Where are you coming from?
ni cóng shémma 'dìfang lái?	What place are you coming from?
wo cóng Zhījiāgē qu.	I'm going from Chicago.

ni cóng Zhǐjiāgē, zuò 'shémma lái?	What (means of conveyance) are you coming from Chicago by?
wo cóng Zhǐjiāgē, zuò fēijǐ qu; wo xiǎng zuò chuán, cóng Ōuzhōu huí lai.	I'm going from Chicago by plane; I think I'll come back from Europe by ship.

11.1.3 dào O "to O"

ni dào 'nǎr qù?	Where are you going?
ni dào shémma 'dìfang qù?	What place are you going to?
wo dào fēijǐchǎng qu.	I'm going to the airport.
wǒ cóng jiāli, dào fēijǐchǎng qu.	I'm going from home to the airport.
wo zuò qìchē, dào fēijǐchǎng qu.	I'm going to the airport by car.
wǒ cóng jiāli, zuò qìchē, dào fēijǐchǎng qu.	I'm going from home to the airport by car.
wǒ zuò qìchē, cóng jiāli, dào fēijǐchǎng qu.	

11.2 -zai and -dao as verbal suffixes. -zai (from zài "be located at") and -dao (from dào "arrive, to") occur suffixed to certain verbs.

11.2.1 V-zai "V at".

ni zhùzai nǎr? -- wo zhùzai chénglǐtou.	Where do you live? I live in the city.
ta zuòzai shémma dìfang?	Where is she sitting?
ta zuòzai zhuōzi qiántou.	She's sitting in front of the table.
ta zuòzai mén wàitou.	She's sitting outside the door.
ta zuòzai jiēshang.	She's sitting on the street.
ta zuòzai wo pángbiār.	She's sitting next to me.

11.2.2 V-dao...lai/qu "V to... (here/there)".

ta jīntian fēidao Xīngǎng lai.	He's flying to New Haven (here) today.

wo yao fēidao Fēizhōu qu.	I want to fly to Africa.
wo yao cóng Xīngǎng, fēidao Fēizhōu qu.	I want to fly from New Haven to Africa.
ta jiù yao kāidao xuéxiào qu.	He only wants to drive to school. (see below, 11.5)
ni 'kéyi bukéyi kāidao women jiā lai?	Can you drive (over here) to our house?
hǎo; wo kāidao nǐmen jiā qu.	OK; I'll drive (over there) to your house.

Notice that with verbs denoting travel or other large-scale motion, lai or qu is regularly present at the end of the sentence. Sometimes, however, if a lai or a qu already appears after V-dao but before the sentence ends (in an embedded sentence, for example) the sentence-final lai or qu may be omitted, to avoid repeating that word. Thus:

wǒ xiǎng fēidao wo yào 'qù de neige dìfang (qu).	I intend to fly to the place that I want to go to.

11.3 Purpose clauses with lái and qù. The purpose of coming or going to a place may be expressed by a V or a V O expression, coming before or after lái or qù. If the lái or qù comes before the purpose clause, it may be repeated after the clause. lái and qù often take the neutral tone.

ta dào 'zhèr lái, zuò shémma?	What is he coming here to do?
ta dào zhèr, zuò 'shémma lái?	
ta dào 'zhèr lái, zuò 'shémma lái?	
ta zuò 'shémma lái?	What is he coming to do ? / By what (means of conveyance) is he coming?
ta lái jiāo shū.	He's coming to teach.
ta zhǎo péngyou qu.	She's going to look up a friend.
ta qu kàn péngyou.	She's going to visit a friend.

ta qu jiē péngyou qu.	She's going to meet a friend.
ta lai xué diar Yīngwén.	He's coming to study some English.
ta cóng Rìběn lái, xué yìdiǎr Yīngwén lai.	He's coming from Japan to study some English.
ta dào xuéxiào qu, kàn Huáng Xs qu.	She's going to the school to see Mr. Huang.
ta dào chéng lǐtou, zuò mǎimai lai.	He's coming into the city to do business.

11.4 le indicating future change of status (imminent action).
With certain adverbs that indicate that the action of the verb is
going to happen soon in the future, such as kuài "quickly, soon" and
jiù "right away", le is added to the end of the sentence. kuài (yào)
V (O) le is less immediate than jiù yào V (O) le.

women kuài yào chī fàn le.	We're just about to eat (in twenty minutes or so).
huǒchē kuài kāi le.	The train is about to leave.
huǒchē jiù yào kāi le.	The train is about to leave (in about five minutes).
tamen jiù yào lái le.	They're just about to come here.

11.5 jiù "immediately". With no le at the end of the sentence,
jiù (yào) expresses an even greater immediacy of the action of the
verb than in the sentences of 11.4.

wǒ jiù lái.	I'm coming right away.
chē jiù dào.	The bus/train will arrive right away.
chē jiù yào kāi.	The bus/train is going to leave right away.

11.6 kuài (alone) with negated verbs.

chá kuài méiyǒu le.	(We'll) soon be out of tea.

wo kuài bùjiāo shū le.   Soon I won't be teaching any more.

tamen kuài méiyou qián le.   They soon will be out of money.

Pyramid drills

            zài pángbiār.
       zuòzai pángbiār.
    zuòzai ni pángbiār.
    zuòzai ni pángbiār de rén.
    zuòzai ni pángbiār de neige rén.
    zuòzai ni pángbiār de neige rén, shi shéi?
    zuòzai wo pángbiār de neige rén, shi wǒ jiějie.

              dào Shànghǎi qu.
cóng Guǎngzhōu, dào Shànghǎi qu.
cóng Guǎngzhōu, dào Shànghǎi qu, duó yuǎn?
cóng Guǎngzhōu, dào Shànghǎi qu, yǒu duó yuǎn?
cóng Guǎngzhōu, dào Shànghǎi qu, you yìqiānduō-gōnglǐ.

              dào Niǔyuē lai.
      zuò fēijī, dào Niǔyuē lai.
              dào Niǔyuē lai de fēijī
cóng Zhījiāgē, dào Niǔyuē lai de fēijī
cóng Zhījiāgē, dào Niǔyuē lai de fēijī, 'duō buduō?
cóng Zhījiāgē, dào Niǔyuē lai de fēijī, duōjíle.

              kuài lái.
         kuài diar lái.
              kuài lái chī fàn.
      kuài diar lái chī fàn.
      kuài diar lái chī fàn lai.

Exercises

Answer the following questions:

nín cháng fēidao Bālí qu ma?

Sītú Tóngxué, jīntian dǎsuan dào Niǔyuē qu, zuò shémma?

nǐ 'néng bunéng cóng Běipíng fēidao Niǔyuē?

nǐ běnlai xiǎng kāidao nǎr qu?

zuò gōnggòngqìchē, dào Niǔyuē de fēijīchǎng, fāng'biàn bufāngbiàn?

ni xiǎng, kāi huǒchē hen róngyi xué ma?

Make up questions to which the following would be likely answers:

bùxíng; wǒmen kuài yào chī fàn le.

hǎo; wǒmen xiàyicì qǐng ta zuò fàn.

xiànzài, Fēizhōude   jiāotōng, hěn fāngbiàn le.

děi zài Bālí, huàn lìngwàiyíjià fēijī, zài fēidao Niǔyuē.

women xué Zhōngguo huà, méiyou hen dà de jìnbù. (This is a polite

  answer.)

Translate into Chinese:

1. The nations of Europe have made great progress in communications.

2. Airplane food isn't much good.

3. What will you go to Chicago to do?

4. How will you get to Chicago?

5. Hurry up, please. We are going to eat soon.

6. First, let's have another bottle of beer.

7. I originally thought I had to change planes in New York before
      flying on to Paris.

8. I still want to buy another pen.

9. For these five or six days, we plan to live in the biggest room
      in the biggest hotel in Paris.

10. He only goes to the most interesting places.

11. The candy's almost gone.

12. The plane is arriving right away.

13. Now she's happy.

14. We'll be able to rest very soon.

15. I'm going to the market to buy some fruit. Are you coming?

Lesson 12

The past tense, completed action,

the shi...de construction, and "when" clauses

Pronunciation

<u>Plain</u>:

<u>a</u>: Fàguo; dà; dàxué "university"; kāfēi; Hǎfó "Harvard"; chá.

<u>e</u>: Déguo; gē "song"; Gélúnbǐyǎ "Columbia"; gēge; kéyi; kěshi; kè "class"; gōngkè "school work"; huǒchē; yánsè; Èguo.

<u>i</u>: lǎoshī; shí; shíhou "time"; zìjǐ; yícì; sì.

<u>ao</u>: bào; dào; gàosong; shǎo; zǎo; Àozhōu.

<u>ou</u>: tóuyicì; gòu; Měizhōu; Jiāzhōu "California"; zǒu; Ōuzhōu.

<u>an</u>: fàn; lánde; tán "chat"; Nánjīng; Hánguo; zhàn; sān.

<u>en</u>: běnlái; nèmma; gēn; zhēn; zěmma.

<u>ang</u>: máng; táng; yìtáng "one (class)"; Xiānggǎng; cháng$_{1,2}$; nóngchǎng. chàng "sing"; shàng kè "go to class".

<u>eng</u>: péngyou; děng "wait"; néng; zhèngzai.

<u>ar</u>: yíbàr; nǎr; xiǎohár.

<u>er</u>: yífèr; nèr; gēr "song"; zhèr; èr.

<u>aor</u>: sháor.

<u>our</u>: shíhour "time".

<u>Frontalized</u>:

<u>ia</u>: Jiānádà; Jiāzhōu "California"; yíjià; xià kè "get out of class"; Yǎzhōu; Gélúnbǐyǎ "Columbia".

<u>ie</u>: tèbié; jièshao; Yélǔ "Yale"; yě.

<u>i</u>: bǐ; Gélúnbǐyǎ "Columbia"; dǐxia; fēijī; hǎojíle; jǐge; jìde "remember"; qǐ; yìqǐ "together"; qìchē; yīshang; yíkuàr "together", yǐzi; yǐjing "already"; yìsi; yìhuěr "a moment".

231

<u>iao</u>: biǎo; yìtiáo; Jiàoshòu; Jiànqiáo "Cambridge"; yào.

<u>iu</u>: niú; Niújīn "Oxford"; Niǔyuē; jiǔ_{1,2}; yǒu.

<u>ian</u>: pángbiān; diǎnxin; shūdiàn; diànhuà "telephone"; yìnián "one year"
niàn; yíjiàn; Jiànqiáo "Cambridge"; yánsè.

<u>in</u>: nín; jīntian; Niújīn "Oxford"; jìn; jìn lai "come in"; jìn qu
"go in"; xīn.

<u>iang</u>: liǎngge; Xiānggǎng; xiǎng.

<u>ing</u>: Běipíng; míngtian "tomorrow"; lìngwài; Nánjīng; Dōngjīng
"Tokyo"; Jīngdū "Kyoto"; Yīngguo.

<u>Labialized</u>:

<u>ua</u>: Huá Shān; huà_{1,2}; diànhuà "telephone".

<u>uo</u>: Hāfó "Harvard"; duō; yìduǒ; guójiā; zhuōzi; zuótian "yesterday";
zuò; wǒ.

<u>u</u>: mǔqin; Jīngdū "Kyoto"; Yélǔ "Yale"; lù; Lù; zhūròu; chū lai
"come out"; chū qu "go out"; shū; shūfu "comfortable"; zúqiú; wǔ.

<u>uai</u>: huài le; wàitou; wàibian "outside".

<u>ui</u>: duìbuqǐ; huí lai; yìhuǐ "a moment"; huì; shuǐ; zuì; wèishemma.

<u>uan</u>: huàn; chuān; suān; Táiwān "Taiwan"; yìwǎn; wǎnfàn "supper";
wǎnshang "evening"; yíwàn.

<u>un</u>: Gēlúnbǐyǎ "Columbia"; yícùn; wèn.

<u>uang</u>: Guǎngzhōu; wǎngqiú.

<u>ong</u>: Dōngjīng "Tokyo"; dōngxi; dǒng; yìgōnglǐ; gōnggòngqìchē; gōngkè
"school work"; zhòng; cōngming; cóng.

<u>uar</u>: fànguǎr; yíkuàr "together"; huār; huàr.

<u>uor</u>: yìduǒr; yìsuǒr.

<u>uer</u>: yìhuěr "a moment".

<u>ur</u>: (none yet)

Frontalized and labialized:

ue: xuéxiào; dàxué "college"; Niǔyuē.

ǚ: lǚguǎn; qù; yǔ "rain"; yùbei "prepare".

Dialogs

I

A: ta zǒu le ma?	Has she left?
B: ta zǒu le.	Yes, she has.
A: ta shi 'něitiān zǒu de?	On what day?
B: ta 'zuótian zǒu de.	Yesterday.
A: zuótian, shémma shíhou zǒu de?	What time yesterday?
B: zuótian 'wǎnshang zǒu de.	Yesterday evening.

II

A: Měizhēn huí lai le ma?	Has Mei-chen come back?
B: ta hái méihuí lai ne.	Not yet.
A: ta shuō, ta shémma shíhou huí lai?	When does she say she's coming back?
B: ta shuō, ta míngtian xiàwu huí lai.	She says she's coming back tomorrow afternoon.

III

A: tamen lái le meiyou?	Have they come yet?
B: hái méilái ne.	Not yet.
A: 'zěmma hái méilái ne? búshi qìchē huài le ba! dǎ yige diànhuà, wènwen tamen lái le meiyou.	How come they haven't come yet? It couldn't be that their car is out of order, could it? Give a call (on the telephone) and ask if they've come yet.

B: wo yǐjing dǎguo diànhuà le.   I've already called. Mrs. Chang
   Zhāng Tt shuō, Guóxīn,   said that Kuo-hsin and Kuo-hsien
   Guóxiān, zhèngzai chī fàn   are just in the middle of eating.
   ne. tamen yǐchīle fàn,   As soon as they have eaten,
   jiù lái.   they'll come right away.

                          IV

A: ni huí lai la. wàibian   You're back. Is it still raining
   hái xià yǔ ma?   outside?
B: búxià le. keshi lù,   No, it's stopped. But the roads
   zhēn bùhǎozǒu.   are a mess.
A: ni shi zěmma huí lai de?   How did you come back?
B: wo zuò yige péngyou de   In a friend's car.
   qìchē huí lai de.

                           V

A: Guóxīn zài jiā ma?   Is Kuo-hsin at home?
B: ta chū qu le.   He's gone out.
A: ta dào nǎr qù le?   Where did he go?
B: ta dào xuéxiào qu dǎ   He's gone to the school to play
   lánqiú qu le.   basketball.
A: Guóxiān ne?   And Kuo-hsien?
B: tamen shi liǎngge rén   They both went together.
   yíkuàr qu de.
A: Guóxiān búshi zuótian shuō,   Didn't Kuo-hsien say yesterday
   ta jīntian bùdǎ lánqiú ma?   that he wouldn't be playing
                                        basketball today?
B: ta zuótian yǒu yidiǎr   He was a bit sick yesterday, but
   bùshūfu. jīntian ta hǎo le.   he's better today.
A: tamen shémma shíhou huí   And when are they coming back?
   lai ne?
B: tamen shuō, tamen huí lai   They said they were coming back
   chī wǔfàn.   for lunch.

VI

A: qǐng jìn lai, 'zuò yìhuěr. Please come in and sit for a while.
B: duìbuqǐ; wo yào shàng kè Excuse me, but I'm going to class.
   qu le.
A: ni xiàle kè, women zài Let's have a chat after you get
   tán ba.   out of class.

VII

A: shū mǎi le ma? (Did you) buy the books?
B: mǎi le. Yes.
A: bǐ ne? And the pens/pencils?
B: bǐ yě mǎi le. Them, too.
A: hái mǎile xie shémma? Did you buy (a little of) anything
                            else?
B: hái mǎile xie zhǐ. (In addition,) I bought a little
                        paper.

VIII

A: kuài yào shàng kè le. It's almost time for class. Let's
   zǒu ba.   go.
B: wo méi kè. wo zài zhèr, I have no class. I'll (stay) here
   yùbei gōngkè. nimen shémma (and) do my homework. When are
   shíhou huǐ lai?   you coming back?
A: women yíxià kè, jiù huí lai. As soon as we get out of class.

IX

A: tamen dōu dào 'nǎr qù le? Where have they all gone?
B: tamen dōu qu chàng gēr They've all gone to sing.
   qu le.
A: 'nǐ zěmma búqù ne? And how come you're not going?
B: tamen chàng 'Èguo gēr. They sing Russian songs, and I want
   wǒ yào chàng 'Zhōngguo gēr. to sing Chinese songs.

A: women zhèngzai xué chàng   We're just now studying how to
    Zhōngguo gēr ne. ni lái gēn   sing Chinese songs. How about
    wǒmen yíkuàr 'xué hǎo buhǎo?   coming to study together with us?
B: hǎojíle.   Great!

X

A: nide Zhōngguo huà, shi   Where did you learn your Chinese?
    zài nǎr xué de?
B: zài Měiguo, Yélǔ Dàxué   At Yale University, in America.
    xué de.
A: shi něinián xué de?   What year?
B: shi yǐ-jiǔ-qī-sān, dào   The two years from 1973 to 1975.
    yǐ-jiǔ-qī-wǔ, neiliǎngnián
    xué de.
A: 'něiwei xiānsheng jiāoguo   Which teacher taught you?
    ni?
B: wo jìde, yǒu yiwei xìng   I remember there was one named Chang,
    Zhāng de; hái yǒu yiwei xìng   and another named Lee.
    Lǐ de.
A: tamen dōu 'hái zài Yélǔ ma?   Are they both still at Yale?
B: tīng shuō, tamen dōu búzài   No, I hear that neither of them
    Yélǔ le.   is at Yale anymore.

XI

A: nimen zuótian méichū qu ma?   Didn't you go out yesterday?
B: méiyǒu. women běnlái   No. We had originally planned to
    dǎsuan dào Niǔyuē qu kàn   go to New York to watch some
    Měiguo zúqiú qu; kěshi   (American) football, but the
    tiānqi bùhǎo; women méiqù.   weather was bad, (so) we didn't
                                     go.

XII

A: ni chīle fàn le ma?   Have you eaten yet?

B: hái méi ne.   Not yet.

A: women yíkuàr qu chī fàn   How about us going to have a meal
    qu, 'hǎo buhǎo?   together?

B: hǎo. qǐng nǐ děng wǒ   Fine. Please wait (for me) a moment.
    yihuěr. wo jiù lái.   I'll come (back) right away.

XIII

A: ni chīguo Zhōngguo fàn ma?   Have you ever had Chinese food?

B: wo chīguo; keshi 'zhèmma   Yes, but I've never had Chinese
    hǎochī de Zhōngguo fàn, wo   food that tasted this good.
    méichīguo.

XIV

A: Lǐ Xs dào 'nǎr qù le?   Where has Mr. Lee gone?

B: ta dào Yīngguo qu le.   He's gone to England.

A: ta dào Yīngguo qu, zuò   What has he gone there to do?
    shémma qu le?

B: ta dào Yīngguo qu, kàn   He's gone to England to see a
    yige péngyou qu le.   friend.

A: ta búdào Fàguo qu ma?   He's not going to France?

B: ta yě yào dào Fàguo qu.   Yes, he's going to go there too.
    ta shuō, ta yě yào zài Fàguo,   He says he wants to see one or
    kàn yǐ-liǎngge péngyou.   two friends in France, too.

A: ta dào Fàguo qùguo ma?   Has he ever been to France?

B: Fàguo, Yīngguo, ta dōu   He's been to neither France nor
    méiqùguo. zhè shi tóuyícì.   England. This is the first time.

New words

míngtian TW   tomorrow

zuótian TW   yesterday

zǎoshang TW	morning
wǎnshang TW	evening
wo zuótian wǎnshang zài jiā.	I was at home yesterday evening.
jīntian zǎoshang, ta zài xuéxiào.	This morning, she was at school.
women míngtian zhōngwu, zài fànguárli chī fàn.	Tomorrow noon, we eat in a restaurant.
shíhou, shíhour TW	time
shémma shíhou?	when?
nimen shémma shíhou chī fàn?	When do you eat?
chī'fàn de shíhou	when eating
chī'fàn de shíhou, bié shuō huà.	Don't speak when you're eating.
wo méiyou'qián de shíhou, wo bàba cháng gěi wǒ qián.	My father often gives me money when I don't have any.
zhè shi ta zuì'máng de shíhou.	This is his busiest time.
wǒ xiǎng zài Běi'jīng de shíhou, kàn jǐge péngyou.	I intend to see some friends when I'm in Peking.
zǎofàn N	(morning meal:) breakfast
zhōngfàn N	(noon meal:) lunch
wǎnfàn N	(evening meal:) supper
ta cháng buchī zǎofàn.	He often doesn't eat breakfast.
wo míngtian zhōngwu, zài Lǐjia chī zhōngfàn.	I'm having lunch tomorrow at the Lee's at noon.
jīntian wǎnshang, wo bùxiǎng zai lǚguǎn chī wǎnfàn.	I don't intend to eat supper in the hotel this evening.
shàngbian, shàngbiar PW[1]	surface, top, above (same as shàngtou)
xiàbian, xiàbiar PW[1]	bottom, below (same as xiàtou, dǐxia)
lǐbian, lǐbiar PW[1]	inside (same as lǐtou)
wàibian, wàibiar PW[1]	outside (same as wàitou)
qiánbian, qiánbiar PW[1]	front (same as qiántou)
hòubian, hòubiar PW[1]	back (same as hòutou)

zhuōzi shàngbiar, you hěn
  duō zhǐ.

chē xiàbiar you yìzhǐ xiǎo
  zhū.

míngzi, zai shū lǐbiar.

ta zài huǒchēzhàn wàibiar,
  mài bào.

wūzi qiánbiar, you yìzhāng
  dà zhuōzi.

wo zuòzai hòubiar ba.

dàxué PW

Yélǔ PW[2]

  ta zài Yélǔ Dàxué niàn shū.

  ta zài Yélǔ xué Fàwén.

yǔ N

xià yǔ VO

  wàitou búxià yǔ le.

kè N (M: -táng)

shàng kè VO

xià kè VO

  ni jīntian shàng 'jǐtáng kè?

  (wo) shàngwu (shàng) liǎngtáng,
    xiàwu méi kè.

  wo yǒu kè.

  wo yǒu yìtáng kè.

  wo yǒu liǎngtáng kè.

  ta yíxià kè, jiu chī diǎnxin.

gōngkè N

  wode gōngkè tài duō le.

  wo děi zuò wode gōngkè.

There's a lot of paper on the
  table.

There's a little pig under the
  wagon.

The name is inside the book.

He sells papers outside the
  railway station.

In the front of the room is a
  big table.

Let me just sit in the back.

(great school:) college, university

Yale

He studies at Yale University.

She's studying French at Yale.

rain

(send down rain:) to rain

  It's stopped raining outside.

class

(go up to class:) go to class

(come down from class:) get out of
  class

How many classes do you have today?

I have two in the morning and
  none in the afternoon.

I have a class.

I have two classes.

As soon as he gets out of class,
  he has a snack.

school work, homework

I have too much (school) work to do.

I have to do my homework.

yùbei V   prepare

   ta zài lóushang, yùbei   At the moment, she's upstairs
    gōngkè ne.   doing her homework.

yǐhuěr, yǐhuǐ TW   in a little while, in a moment

   yǐhuěr ta jiu huí lai.   She'll be back in a minute.

   wo yǐhuěr qù.   I'll go in a little while.

   qǐng nǐ zuò yihuer.   Please sit for a while.

děng V   wait

   qǐng 'děng yǐhuěr.   Please wait a little while.

   wo búyào děng ta.   I won't wait for him.

gēr, gē N   song

chàng V   sing

chàng gēr/gē VO   sing

   ni xǐhuan chàng gēr ma?   Do you like to sing?

   wo xǐhuan chàng 'Zhōngguo gēr. I like to sing Chinese songs.

diànhuà N   (electric speech:) telephone

dǎ diànhuà VO   (operate a telephone [with the
                       hands]:) make a call on the
                       telephone

   zuì hǎo, xiān dǎ ge diànhuà.   It would be best to telephone
                       first.

tán V   chat, discuss

-táng M   (class [as a period of time])

-nián M   year

   ni xiǎng něinián zài dao   What year do you plan to go
    Běijīng qu?   again to Peking?

   wo yī-jiǔ-qī-bā-nián zài qù.   I'll go again in 1978.

yǐjing A   already

   tamen yǐjing lái le.   They've already come.

   wo yǐjing gàosong ta le.   I've already told her.

   ta yǐjing 'qǐng wǒ le.   He's already asked me.

yíkuàr, yìqǐ A   together

  bié yíge rén qù; women yíkuàr   Don't go alone; let's go together.

    qù ba.

  tāmen liǎngge rén, yào yíkuàr   Those two are going to sing

    chàng gēr.   together.

-- PW   together, one place

  wǒ gēn wǒ gēge, zhùzai yíkuàr.   I live (together) with my (older)

     brother.

yǒu yìdiǎr, yóu diar A   a bit

  ta jīntian yóu diar bùgāoxìng.   She is a bit upset today.

gēn CV   with, accompanying

  wo 'kéyi bukéyi gēn nǐ huí qu?   Can I go back with you?

  wo bùgēn ta shuō huà le.   I'm not speaking to him any more.

  wo bùxiǎng zài gēn ta chàng   I don't think I'll sing with her

    gēr.   any more.

dào CV[3]   to (a place; 1l); until (a time)

  wo dào míngtian, hái zai   I'll be in Hong Kong until

    Xiānggǎng.   tomorrow.

  wo cóng zuótian zǎoshang, dào   I was in New Haven from yesterday

    jīntian zhōngwu, dōu zài   morning until noon today.

    Xīngǎng.

shūfu SV   comfortable

  zhèibǎ yǐzi, hěn shūfu.   This chair is comfortable.

bùshūfu SV   uncomfortable; (slightly) sick

  zhèibǎ yǐzi, hěn bùshūfu.   This chair is uncomfortable.

  wo jīntian yóu diar bùshūfu.   I'm a bit ill today.

zǒu V   take (a road; 10); depart

  women míngtian zǒu ba.   Let's leave tomorrow.

  ta zuò huǒchē zǒu.   She's leaving by train.

chū V   emerge, exit (with lai and qu)

  women jīntian wǎnshang, chū   Let's go out to eat this evening.

    qu chī fàn ba.

jìn V   enter (with <u>lai</u> and <u>qu</u>)
  qǐng jìn lai.   Please come in.
jìde V   remember
  wo bújìde ta xìng shémma le. I don't remember anymore what
                                                    his surname is.

  wo jìde, ta zhùzai xuéxiào   I remember that he lives in a
    hòubiar de yisuo xiǎo fángzi-   a small house behind the school.
    li.
le VS   (<u>liǎo</u>: finish:) so that the action
                                                of the verb has been completed
  ta yìchīle fàn, jiù lái.   She'll come as soon as she's
                                                    eaten.
  ta mǎile ge biǎo.   He bought a watch.
-guo VS   (<u>guò</u>: pass by, experience:) with
                                                the result that at least one
                                                instance of the action of the
                                                  verb has occurred
  ta dào Ōuzhōu qùguo.   She has gone to Europe (at least
                                                  once before now).
le P   (indicates action completed in the
                                                past, having occurred as of the
                                                present)
  ni chī fàn le ma?   Have you eaten yet?
-guo, -guò VS   (<u>guò</u>: pass by, experience:) so that
                                                the action of the verb has been
                                              completed
  wo dǎguo diànhuà le.   I have phoned (already).
méi(you) A   have not
  ta méimǎi biǎo.   He hasn't bought a watch.
  ta méiyou mǎi biǎo.
  wo méiqu.   I didn't go.
  ta méidào Ōuzhōu qùguo.   She hasn't been to Europe (ever).
  wo méidǎguo diànhuà.   I haven't phoned (yet).

méiyǒu? V	(the negative verb used in choice-type questions asking about experience, or completed action)
ta mǎi 'biǎo le méiyǒu?	Has he bought a watch?
ni chī 'fàn le méiyǒu?	Have you eaten?
ta dào Ōuzhōu 'qùguo méiyǒu?	Has she (ever) been to Europe?
nǐ dǎguo diàn'huà méiyǒu?	Have you phoned (yet)?
hái méi...ne.	have not...yet, still not...
ta hái méimǎi biǎo ne.	he hasn't bought a watch yet.
wo hái méichī fàn ne.	I haven't eaten yet.
ta hái méidào Ōuzhōu qùguo ne.	She still hasn't ever been to Europe.
wo hái méidǎ diànhuà ne.	I haven't phoned yet.
a P	(question particle: Lesson 9); (exclamatory particle)
nà hǎo a.	That's just fine.
la P	(fusion of le and a)
ni huí lai la.	Ah, you've come back.

Notes

[1] The suffix -bian or -biar (Lesson 10) is interchangeable with -tou in these placewords. xiàbian (xiàbiar) is interchangeable with dǐxia and xiàtou.

[2] Yélǔ is a sound borrowing from English "Yale". Names of some other universities are:

Niújīn Dàxué	(ox ford:) Oxford University
Jiànqiáo Dàxué	(The first syllable is pronounced gim in Cantonese, and is a sound borrowing from the first syllable of the English name: "Cam-". qiáo means "bridge".) Cambridge University

Hǎfó (Hāfó) Dàxué	(Hǎfó and Hāfó are sound borrowings:) Harvard University
Gēlúnbǐyǎ Dàxué	(Gēlúnbǐyǎ is another sound borrowing:) Columbia University
Zhījiāgē Dàxué	University of Chicago
Jiāzhōu Dàxué	(Jiā stands for the first syllable of "California"; zhōu is "state":) University of California
Běijīng Dàxué	Peking University
Táiwān Dàxué	(National) Taiwan University
Xiānggǎng Dàxué	Hong Kong University
Dōngjīng Dàxué	(eastern capital:) Tokyo University
Jīngdū Dàxué	(capital metropolis:) Kyoto University

These names are often shortened to a one-syllable version of
the first word plus Dà, short for Dàxué. Thus:

Gē Dà	Columbia
Běi Dà	Peking U., Pei Ta
Tái Dà	Taiwan U., T'ai Ta
Jīng Dà	Kyoto U., Kyō Dai

[3]dào in the meaning "until" is followed by a time word. Notice
that both time words and place words may follow dào, but that only
place words can follow dào in the pattern dào PW qu.

More notes on grammar

12.1 The sentence particle le, used to express action completed
in the past. The sentence particle le has been introduced as expressing "change of status" (Lesson 9, "New words, notes 10 and 11; 9.2;
11.4, and 11.6). It is also used to express "completed action", that
is, action undertaken and completed in the past. Sometimes, especially when the verb has a measured (but unspecified) object, the sentence

particle _le_ expresses the idea that the action of the verb has
occurred to the extent expressed in the NU-M phrase modifying the
object "so far" (i.e. up to the present time). Compare these
sentences ending in the sentence particle _le_:

zuótian, tiānqi buhǎo; xiànzài hǎo le.	The weather was bad yesterday; it has gotten better today.
women kuài yào chī fàn le.	We're just about to eat.
tamen chī fàn le.	They have begun to eat (rice). / They have eaten. (Cf. _tamen_ _chīle fàn le_. "They have eaten." -- the only meaning.)
ta hēle liǎngbēi jiǔ le.	He has drunk two glasses of wine, so far.

12.1.1 "Completed action" negated with méi(you).

nǐmen chī táng le ma?	Have you eaten (some) candy?
women méichī.	No, we haven't.
women méiyou chī.	

ta xiūli chē le ma?	Has he fixed the car?
méiyǒu.	No.

ni kàn bào le ma?	Have you read the paper?
méiyǒu.	No.
méikàn.	
méiyou kàn.	
méiyou kàn bào.	
wo méiyou kàn bào.	

12.1.2 "Completed action" and non-content questions. In addi-
tion to questions ending in _ma_? choice-type questions occur with
"completed action" sentences, where the negative choice takes the
form _méiyǒu_? or _méi-V_? always at the end of the sentence.

ni yùbei nide gōngkè le ma?   Have you done your school work?

ni yùbei nide gōng'kè le méiyǒu?

ni yùbei nide gōng'kè le méiyùbei?

yùbei le.   Yes, I have.

ta shàng kè le ma?   Has he gone to class?

ta shàng 'kè le méiyǒu?

ta shàng 'kè le méishàng?

shàng kè le.   Yes, he has.

tamen xià kè le ma?   Have they gotten out of class yet?

tamen xià 'kè le méiyǒu?

tamen xià 'kè le méixià?

xià le.   Yes, they have.

ta méidǎ diànhuà ma?   Hasn't she phoned?

méiyou.   No.

12.2 <u>The verbal suffix</u> -guo (-guò), <u>used to express action</u>
<u>completed in the past</u>. When used in conjunction with the sentence
particle <u>le</u>, the verbal suffix -<u>guo</u> expresses "completed action in
the past". This -<u>guo</u> is derived from a verb, <u>guò</u> "pass by, exceed,
experience", and adding it to the verb in sentences ending with the
"completed action" sentence particle <u>le</u> carries something of the
meaning of the original verb: dǎguo wǎngqiu le. "(I) have undergone
the experience of playing tennis."; but this meaning is weakened, so
that dǎ wǎngqiú le and dǎguo wǎngqiu le are virtually synonymous.
This completed action -<u>guo</u> is not generally added to verbs that end
in a syllable carrying the neutral tone.

When a sentence with this "completed action" -<u>guo</u> is negated,
<u>méi(you)</u> is used before the <u>V-guo</u> expression. Choice-type questions
are made with <u>méiyou</u> only, placed at the end of the sentence.

nǐmen dǎguo wǎngqiú le ma?   Have you played tennis?

wǒmen méidǎ.   No, we haven't.

wǒmen méiyou dǎ.

ni kànguo'bào le méiyǒu?   Have you read the paper?
méiyǒu.   No.
méikànguo.
méiyou kànguo.
méiyou kànguo bào.
wo méiyou kànguo bào.

    12.3 <u>The verbal suffix -le</u>, <u>used to express action completed</u>
<u>at any time</u>. When used in conjunction with the (homophonous)
sentence particle <u>le</u>, the verbal suffix <u>-le</u> expresses "completed
action in the past", and is virtually synonymous with the -<u>guo</u> (or
-<u>guò</u>) described in 12.2 above. Thus, the first three sentences
below are virtually equivalent in meaning:

ni chī fàn le ma?   Have you eaten?
ni chīguo fàn le ma?
ni chīle fàn le ma?

wo méichī.   No, I haven't.
wo méiyou chī ne.

ni kànle bào le ma?   Have you read the paper?
méiyou.   No.
méikàn.
méiyou kàn.
méiyou kàn bào.
wo méiyou kàn bào.

tamen xià kè le ma?   Have they gotten out of class yet?
tamen xiàle 'kè le méiyǒu?
tamen xiàle 'kè le méixià?
xià le.   Yes, they have.

    12.4 le <u>and object-less functive verbs</u>. Among the functive
verbs that often occur without a direct object are verbs of motion,

such as <u>lái</u>, <u>qù</u>, and <u>zǒu</u>. They occur with the "completed action"
verbal suffix <u>-guo</u>, combined with the sentence particle <u>le</u>: <u>wo</u>
<u>qùguo le</u>. "I have gone (there). " (cf. <u>wo chīguo fàn le</u>. "I've
eaten.") But the verbal suffix <u>-le</u> and the sentence particle <u>le</u>
do not both occur after such verbs: <u>wǒ qù le</u>. "I have gone (there)."
(cf. <u>wo chīle fàn le</u>. "I've eaten.")

ta lái le.	She's come (here).
ta qù le.	She's gone.
ta zǒu le.	She's left.
ta méilái.	She hasn't come (here).
ta méiqù.	She hasn't gone.
ta méizǒu.	She hasn't left.
ta huí lai le.	He's come back.
ta méihuí qu.	He hasn't gone back.
ta jìn lai le.	He has come in.
ta méichū qu.	He hasn't gone out.
ta lái le ma? -- méilái.	Has she come (here)? -- No.
ta qù le méiyǒu? -- méiyǒu.	Has she gone? -- No.
ta 'huí lai le méiyou? -- méiyǒu.	Has she come back? -- No.
ta 'jìn qu le méijìn qu? -- méijìn qu.	Has she gone in? -- No.
ta 'chū lai le méiyǒu? -- méiyou.	Has she come out(side)? -- No.

12.5 <u>Reinforcing adverbs</u> yǐjing <u>"already" and</u> hái méi- ...ne
<u>"not yet"</u>.

nǐ yǐjing chī fàn le ma?	Have you already eaten?
ni yǐjing chīguo fàn le ma?	
ni yǐjing chīle fàn le ma?	
wo hái méichī fàn ne.	No, not yet.
wo hái méichī ne.	

wo hái méiyǒu chī ne.	Not yet.
hái méiyǒu ne.	
hái méi ne.	
tamen yǐjing shàng kè le ma?	Have they already gone to class?
tamen yǐjing shàng 'kè le méiyǒu?	
tamen hái méiyou shàng kè ne.	No, not yet.
tamen hái méiyǒu ne.	
hái méi ne.	
ta yǐjing jìn lai le ma?	Has she already come in?
ta hái méijìn lai ne.	Not yet.
tamen yǐjing chū qu le ma?	Have they already gone out?
yǐjing chū qu le.	Yes.

12.6 <u>The sentence particle</u> le <u>with coverbs, and with purpose</u> <u>clauses</u>. Sentence particle <u>le</u> comes after the last verb. In purpose clauses the second <u>lai</u> or <u>qu</u> must be present.

ta dào xuéxiào qu le.	He's gone to the school.
ta dào Hāfó Dàxué lai le.	He's come to Harvard.
ni dào Gē Dà qu le ma?	Have you gone to Columbia?
wo hái méidào Gē Dà qù ne.	Not yet.
ta lái niàn shū lai le.	She came to study.
ta xiūli qìchē qu le.	He's gone to have the car fixed.
ta huí lai zuò fàn lai le.	He's come back to cook.
ta jìn qu kàn péngyou qu le.	He's gone in to see a friend.
tamen dào Niújīn qu, kàn Měiguo zúqiú qu le.	They've gone to Oxford to watch some (American) football.
ta dào huǒchēzhàn qu, zuò shì qu le.	He's gone to the railway station to work.
wo zuótian wǎnshang dào Zhāngjia qu, kàn Zhāng Tt qu le.	Yesterday evening, I went to the Chang's to see Mrs. Chang.

12.7 <u>The verbal suffix -le in sentences that do not require the</u>
<u>sentence particle</u> le. The verbal suffix -<u>le</u> occurs with unmeasured
objects (i.e. not preceded by a specifier or a measure) in a
main clause only if followed by a sentence particle <u>le</u>: wo chīle fàn
<u>le</u>. This suffix occurs without the sentence particle in subordinate
clauses: wo chīle fàn, jiù kàn bào. "I'll read the newspaper after
I have eaten.": or if the object is measured: wo hēle liǎngbēi jiǔ.
"I've had two glasses of wine."

12.7.1 <u>V</u>-le (<u>O</u>), jiù...: <u>non-past</u>. If there is no sentence
<u>le</u> after the clause that has <u>jiù</u>, the sentence is non-past: present
or future.

wo chīle fàn, jiù kàn bào.   I'll read the newspaper after I
                                    have eaten.

ta dàole lǚguǎn, jiù chī fàn.   She'll eat after she arrives at
                                    the hotel.

ta xiàle kè, jiù zuò gōngkè.   He does his school work after he
                                    gets out of class.

12.7.2 <u>V</u>-le (<u>O</u>), jiù...le: <u>past</u>. A sentence <u>le</u> ending the
clause that has <u>jiù</u> puts the sentence in the past tense.

ta kànle bào, jiù shàng kè le.   He went to class after he read the
                                    newspaper.

ta zuòle gōngkè, jiù xiūxi le.   She rested after she did her school
                                    work.

ta dàole Niǔyuē, jiù qu kàn   After he got to New York, he went
   péngyou qu le.   to see some friends.

12.7.3 <u>V</u>-le (<u>SP-NU-</u>)M O: <u>ordinary past</u>. If there is no sentence <u>le</u> at the end of a sentence that has a verbal suffix <u>le</u> and a
measured object, the tense of the sentence is past, and there is no
special modification of this past-tense idea.

ta hēle liǎngbēi jiǔ.	He drank two glasses of wine.
ta mǎile sānzhǐ gāngbǐ.	He bought three pens.
ta hái mǎile xiē zhǐ.	In addition, he bought some paper.

12.7.4 V-le (SP-NU-)M O le: past, "up to now". If the sentence that has a verbal suffix -le and a measured object also ends with the sentence particle le, there is added the idea that the action of the verb has happened to the extent indicated in the measuring phrase "up to now", or "so far".

ta hēle liǎngbēi jiǔ le.	So far, he has drunk two glasses of wine.
wo jīntian xiūlile liǎngliàng qìchē le.	I've repaired two cars today, so far.
wo jīntian shàngle sāntáng kè le.	I've gone to three classes so far today.

12.8 The verbal prefix yì- "once, as soon as" with the verbal suffix -le. Adding the verbal suffix -le to a verb with the yì-prefix, together with sentence le in the second clause indicates change of status (see Lesson 9, "New words, note 10), either past or habitual.

wo yíkàn yizhang huàr, jiu yào mǎi.	As soon as / whenever I look at a painting I want to buy it.
wo yíkànle zhèizhāng huàr, jiu yào mǎi le.	As soon as I saw this painting, I want(ed) to buy it./Whenever I saw...
ni yíkàn bào, jiu jìde le.	As soon as you read the newspaper, you'll remember.
wo yíkànle bào, jiu jìde le.	As soon as I read the newspaper, I remembered. /Whenever I read...

wo yídào Bālí, jiu xiǎng chī	As soon as / whenever I arrive in
Fǎguo fàn le.	Paris, I begin to think about
	eating French food.
wo yídàole Bālí, jiù xiǎng	As soon as I arrived in Paris, I
chī Fǎguo fàn le.	began to think about eating
	French food.

12.9 <u>The experiential verbal suffix</u> -guo. This suffix indicates
that the action of the verb to which it is suffixed happened at least
once in the past. It differs from the past tense verbal suffix <u>-guo</u>
(<u>-guò</u>) in always carrying the neutral tone and in never occurring with
the sentence particle <u>le</u> that means "action completed in the past".
It is negated with <u>méi</u>-.

ni dào Ōuzhōu 'qùguo méiyǒu?	Have you ever been to Europe?
wo méiqùguo.	No, I haven't.
ni chīguo Zhōngguo fàn ma?	Have you ever eaten Chinese food?
wo chīguo. women cháng chī	Yes, I have. We often eat Chinese
Zhōngguo fàn.	food.
ni zài nóngchǎng 'zhùguo	Have you ever lived on a farm?
méiyou?	
wo méizài nóngchǎng zhùguo.	No, I never have.
ni zuòguo fēijī ma?	Have you ever ridden an airplane?
méizuòguo.	No.
ni gēn Cáo Xj dǎguo wǎngqiú	Have you ever played tennis with
ma?	Miss Ts'ao?
wo hái méigēn ta dǎguo ne.	No, I never have, yet, with her.

12.10 <u>Follow-up sentences with</u> shi...de <u>concerning past action</u>.
After an opening question or statement which establishes the fact
that action in the past is being asked about or talked about, follow-
up questions and statements concerning circumstances attending the

action discussed use the <u>shi...de</u> pattern, where the expression
denoting the attendant circumstances follows <u>shi</u>; and <u>de</u> follows the
verb, and precedes any object.   The <u>shi</u> is sometimes omitted in
positive sentences.   Cf. 9.1.7.

ni zuótian dào shémma dìfang qu le?	Where did you go yesterday?
wo dào chénglitou qu le.	I went into the city.
shi cóng jiāli qù de ma?	Did you go from home?
búshi cóng jiāli qù de; shi cóng xuéxiào qu de.	No, not from home, from school.
ni zuò shémma chē qu de?	How did you go?
wo zuò gōnggòngqìchē qu de.	By bus.
ni shi yíge rén qu de ma?	Did you go alone.
búshi yíge rén qu de; wo gēn yige péngyou yíkuàr qu de.	No; I went along with a friend.
nimen qu zuò shémma qu de?	What did you go to do?
women qu mǎi shū qu de.	We went to buy some books.
zai 'nèige shūdiàn mǎi de?	At which bookstore did you buy them?
shi zài huǒchēzhàn pángbiār de nèijiā shūdiàn mǎi de.	At the bookstore next to the rail-way station.
neixie shū, yígòng shi duōshao qián mǎi de?	How much did the books cost all told?
yígòng, sānkuài wǔ.	Three fifty.
shi nǐ gěi de qián ma?	Did you pay?
búshi; shi wǒ péngyou gěi de qián.	No, my friend did.
nimen shi shémma shíhou huí lai	When did you come back?
women shi wǎnshang huí lai de.	In the evening.

12.11 <u>X de shíhou</u>: "when X". Time phrases denoting "when"
something takes place often take the form of a noun clause formed by
<u>shíhou</u> "time", preceded by modifiers: <u>chī 'fàn de shíhou</u> is thus

"the time of eating / the time when one eats", which, when it occupies a time-word position in a sentence, means "when one eats".
The tone on <u>shíhou</u> is often weakened to a neutral tone.

ta shàng 'kè de shíhou kàn bào.   She reads the newspaper while in
                                          class.

wo (shi) shàng 'kè de shíhou,   I read the newspaper when I was
   kàn de bào.   in class.

women chī zhōng'fàn de shíhou,   Let's have a chat when we eat
   tántan ba.   lunch.

women (shi) shàng 'kè de shíhou,   We learned this character in
   xué de zhèige zì.   class.

women (shi) zài Yélǔ Dàxué, xué   We got acquainted when we were
   Zhōngguo 'huà de shíhou, rènshi   studying Chinese at Yale.
   de.

Exercises

Answer the following questions:

ni chī zǎofàn de shihou, hái zuò shémma?

nide gōngkè shi shéi yùbei de?

ni gen Zhāng Tt shuōguo huà ma?

ni jīntian gen Zhāng Tt shuōguo huà le ma?

ni yídào Táiběi, jiu xiǎng zuò shémma?

ni dǎle diànhuà, jiu zuò shémma?

ni xiǎng, míngtiande tiānqi, hái nemma bùhǎo ma?

ni jīntian shàngle 'jǐtáng kè le?

ni míngtian dàole Niǔyuē, jiu dǎsuan zuò shémma?

ni zuótian wǎnshang, dàole shūpù, jiu zuò shémma le?

ni zuótian dào Wángjia qu zuò shémma qu le?

ni zuótian zuò shémma dao Wángjia qu de?

ni jīntian zǎoshang yǐjing chīguo zǎofàn le ma?

Zhāng Tt jìn lai zuò shémma lai le?

'zěmma Zhèng Xs hái méilái ne?

nide gōngkè dōu yùbei le ma?

nǐ xiǎng, kuài yào xià yǔ le ma?

wo tīng shuō, Wáng Xj kuài yao dao Měiguo lai le; ta 'shémma shíhou
lái ne?

ni 'jìde bujìde, jiāo ni Zhōngguo huà de neixie xiānsheng, dōu xìng
shémma?

ni zài Zhōng-Měi Fànguǎr chīguo fàn ma?

Translate into Chinese:

1. She's come back already.

2. She hasn't come back yet.

3. After eating breakfast, he often reads the newspaper.

4. After she got out of class yesterday morning, she did her school
   work.

5. I don't remember anymore what this character means.

6. Have you ever been to Harvard?

7. I've had three cups of tea so far today.

8. He's come to America to learn English.

9. She has already gone back to Japan. She went by boat from New
   York. She went with an American friend. The friend went to Japan
   to study Japanese.

10. As soon as I looked at the character she had written, I knew I
    didn't know it.

11. She eats candy when she writes.

Lesson 13

Time when and time spent

Pronunciation

<u>Plain</u>:

<u>a</u>:   Fàguo; dà; dàhòutian "day after the day after tomorrow"; dàqiántian "day before the day before yesterday"; Hāfó; chá.

<u>e</u>:   tèbié; gōngkè; mǎchē; yánsè; Èguo.

<u>i</u>:   shìde; Bōshìdùn "Boston"; Rìběn; xīngqīrì "Sunday"; zìjǐ.

<u>ai</u>: báide; yìbǎi; lǐbài "week"; Táiwān; Shànghǎi; gāngcái "just a moment ago"; cài; ài.

<u>ei</u>: měige "each one"; Měiguo; děi; hēide; shéi.

<u>ao</u>: yìmáo; lǎoshī; yíhào; shǎo; zǎofàn.

<u>ou</u>: lóu; hòutou; hòutian "day after tomorrow"; hòunian "year after next"; Jiāzhōu; zhōumò "weekend"; zǒu; Ōuzhōu.

<u>ang</u>: fángzi; yìtáng; yítàng "one (journey)"; gāng; gāngcái "just a moment ago"; Xiānggǎng; yìzhāng.

<u>eng</u>: péngyou; děng; zhèng.

<u>Frontalized</u>:

<u>ia</u>: xià kè; Gēlúnbǐyǎ.

<u>ie</u>: tèbié; xiě; Yélǔ; yě; yèzi "leaf"; hóngyè "red leaves".

<u>i</u>:   píjiǔ; Bālí; yìlǐ; lǐtou; xiūlǐ; lǐbài "week"; lǐbàitiān "Sunday"; qī; xīngqī "week"; xīngqīrì "Sunday"; yìqǐ; qìchē; yíkuàr; yìhuěr.

<u>iao</u>: biǎo; yìtiáo; jiāotōng; jiàoshòu; yào; yàoshi "if".

<u>iu</u>: liù; jiǔge; píjiǔ; jiǔ "long (time)"; yǒude.

<u>ian</u>: fāngbiàn; diǎnxīn; diànyěngr "movie"; diànhuà; yìtiān; lǐbàitiān "Sunday"; qiántian "day before yesterday" qiánnian "year before last" yìjiān; yíjiàn; jiàn "see"; yánsè.

<u>in</u>: nín; jīntian; jīnnian "this year"; yīnwei "because".

256

iang: yíliàng; Cháng Jiāng.

ing: míngtian; míngnian "next year"; yídìng; gāoxìng; Yīngwén; diànyǐng
"movie".

iangr: (none yet)
iengr: diànyěngr "movie".

Labialized:

ua: Huá Shān.

uo: Bōshìdùn "Boston"; Hāfó; zhōumò "weekend"; duōshao; shuǐguǒ;
zuótian; búcuò; wǒ.

u: jìnbù; Jīngdū; shūfu; zúqiú; wūzi.

uan: huàn; chuán; suān; Táiwān; wán "have fun"; yìwǎn; wǎnfàn; yíwàn.

un: Lúndūn "London"; Bōshìdùn "Boston"; yícùn; wèn.

uang: Huáng Hé; wǎngqiú.

ong: gōngfu "free time"; gōnglǐ; gōnggòngqìchē; gōngkè; yígòng; hóngde;
hóngyè "red leaves".

uar: fànguǎr; yíkuàr; huār; huàr; wár "have fun".

uor: yìduǒr; yìsuǒr.

uer: yìhuěr.

ur: (none yet)

Frontalized and labialized:

ue: juéde; Niǔyuē; yuè "month".

ü: nǚde; lǚguǎn; júzi; qù; qùnian "last year"; xià yǔ; yùbei.

Dialogs

I

A: yìnián, yǒu 'dūoshaotiān?   How many days are there in a year?

B: yìnián, yǒu sānbǎi-liùshi-   There are 365 days in a year.
   wǔtiān.

A: yìnián yǒu 'dūoshaoge yuè?   How many months are there in a year?

B: yìnián, yǒu shí'èrge yuè.   There are 12 months in a year.

A: yíge yuè, yǒu 'dūoshaotiān?   How many days are there in a month?

B: yǒude yǒu 'sānshitiān;   Some have thirty days; others have
   yǒude yǒu sānshi'yītiān.   thirty-one.

A: èryuè, yě yǒu 'sānshitiān   Does February have as many as thirty
   nèmma dūo ma?   days too?

B: méiyou. èryuè, jiù yǒu   No, February has only twenty-eight
   èrshibātiān.   days.

A: yìnián, yǒu 'jǐge xīngqī? *   How many weeks are there in a year?

B: yíge yùe, yǒu 'sìge xīngqī.   There are four weeks in a month,
   yìnián, yǒu wǔshi'èrge xīngqī.   fifty-two in a year.

A: měiyige xīngqī, yǒu jǐtiān   And how many days are there in a week?
   ne?

B: měige xīngqī, yǒu qītiān.   Seven.

A: jīntian shi xīngqījǐ?   What day of the week is it today?

B: jīntian shi xīngqīyī.   It's Monday.

A: zuótian ne?   And what about yesterday?

B: zuótian shi xīngqīrì.   Yesterday was Sunday.

A: qiántian ne?   And what about the day before yesterda

B: qiántian shi xīngqīliù. *   That was Saturday.

A: jīnnian shi yìqiān-jǐubǎi-   This year is 1970-what?
   qīshi 'jǐnián?

B: jīnnian shi yìqiān-jǐubǎi   It's 1975.
   qīshi'wǔnián.

A: zhèige yuè shi 'jǐyuè?   What month is it?

B: zhèige yuè shi shí'yíyuè.   It's November.

A: jīntian, 'jǐhǎo?   What day (of the month) is it?

B: jīntian shi shíyíyuè,   It's the 25th of November.
   èrshi'wǔhǎo.

*Repeat the material from here to the next sentence with an
asterisk, substituting <u>lǐbài</u> for <u>xīngqī</u>, and <u>lǐbàitiān</u> for <u>xīngqírì</u>.

                                II

A: xīngqi'tiān zhèige 'tiān zì,   Isn't the <u>tiān</u> of <u>xīngqitiān</u> just the
   'shì bushì, jiùshi tiānqi de   same as the <u>tiān</u> of <u>tiānqi</u>.
   'tiān zì?

B: shì. shi tiānqi de 'tiān   Yes. It's the <u>tiān</u> in <u>tiānqi</u>; its
   zì; yě shi jīntian, míngtian   also the <u>tiān</u> of <u>jīntian</u>, <u>míngtian</u>
   zuótian, 'qiántian, 'hòutian,   <u>zuótian</u>, <u>qiántian</u>, <u>hòutian</u>, <u>dàqián-</u>
   dà'qiántian, dà'hòutian de   <u>tian</u>, and <u>dàhòutian</u>.
   'tiān zì.

A: nǐ gāngcái shuō, měige   You said a moment ago that the first
   xīngqī de dìyìtiān, shi xīng-   day of every week was Sunday, didn't
   qītiān, 'shì bushi?   you?

B: shì.   Yes.

A: yàoshi xīngqītiān, shi   If Sunday is the first day of the
   měiyige xīngqī de dìyìtiān,   week, (in) that (case) how can you
   nà 'zěmma néng shuō <u>Monday</u>   say that "Monday" is <u>xīngqīyī</u> and
   shi xīngqīyī, Tuesday shi   "Tuesday" is <u>xīngqīèr</u>?
   xīngqīèr ne?

B: nà shi yīnwei wàiguode   That's because the foreign week goes
   xīngqī, shi cóng xīngqītiān,   from Sunday to Saturday; the Chinese
   dào xīngqīliù; Zhōngguode   week goes from Monday to Sunday.
   xīngqī, shi cóng xīngqīyī, dào
   xīngqītiān.

   *Repeat the dialog, substituting <u>lǐbài(tiān)</u> for <u>xīngqī(tiān)</u>

III

A: ni fùmǔ shémma shíhou dào   When do your parents come to
   Měiguo lái?   America?

B: tamen míngnian lái.   Next year.

A: míngnian shémma shíhou lái?   When, next year?

B: míngnian sì-wǔyuè de shihou   (Some)time around April or May.
   lái.

A: tamen dǎsuan zài Měiguo zhù   How long do they plan to stay in
   duó jiǔ?   America?

B: zhù yì-liǎngge yuè.   For one or two months.

A: tamen shi tóuyícì dào   Is it true that they are coming to
   Měiguo lái ma?   America for the first time?

B: bùshi. tamen láiguo   No. They've come twice before.
   liǎngcì le.

IV

A: ni kànguo Zhōngguo diàn-   Have you ever seen a Chinese movie?
   yěngr ma?

B: méikànguo.   No.

A: míngtian wǎnshang you yige   Tomorrow evening there's a Chinese
   Zhōngguo diànyěngr. ni   movie. Do you want to see it?
   yuànyi qu kànkan ma?

B: míngtian wǎnshang wo méiyou   I don't have time tomorrow evening.
   gōngfu. hòutian wǎnshang hái   Will it still be there day after
   yǒu ma?   tomorrow evening?

A: yǒu.   Yes.

B: women hòutian wǎnshang   Let's go together day after tomorrow
   yíkuàr qu kàn ba, 'hǎo   evening. OK?
   buhǎo?

A: hǎo.   Fine.

B: neige diànyěngr, ni bùshi   Haven't you already seen the movie
   kànguo yícì le ma?   once?

A: wo kànguo yícì; kěshi nèige   Yes, but it's really good. I'd
   diànyěngr zhēn hǎo. wo hái   still like to see it one more
   yào zài kàn yícì.   time.

V

A: nín dào Lúndūn qùguo ma?   Have you ever been to London?
B: qùguo.   Yes, I have.
A: nín zài nèr zhùguo duó jiǔ?   How long did you stay there?
B: zhùguo liǎngnián.   For two years.
A: nín zhèiyicì dǎsuan zhù duó   How long do you plan to stay this
   jiǔ?   time?
B: zhèicì, jiù dǎsuan zhù   This time I plan to stay just a few
   yì-liǎngge yuè.   months.
A: nín búdào Fàguo qu kànkan   Aren't you going to France to have
   ma?   a look around / to visit?
B: duì le. wo zhèicì yào dào   Right. This time I'm also going to
   Fàguo qu kànkan, yě yào dào   France for a visit, also to
   Déguo qu kànkan.   Germany.

VI

A: ni xuéguo Zhōngguo huà ma?   Have you ever studied Chinese?
B: wo qùnian xuéguo yìdiǎr.   Last year I studied a little.
A: ni jīnnian xuéle duóma jiǔ   How long have you studied so far
   le?   this year?
B: wo jīnnian xuéle shíge lǐbài   Up to now, I've studied Chinese for
   de Zhōngguo huà le.   ten weeks this year.
A: nimen xué xiě zì ma?   Are you learning to write?
B: women gāng xué xiě zì.   We've just started to learn to write.
A: ni huì xiě nǐde míngzi ma?   Do you know how to write your name?
B: wo 'jiù huì xiě wǒde míngzi.   I can only write my name. / Yes, but
                                      that's all.

VII

A: ni zhèiliàng chē, shi   When did you buy your car?
   'něinián mǎi de?

B: shi yī-jiǔ-liù-bā mǎi de.   In 1968.

A: zǒule 'duōshaolǐ le?   How many miles has it gone so far?

B: zǒule kuài shíwànlǐ le.   Close to 100,000 miles.

A: wǒde, yě zǒule kuài wǔwànlǐ   Mine has also gone close to 50,000
   le. wǒde shi 'qiánnian mǎi   miles. I bought it year before
   de.   last.

B: nǐde chē, 'zěmma zǒule   How come your car has gone so many
   'nèmma duō lǐ ne!*   miles?

A: wo zhèijinián, zài zhèr niàn   The last few years I've been study-
   shū. wo fùmǔ zhùzai 'Jiāzhōu. ing here. My parents live in
   wo měinián dou huí qu liǎng-   California. I go back there twice
   tàng. yítàng, jiushi sānqiān- a year. One trip is over three
   duōlǐ.   thousand miles (one way).

VIII

A: zài chī kuai táng ba.   Have another piece of candy.

B: buchī le.   I won't have any more (thanks).

A: zài chī yíkuài ba.   Oh, come on.

B: bùchī le, xièxie. wo   No more, thanks. I've already eaten
   yǐjing chīguo hǎojǐkuài le.   quite a few pieces up to now.

IX

A: nimen zhèige zhōumò, dǎsuan   Where do you plan to go this weekend
   dào 'nǎr qu wár?   (to have fun)?

B: tīng shuō, zheige zhōumò de   They say that the leaves will be at
   hóngyè, zhèngshi hǎokàn de   their prime this weekend. We
   shihou. women dǎsuan míngtian plan to drive to Boston tomorrow
   zǎoshang kāi chē, dào Bōshìdùn morning. Will you come along?
   qu. ni 'qù buqù?

─────────────────────

*Expressions with duo such as nèmma duō (but not duō alone) are
like numbers in that they sometimes occur directly before measures.

A: wo xiǎng qù.   I think I will.

B: hǎo. nèmma ni míngtian   Fine. In that case, tomorrow morning,
   zǎoshang dào women jiā lai,   you come to our place and we'll go
   yíkuàr qu ba.   together.

A: hǎojíle. míngtian zǎoshang   Great. See you tomorrow morning.
   jiàn.

                              X

A: ni dàhòutian 'néng bunéng   Can you go with us in three days to
   gēn wǒmen dào Zhījiāgē qu wár?   Chicago to have a good time?

B: děng wǒ kànkan. jīntian,   Let me think. What day is today?
   jǐhào?

A: jīntian, shíjiǔhào.   It's the nineteenth.

B: yàoshi jīntian, shi shí'jiǔ-   If today's the nineteenth, tomorrow's
   hào; míngtian, 'èrshihào; hòu-   the twentieth, the day after tomor-
   tian, èrshiyīhào; dàhòutian shi   row's the twenty-first, and the day
   èrshièrhào. wo nèitian bunéng   after that is the twenty-second.
   qù. nèitian shi wǒde shēngrì.   I can't go that day. That's my
   nèitiān 'wǎnshang, wo yào gēn   birthday. That evening, I'll be
   wo jiāliren yíkuàr chī wǎnfàn.   having dinner with my family.

A: o? nèitian shi nide shēngrì   Oh, so that's your birthday? In
   ma? ni shi 'něinián shēng de?   what year were you born?

B: wo shi yī-jiǔ-wǔ-língnián   In 1950.
   shēng de.

A: wo yě shi nèinián shēng de.   I was born that year, too. We
   wǒmen shi tóngnián.   share the same year (of birth).

                        New words

yuè N   month
   yíge yuè   one month
   'něige yuè?   which month?
   shàngyuè / shàngge yuè   last month
   yígeduō yuè   more than one month

wǔge yuè líng yìtiān	five months and one day
xīngqī N	(star period) week
lǐbài N	(worship) week
sānge xīngqī/sānge lǐbài	three weeks
zhèige xīngqī/zhèige lǐbài	this week
xiàxīngqī / xiàge xīngqī	next week
sāngebàn xīngqī/sāngebàn lǐbài	three and a half weeks
liǎngge xīngqī líng yìtiān	two weeks and one day
-yuè M	(in names of months)
yīyuè, yíyuè TW	January
èryuè TW	February
sānyuè TW	March
sìyuè TW	April
wǔyuè TW	May
liùyuè TW	June
qīyuè, qíyuè TW	July
bāyuè, báyuè TW	August
jiǔyuè TW	September
shíyuè TW	October
shí'yīyuè, shí'yíyuè TW	November
shí'èryuè TW	December
'jǐyuè TW	What month?
sānyuèli	in March
wǔ-liùyuèli	in May or June
ta shi 'jǐyuè lái de?	What month did she come here?
ta shi shí'èryuè lái de.	In December.
xīngqīyī/lǐbàiyī TW	Monday
xīngqīèr/lǐbàièr TW	Tuesday
xīngqīsān/lǐbàisān TW	Wednesday
xīngqīsì/lǐbàisì TW	Thursday
xīngqīwǔ/lǐbàiwǔ TW	Friday
xīngqīliù/lǐbàiliù TW	Saturday
xīngqītiān/lǐbàitiān TW	Sunday

shàngxīngqīsān / shàngge xīngqīsān	last Wednesday
xiàxīngqīwǔ / xiàge xīngqīwǔ	next Friday
xīngqīrì, xīngqītiān TW	Sunday
-hào M	number (6); day (of month)
jīntian, jǐhào?	What day of the month is it?
jīntian, shíwǔhào.	It's the fifteenth.
shí'jǐhào?	What day (between the 11th and the 19th)?
shí'wǔhào.	The fifteenth.
ni shuō, 'duōshaohào?	What day, did you say?
wo shuō 'shí, 'wǔ, 'hào.	I said, the FIFTEENTH.
ta shi 'jǐhào lái de?	On what day did she come?
ta shi èrhào lái de.	On the second.
-nián M	year (12)
bànnián	half a year
yìniánbàn	a year and a half
sānniánduō	three years plus
yìnián líng yíge yuè	a year and one month
zhèiliǎng-sānnián	the last two or three years
něinián	which year?
yī-jiǔ-líng-sānnián	1903
yī-jiǔ-wǔ-jǐnián?	195?
jīnnian TW[1]	this year
míngnian TW[1]	next year
hòunian TW[1]	year after next
qùnian TW[1]	last year
qiánnian TW[1]	year before last
dàqiànnian TW[1]	three years ago
dàhòunian TW[1]	three years from now
qiántian TW[1]	day before yesterday
dàqiántian TW[1]	day before the day before yesterday

hòutian TW[1]   day after tomorrow

dàhòutian TW[1]   day after the day after tomorrow

diànyěngr, diànyǐng N   (electric shadow:) movie, film

  kàn diànyěngr VO   see a movie

  qiánnián zuò de diànyěngr   a movie made year before last

gōngfu N   free time; time

  ni 'yǒu meiyǒu gōngfu kàn   Do you have time to see a movie?

    diànyěngr?

  wo méiyou gōngfu.   I have no time.

  liǎngniánde gōngfu   two years(' time)

  xué Zhōngguo huà, zuì shǎo, It takes at least two years to

    děi liǎngniánde gōngfu.   study Chinese (so that you know

              it).

zhōumò N   weekend

  wo zhèige zhōumò niàn shū.   I'm studying this weekend.

Lúndūn PW   London

  ta zài Lúndūn Dàxué niànguo She's studied at the University

    shū.   of London.

Bōshìdùn   Boston

  ta zài Bōshìdùn Dàxué xuéguo He's studied Japanese at Boston

    Rìwén.   University.

yèzi N   leaf (of a tree, etc.)

  hóng yánsè de yèzi   red leaves

hóngyè N   red leaves, colored leaves (of autumn)

  kàn hóngyè   look at the colored leaves

měi- SP   each, every

  měige rén   each person

  měisānge rén kàn yìběn.   Every (group of) three persons reads

              one book.

  měidìsānge rén kàn yìběn.   Every third person reads one book.

  měinián   every year

  měisānnián   every three years

  měiliǎngtiān   every two days / every other day

měiliǎngge xīngqī	every two weeks / every other week
měiliǎngge yuè	every two months / every other month
měige èryuè	every February
měinián èryuè	every February
měitiān zǎoshang	every morning
měijǐtiān	every few days
-tàng M	(journeys, trip)
wo měige lǐbài, kāi liǎngtàng chē, dao Niǔyuē qu.	Every week I take two trips to New York by car
yīnwei CA^2	because
ni wèishemma yào dao Zhōngguo qu? — yīnwei wo yào xué Zhōngwén.	Why do you want to go to China? — Because I want to study Chinese.
gāngcái TW	just a moment ago
gāngcái ta lái le; xiànzài ta zǒu le.	He came just a moment ago; (but) now he is gone.
ta gāngcái méilái.	He hadn't come a moment ago.
ta gāngcái búyuànyi lái, xiànzài ta lái le.	Just a moment ago she didn't want to come, but now she has come.
ta gāngcái chàngle yige gēr.	He just sang a song.
gāngcáide gēr, méiyìsi.	The song of just a moment ago was dull.
ta gāngcái búzai zhèr.	She wasn't here a moment ago.
ta gāngcái méizai zhèr.	She wasn't here a moment ago.
nèmma CA	in that case
nèmma, wǒmen zhèmma zuò ba.	In that case, lets do it this way.
jiù A^3	only (4); then, afterwards (9); right away (11); then
tā bulái, wǒ jiù lái.	(If) she doesn't come, then I will.
yàoshi MA^3	if
yàoshi ta qù, wǒ yě qù.	If she goes, I'll go too.
ta yàoshi bumǎi, wǒ mǎi.	If he doesn't buy it, I will.

jiǔ SV

  duó jiǔ?

  nǐ dǎsuan zhù duó jiǔ?

  bùhěn jiǔ.

kuài A⁴

  kuài shíwànlǐ le

  ta hēle kuài shíbēi jiǔ le.

  ta zài Bālí zhùle kuài sān-
    nián le.

jiùshi A V

  Měiguo de 'měi zì, jiùshi
  Měizhēn de'měi zì.

zhèngshi A V

  ta lái de shihou, zhèngshi
    wo zuì máng de shihou.

kàn V

  wǒ xiǎng, zhèige zhōumò, dao
    Niǔyuē qù kànkan.

wár, wán V

  háizimen dōu zai wàibiar wár
  ne.

  háizimen dōu xǐhuan wár.

  ta xǐhuan wár shémma?

  ta xǐhuan wár xiǎo chuán.

  chū qu wár ba.

---

long (time)

  how long (a time)?

  How long do you plan to stay?

  Not long.

close, soon (11); close to, nearly

  close to 100,000 miles so far

  She's had close to ten cups of
    wine, so far.

  He's lived in Paris for nearly
    three years.

(only is:) is just, is exactly

  The character for the měi in
    Měiguo is (exactly) the (same as
    the) one for the měi of Měizhēn.

(is right in the process of being:)
  is just (during), is exactly
  (during)

  He came just when I was busiest.

read (2); look at (9); have the opinion
  that (9); visit (someone) (11); visit
  (a place), look around

  This weekend, I think I'll go to
    New York to take a look around.

play, have fun, have a good time, play
  with

  The children are all playing outside

  Children all like to play.

  What does she like to play with?

  She likes to play with little boats.

  Go out and play.

wǒ xiǎng hòutian dào Bōshìdùn qu wár.	Day after tomorrow, I think I'll go to Boston and have some fun.
ta gēn shéi wár ne?	Who's he playing with?
ta gēn yige xiǎo péngyou wár ne.	He's playing with one (of his) little friends.
zài lái wár.	Come again (for a good time).
shēng V	be born
nǐ shi 'něinián shēng de?	What year were you born in?
wǒ shi yi-jiǔ-wǔ-liù shēng de.	In 1956.
shēngrì N	birthday
nide shēngrì, shi 'jǐyuè, 'jǐhào?	What's the date of your birthday?
wo de shēngrì, shi shí'èryuè, 'qíhào.	It's the seventh of December.
jiàn V[5]	see, meet
ni qu jiàn shéi?	Whom are you going to see?
wo qu jiàn wo lǎoshī.	I'm going to see my teacher.
wo méijiànguo ta.	I've never met her.
zài jiàn.	See you later.
yìhuěr jiàn.	
míngtian jiàn.	See you tomorrow.
xīngqīyī jiàn.	See you Monday.

Notes

[1]The time words that are relative to the time "now" introduced so far are:

dàqiántian	dàqiánnian
the day before	three years ago
the day before yesterday	
qiántian	qiánnian
the day before yesterday	the year before last

zuótian	shàng(ge) xīngqī	shàng(ge)yuè	qùnian
yesterday	last week	last month	last year
jīntian	zhèige xīngqī	zhèige yuè	jīnnian
today	this week	this month	this year
míngtian	xià(ge) xīngqī	xià(ge)yuè	míngnian
tomorrow	next week	next month	next year
hòutian			hòunian
the day after			the year after ne
tomorrow			
dàhòutian			dàhòunian
the day after			three years from
the day after			
tomorrow			

[2]"CA" stands for "conjunctive adverb", which is the third kind of adverb, different from a fixed adverb (which only occurs after any topic) and a movable adverb (which may come before or after the topic). A conjunctive adverb only occurs before any topic. In an answer to a question with wèishemma, yīnwei is a conjunctive adverb.

[3]The "if" clause precedes the conclusion. jiù "then" may appear in the conclusion and yàoshi may appear in the "if" clause:

tā búqù, wǒ qù.	He doesn't go along: I do. / If he doesn't go along, I will.
tā yàoshi búqù, wǒ qù.	If he doesn't go along, I will.
tā yàoshi búqù, wǒ jiu qù.	If he doesn't go along, then I will.
ta búqù, wǒ jiu qù.	He doesn't go along: then I do. / If he doesn't go along, I will.

[4]kuài, like yígòng, may modify a nominal comment (6.3), and like yígòng, a verb may follow the adverb. The verb that may follow kuài is yǒu.

wǒ de chē zǒule kuài you sān-qiānlǐ le.	My car has gone close to three thou-sand miles.

⁵jiàn implies a more formal meeting than kàn "visit"; compare
these verbs with jiē:

wǒ xiǎng qu kàn Guóxiān.	I intend to go see Kuo-hsien.
wǒ děi qù jiàn wǒ lǎoshī.	I must go meet with my teacher.
wǒ děi dào huǒchēzhàn qu jiē Zhēnzhēn.	I have to go to the railway station to meet Chen-chen.

More notes on grammar

13.1 **Time when.** The time when the action of the verb takes
place is expressed as a time expression: a time word, or a "when"
clause ending in de shíhou, de nèitiān, de nèige yuè, de nèinián,
and the like. Such time expressions are topics and act like movable
adverbs: they occur before the verb, and before or after any other
topic. Notice that the corresponding English expression often occurs
last.

xiàlǐbàiyī, wo xiǎng qu kàn ta.	I intend to go see her next Monday.
shàngxīngqīrì, wo qu kàn ta le.	I went to see her last Sunday.
ta zhèige xīngqī bùlái.	He's not coming this week.
ta zhèige xīngqī méilái.	He hasn't come this week.
xiàlǐbài, wo búniàn shū le.	I won't be studying anymore next week.
shànglǐbài, wo méiniǎn shū.	I didn't study last week.
zhèige lǐbàisān, wo bùhē jiǔ le.	I stop drinking this Wednesday.
zhèige lǐbàisān, wo méihē jiǔ.	I didn't drink Wednesday of this week.
zhèige lǐbàisān, wo bùhē jiǔ.	I won't drink this Wednesday.
ta jīnnian měige xīngqīsān jiāo shū.	She teaches every Wednesday this year.
ta qùnian, měige xīngqīsān jiāo shū.	She taught every Wednesday last year.
ta qùnian jiāo shū le.	She began teaching last year.
ta qùnian jiāoguo shū.	She taught (at least once) last year.
ta qùnian jiāo shū le.	She taught last year.

qùnian, ta dào Yīngguo qu le.   He went to England last year.

yī-jiǔ-líng-wǔnián, wo bàba   In 1905, my father went to New York
zuò chuán, cóng Shànghǎi,   from Shanghai by boat.
dào Niǔyuē qù le.

ta qùnian cháng qù.   She often went, last year.

wo shàngyuè cháng qù kàn diàn-   Last month I often went to the movies,
yěngr; wo zhèige yuè búqù le.   but this month I've stopped going.

zhèiliǎngnián, women zuì máng.   These last two years have been busiest
                                             for us.

ta gāng dào Yélǔ lái de shihou,   He often thought of going out, when he
cháng xiǎng chū qu wár.   first came to Yale.

nèisāntiān, wo méizuò shì.   I didn't work those three days.

zhèisāntiān, wo méizuò shì.   I haven't worked for the last three
                                             days.

nèisāntiān, wo búzuò shì.   I'm not working those three days.

nèisāntiān, wo búzuò shì le.   I won't be working any more those
                                             three days.

qùnián, èryuè, tā yǐjing zǒu le. She had already left by February of
                                             last year.

wo yíyuè, yíhào, xiǎng gēn wo   I intend to have a meal with my
jiāliren yíkuàr chī fàn.   family on January first.

jīnnian sān-sìyuèli, wo méizuò   This March and April I didn't cook.
fàn.

míngnian, ta yào zuò shémma?   What is she going to do next year?

ta míngnian yào dào Dōngjīng   She's going to Tokyo next year to
qu xué diar Rìwén.   study a little Japanese.

ta shi 'qùnian zǒu de, shi 'jīn- Did he leave last year or this year?
nian zǒu de?

ta qùnian zǒu de.   Last year.

ta shi 'shànglǐbài gěi wǒ de,   She gave it to me last week, not
búshi 'zhèilǐbài gěi wǒ de.   this week.

zhèiběn shū, shi 'sānyuè xiě   This book was written in March, not
de, búshi 'sìyue xiě de.   in April.

nín shi 'něinián dào Měiguo lái de?	What year did you come to America?
ta shi 'něige xīngqīsì dào de?	What Thursday did she arrive?
tamen shi 'jǐyuè dào de?	What month did they arrive?
měinián, dōu yǒu rén dào Xiānggǎng qu.	There are people going to Hong Kong every year.
měige yuè, ta dōu qǐng péngyou.	She invites friends every month.
měige lǐbàitiān, wo dōu búshàng kè.	I don't go to class any Sunday.
qùnian, wo měige lǐbàiliù, dōu búshàng kè.	Last year, I didn't go to class any Saturday.
zhèr měitiān wǎnshang, dōu xià yǔ ma?	Does it rain every evening here?
qùnian, wo zài Zhōngguo jiāo shū.	Last year, I was teaching in China.
shàngge yuè, ta jiějie zài Niǔyuē chàng gēr.	Last month, his elder sister was singing in New York.
qùnian, wo bú / méizài Zhōngguo.	I wasn't in China last year.
shàngge yuè, ta bú / méizài Niǔyuē.	She wasn't in New York last month.
qùnian, wo méizài Zhōngguo jiāo shū.	I wasn't teaching in China last year.
shàngge yuè, ta méizài Niǔyuē chàng gēr.	She wasn't singing in New York last month.
wo qùnian, cháng gēn tāmen shuō huà.	I often spoke to them last year.
wo qùnian, yǒude shíhou jiāo shū.	Sometimes I taught last year.
wo zuótian gàosong ta, wo méiyou gōngfu kàn diànyěngr.	I told him yesterday that I had no time to see movies.
wo zuótian gēn ta shuō, wo méiyou gōngfu chū qu wár.	I said to her yesterday that I had no time to go out.

wo zuótian xiǎng zuò diar
  Zhōngguo cài.

Yesterday I thought I'd cook some
  Chinese dishes.

wo zuótian wèn ta 'yǒu meiyǒu
  gōngfu tántan. ta shuō ta
  méiyǒu.

I asked him yesterday if he had
  time to have a chat. He said
  that he hadn't.

wo zuótian gàosong ta le.

I told him yesterday.

wo zuótian gēn ta shuō le.

I spoke to him (about it) yesterday.

N.B. In positive statements, verbal or co-verbal zài does not take completed action particles or suffixes, even though the action of the sentence may take place in the past. But if a past-action sentence with zài is negated, the negative adverb is regularly méi- if zài is functioning as a co-verb, and either méi- or bú- if zài is functioning as a verb.

Completed action particles or suffixes are avoided if habitual or frequent action is being referred to, even if that action takes place in the past. Also, these particles and suffixes are avoided with the verbs xiǎng and wèn. They are also avoided with gàosong and shuō if these verbs are followed by a sentence; otherwise these particles and suffixes do occur with these verbs.

13.2 Time spent. The "money spent" pattern has already been briefly introduced (see 8.1.5): wo xiǎng mǎi sānkuài qián de zhǐ. "I intend to buy three dollars' worth of paper." The "time spent" pattern is similar: wo xiǎng zuò sānge lǐbài de chuán. "I intend to take three weeks' time of ship. / I intend to take a three-week trip on a ship." Such time spent expressions always take the form NU-M (and its variations); they follow the verb, and constitute a variety of the "measured object" with sentence and verbal le, and -guo, occurring with the same meaning as they do with other measured objects (see 12.7.3 and 12.7.4):

ta hēle liǎngbēi jiǔ.

He drank two glasses of wine.

ta kāile liǎngtiān chē.

He drove for two days.

ta hēle liǎngbēi jiǔ le.	So far, he has drunk two glasses of wine.
ta kāile liǎngtiān chē le.	So far, he has driven for two days.

When the NU-M expression denotes "time spent", it is optionally followed by de..

nǐ zuòle 'jǐtiān(de) fēijī?	How many days did you fly?
wo jiù zuòle yìtiān(de) fēijī.	Just one day.
wo xiǎng zuò yìtiān(de) fēijī.	I plan to take a trip on a plane for one day.
ta zuòle yìtiān(de) fēijī le.	She has traveled one day on a plane so far.
nǐ míngnián dǎsuàn shàng dūoshaoge xīngqǐ(de) kè?	How many weeks of class do you plan to attend next year?
wǒ dǎsuàn shàng èrshiliùge xīngqǐ(de) kè.	I plan to attend twenty-six weeks of class.
wǒmen shàngle shíge xīng- qǐ(de) kè.	We've attended 10 weeks of class.
wǒmen shàngle shíge xīng- qǐ(de) kè le.	So far, we've attended 10 weeks of class.
ta jiāo sìge yuè(de) Yīngwén.	She teaches English for four months.
ta jiāoguo sìge yuè(de) Yīngwén.	She has taught English for four months.
ta jiāoguo sìge yuè(de) Yīngwén le.	So far, she's taught English for four months.
ta fùmǔ yào gěi ta sānniánde* qián.	His parents are going to give him money for three years.
ta fùmǔ gěile ta sānniánde* qián.	His parents have given him money for three years.
ta fùmǔ gěile ta sānniánde* qián le.	His parents have given him money for three years so far.

---

*-de is obligatory here; sānniánqián also means "three years before/ ago", and adding -de clears up the ambiguity.

13.3 <u>Time spent expressions after intransitive verbs</u>. After such verbs as <u>lái</u>, <u>qù</u>, <u>zǒu</u> and <u>zhù</u>, time expressions may occur denoting the length of time of the action of the verb.

ni (yào) lái duó jiǔ?	How long will you be here?
wo (yào) lái liǎngtiān.	For two days.
ta láile liǎngtiān.	He was here for two days.
ta láile liǎngtiān le.	He's been here for two days, so far.
ta (yào) lái bùshǎo shíhou.	She'll be here quite a while.
ta láile bùshǎo shíhou.	She was here for quite a while.
ta láile bùshǎo shíhou le.	She's been here quite a while, so far.
ta (yào) zǒu duōshao shíhou?	How long will he be away?
ta (yào) zǒu wǔshiduōtiān.	For over fifty days.
ta zǒule wǔshiduōtiān.	He was away for over fifty days.
ta zǒule wǔshiduōtiān le.	He's been away for over fifty days, so far.
tā (yào) qù yígeduō xīngqī.	He'll be gone for over a week.
tā qùle yígeduō xīngqī.	He's been gone for over a week.
tā qùle yígeduō xīngqī le.	He's been gone for over a week, so far.
ni dǎsuan zài Zhōngguo, zhù duó jiǔ a?	How long do you plan to stay in China?
wo dǎsuan zhù yìniánduō.	For over a year.
wo zhùle yìniánduō.	I lived (here) for over a year.
wo zhùle yìniánduō le.	I've lived (here) for over a year, so far.

13.4 <u>Words identifying particular times</u>. When a time word is identified as such-and-such a day of the week or month, such-and-such a month, or such-and-such a year, the verb <u>shì</u> occurs optionally between the two terms.

jīntian, 'jǐhào?	What day (of the month) is it today?
jīntian, shi 'jǐhào?	

jīntian, shí'jǐhào?	What day (between the 11th and the
	19th) is it today?
jīntian, shi shí'jǐhào?	
jīntian, shí'wǔhào.	It's the fifteenth.
jīntian, shi 'wǔhào.	It's the fifth.
jīntian, xīngqī'jǐ?	What day of the week is it?
jīntian, shi xīngqītiān.	Sunday.
jīnnian, shi 'něinián?	What year is it?
jīnnian, shi yī-jiǔ-qī-wǔ.	It's 1975.

13.5 **The whole before the part.** When a place or a time is identified by two or more terms, the term expressing the larger entity precedes the one that expresses the smaller entity.

Měiguo, Yélǔ Dàxué	Yale University, America
wo shi zài 'Měiguo, Yélǔ Dàxué,	I studied Chinese at Yale University,
xué de Zhōngwén.	in America.
ta zai Fàguo, Bālí, zhùguo	She's lived in Paris, France, for
liǎngnián.	two years.
ta zai Rìběn, Dōngjīng, zuò	He does business in Tokyo, Japan.
mǎimai.	
ta shi yíyuè, shíjiǔhào lái de.	She came on the nineteenth of January.
wo yī-jiǔ-qī-sì, wǔyué, shíhào,	I arrived in Canton on the tenth of
dào de Guǎngzhōu.	May, 1974.

13.6 **yǒu X nemma SV: "be as SV as X".** Equal comparison is expressed as "to have the quality of the stative verb in that (same) (way:), degree that X has".

nèige háizi, xiànzài, yǒu ta	That child has now gotten to be as
bàba nemma gāo le.	tall as his dad.
zhèifèr bào, méiyou nèiběn shū	This newspaper is not as expensive
nemma guì.	as that book.

zhèijiàn yīshang, yǒu nèijiàn nemma chǎng.	This dress is as long as that one.
nǐner, yǒu wǒzher zhemma fāngbiàn ma?	Is where you are as convenient as where I am?
wo zhèijiān wūzi, méiyou nǐ nèijiān nemma hǎokàn.	This room of mine is not as good-looking as that one of yours.
èryuè méiyou sānshitiān nemma duō.	There aren't as many as thirty days in February.
qìchē méiyou huǒchē nemma kuài.	An automobile is not as fast as a train.

Exercise

Answer the following questions:

nide shēngrì shi 'jǐyuè 'jǐhào?

ni shi něiniǎn shēng de?

ni zhèixīngqīwǔ wǎnshang, xiǎng zuò shémma?

ni shàngyuè, chǎng chū qu wár ma?

ni zài Xīngǎng zhùle 'jǐge yuè le?

ni fùmǔ dào Xīngǎng láiguo ma?

zài Xīngǎng zhùle duóma jiǔ a?

tamen shàngyicì lái de shihou, ni gēn tamen yíkuàr chū qu chī fàn qu le ma?

ni dàqiántian kàn diànyěngr le ma?

ni zhèige zhōumò yǒu gōngfu chū qu wár ma?

xiànzài, hóngyè hǎi hěn hǎokàn ma?

nǐ qùnian, měixīngqītiān dōu zai 'nǎr chī zhōngfàn?

ni zuótian zài 'nǎr chī de zhōngfàn?

ni chīguo zhōngfàn le ma?

ni 'wèishemma bùgēn Wáng Xj shuō huà?

Wáng Xj gāng yào zǒu de shihou, 'zěmma ni méigēn ta shuō, bié zǒu?

ni yàoshi bùxĭhuan Wáng Xj, wèishemma ni cháng qĭng ta lái gēn ni

    yíkuàr chī fàn ne?

gāngcái ni yào zuò shemma le?

ni dăsuan zài Xīngăng zhù duó jiŭ?

Guóxīn de xīn zi, shi nĕige zì?

women 'shémma shíhou zài jiàn?

zuòzai ni pángbiār de neige rén, shi Mĕiguo 'shémma dìfang de rén?

ni jiāli de qìchē, zŏule duōshaolĭ le?

jīntian shàng Zhōngwén kè de shihou, zhèngshi ni zuì xiăng shuō huà

    de shihou ma?

ni 'shémma shihou xiăng dào Dōngjīng qu kànkan qu?

ni dào Niŭyuē qùguo ma?

ni dào Niŭyuē qùguo 'jĭcì le?

ni qùnián dào Niŭyuē qùguo 'jĭcì ne?

Lesson 14

Indefinites; "before" and "after"

Pronunciation

Plain:

a: māma; ná "take"; náli; kāfēi; chāzi "fork"; chá.

e: Déguo; kèqi "polite"; gōngkè; chē; diànchē "trolley"; yánsè; Éguo.

i: shìqing; diànshì "television"; sì.

ai: mǎi; Táiwān; yìtái "one station"; hái; háishi "or"; gāngcái; ài.

ei: Fēizhōu; nèizhāng; gěi; zhèibǎ.

ao: bào; dāozi "knife"; dào; gàosong; zǎoshang; Àozhōu.

ou: lóushàng; hòutou; yǐhòu "afterward"; Fēizhōu; shōuyīnjī "receiving set"; zǒu; Ōuzhōu.

an: shàng bān "go to work"; yíbàn; tán; kàn; yízhàn; sān.

en: běnlái; nèmma; gēn; zhēn.

ang: yìfānglǐ; Xiǎofāng; tāng; Xiānggǎng; shàngtou.

eng: péngyou; yìfēng "one letter"; néng; chéng; yìcéng "one layer".

Frontalized:

ia: xiàtou; Yǎzhōu.

ie: bié; biéde "other"; xièxie; yèzi.

i: bǐ; búbì "not necessary"; dìfang; fēijī; shōuyīnjī "receiving set"; diànshìjī "television set"; yìqǐ; yǐzi; yǐhòu "afterward"; yǐqián "beforehand".

iao: biǎo; yóupiào "postage stamp"; diào yú "angle for fish"; yìtiáo; jiāo; jiào₁; jiào₂ "call"; xiǎohár; Xiǎofāng; yào.

iu: niúchē; qiú; yóupiào "postage stamp"; yǒu.

ian: wúxiàndiàn "radio"; diànchē "trolley"; diànshì "television"; diànyǐngr; yǐqián "beforehand"; xiān; yánsè.

280

in: nín; xīn; xìn "letter"; yīnwei.

Labialized:

ua: diànhuà.

uo: Hāfó; yìduǒ; huǒchē; zuótian; búcuò; suóyi "therefore"; yìsuǒ; wǒ.

u: búbì "not necessary"; jìnbù; Yélǔ; Zhū Jiāng; zúqiú; wúxiàndiàn "radio"; wǔ.

uai: kuài; kuàizi "chopsticks"; wài "hello"; wàitou.

ui: duì; huì; shuǐ; zuì; yíwèi.

uang: yìshuāng "one pair"; Huáng Hé; wǎngqiú.

ong: tóngzhì; yígòng; zhōngfàn; yìzhǒng "one kind"; cōngming.

Frontalized and labialized:

ue: juéde; xià xué "get out of school"; xià xuě "to snow"; yíyuè.

u: lǜde; qùnian; yú "a fish"; xià yǔ; yùbei.

iong: xiōngdì; yòng "use"; búyòng "no use in...".

Dialogs

I

A: wo xiǎng, jīntian wǎnshang qu chī Zhōngguo fàn. ni 'qù buqù?

I think I'll go and have some Chinese food this evening. Do you want to come along?

B: wo kànkan, wo 'néng bunéng qu. o. duìbuqǐ. wo jīntian wǎnshang yǒu shì, bùnéng qù.

Let me see if I can. Oh. I'm sorry, but I have something to do this evening, so I can't go.

C: wo méichīguo Zhōngguo fàn. wo gēn ni qù, 'hǎo buhǎo?

I've never eaten Chinese food. Is it OK if I go with you?

A: hǎo. ni huì ná kuàizi ma?

Fine. Do you know how to use chopsticks?

C: wǒ búhuì. 'shì bushì,   No. Is it true that if you don't
   búyòng kuàizi, jiu bùnéng   use chopsticks, you can't eat
   chī Zhōngguo fàn a?   Chinese food?

A: bùshi. ni zhēn búhuì yòng   No, it's not. You really can't use
   kuàizi ma?   chopsticks?

C: wo zhēnshi búhuì.   No, I really can't.

A: búyàojǐn. ni kéyi yòng   Never mind. You can eat with knife
   dāozi chāzi chī. fànguǎrner   and fork. They have knives and
   you dāozi chāzi. ni yàoshi   forks at the restaurant. If you
   yuànyi xué 'zěmma ná kuàizi,   want to learn how to use chopsticks,
   wo kéyi jiāo ni.   I can teach you.

C: ná kuàizi, 'shì bushì hěn   Is it true that it's hard to learn
   nánxué ya?   to use chopsticks?

A: bùnánxué. 'yìdiǎr 'dōu   No, not at all.
   bùnánxué.

C: nǐ shi shémma shíhou xué de? When did you learn?

A: wo shi dàqiánnián, zài   Three years ago, in Taiwan.
   Táiwān xué de.

C: ni gēn 'shémma rén xué de?   Whom did you learn from?

A: wo gēn yige Zhōngguo péngyou From a Chinese friend.
   xué de.

C: děi xué duóma jiǔ a?   How long does it take?

A: o, ni zhèmma cōngming,   Oh, (with) someone as clever as you,
   yìxué jiu huì le.   (as soon as you start learning
                                    you'll know how:) you'll learn in
                                    no time.

C: hǎo shuō, hǎo shuō...   Oh please... What restaurant are
   women dào 'něige fànguǎr qu   we going to eat at?
   chī fàn a?

A: chéng wàitou, you yige xīn   There's a Chinese restaurant that
   kāi de Zhōngguo fànguǎr.   opened recently outside the city.
   tīng shuō, nèrde cài búcuò.   They say that the dishes there are
                                    pretty good.

C: wǒmen jiu dào nèr qù, 'hǎo   Let's go there then, OK?
   buhǎo?

(zài fànguǎrli.)

A: ni xǐhuan chī shémma?

C: wo zuì xǐhuan chī yú.

A: nèmma women jiù chī yú ba.
    women yào yige shémma tāng ne?

C: wo 'zěmma zhīdao ne? qǐng
    ni gàosong wo 'něige tāng
    hǎohē; wǒmen jiu yào 'nèige
    tāng, 'hǎo buhǎo?

A: ni shuō de Zhōngguo huà,
    'nèmma hǎo, suóyi wo bújìde
    ni méichīguo Zhōngguo fàn.
    hǎo. wo xiǎng, qīngcài niúròu
    tāng, hěn hǎohē. women yào
    nèige tāng, 'hǎo ma?

C: hǎojíle.

A: yíge cài búgòu ba.
    women zài yào yige zhūròu ba.

C: búbì le. gòu le, gòu le.

(guòle yìhuěr.)

A: 'yào buyào jiào tamen ná
    dāochā lái?

C: búbì le, búbì le.

(chīle fàn yǐhòu.)

C: jīntian, wǒ gěi qián.

A: búyào kèqi. women liǎngge
    rén gěi. nǐ gěi yíbàn, wǒ
    gěi yíbàn.

(At the restaurant.)

What do you like to eat?

I like fish best.

In that case, let's have some fish.
And what soup shall we order?

And how would I know? Tell me
what soup is good and we'll
order that one, OK?

Because the Chinese you speak is so
good, I didn't remember that you
hadn't ever eaten Chinese food.
OK. It seems to me that the beef
and vegetable soup would be good.
Shall we order that one?

Fine.

One dish isn't enough, is it?
Let's order a pork dish, besides.

That's not necessary. It's enough,
as it is.

(After awhile.)

Shall we ask them to bring knife and
fork?

No, it's not necessary.

(After having eaten.)

Today, I'll pay.

(Don't be polite.) We'll both pay.
You pay half, and I'll pay half.

II

A: wài. ni shi Wángjia ma?   Hello? Is this the Wang's?

B: shì.   Yes.

A: o. nǐ shi Xiǎofāng a?   Oh, it's Hsiao-fang?

B: shì.   Yes.

A: bàba zài jiā ma?   Is your daddy home?

B: bàba shàng bān qu le.   Daddy's gone to work.

A: lǐbàiliù, ta yě shàng bān   He goes to work even on a Saturday?
   ma?

B: shì; ta shàng bān qu le.   Yes, he's gone to work.

A: māma ne?   What about your mother?

B: māma mǎi dōngxi qu le.   She's gone shopping.

A: gēge ne?   And your (older) brother?

B: gēge shàng xué qu le.   He's gone to school.

A: lǐbàiliù, ta yě shàng xué   He goes to school even on a Saturday?
   ma?

B: shì; ta shàng xué qu le.   Yes; he's gone to school.

A: ni yíge rén zài jiāli zuò   And what are you doing, all by
   shémma ne?   yourself at home?

B: wo zhèngzai kàn diànshì   I'm just (in the process of) looking
   ne.   at television.

A: ni gěi wǒ zuò yìdiǎr shì,   How about doing something for me?
   'xíng buxíng?

B: shémma shì?   What?

A: ni zhīdao wo shi shéi ma?   Do you know who I am?

B: wo zhīdao, ni shi Zhāng Xs.   I know that / Yes, you're Mr. Chang.

A: ni gàosong ni bàba, wo   Tell your father that I'll come to
   míngtian lái kàn ta. yǒu   see him tomorrow, to discuss
   diǎr shìqing gen ta tányitan.   something with him a bit. If he
   yàoshi ta méiyou gōngfu, qǐng   won't have the time, ask him to
   ta gěi wǒ dǎ ge diànhuà.   call me.

B: hǎo, wo gàosong ta.   All right, I'll tell him.

A: xièxie. zàijiàn.   Thank you. Good-bye.

B: zàijiàn, zàijiàn.   Good-bye.

III

yǒu yícì, wo zài Fàguo mǎi
yóupiào. wo yòng Yīngwén gen
mài yóupiào de rén shuō. mài
yóupiào de bùdǒng Yīngwén, wǒ
bùdǒng Fàwén.

Once, I was in France buying
stamps. I was using English to
talk to the stamp seller. But he
didn't understand English, and I
didn't understand French.

yǒu yige rén, zài pángbiār xiān
yòng Yīngwén gēn wǒ shuō, wèn
wǒ yào mǎi duōshaozhāng yóupiào; ta jiu yòng Fàwén gēn
neige mài yóupiào de shuō.

A person next to us first spoke to
me in English and asked me how
many stamps I wanted to buy; then
she spoke to the stamp seller in
French.

wǒ wèn ta, nǐ shi cóng 'nǎr
lái de?

I asked her, "Where are you from?"

ta shuō, wǒ shi cóng Jiānádà
lái de.

She said, "I'm from Canada."

wǒ shuō, nǐde Fàguo huà, zhēn
hǎo.

I said, "Your French is really good."

tā shuō, wǒmen nèr, 'yě shuō
Yīngwén, 'yě shuō Fàwén;
suóyi wo 'liǎngzhǒng huà, dōu
huì.

She said, "Over there, we speak both
English and French, which is why I
know them both."

IV

A: yǒu yìzhǒng diànchē, yǒu
lóushàng lóuxià de; ni
zuòguo ma?

There's a kind of trolley that has
an upper and lower level. Have
you ever ridden in one?

B: wǒ zuòguo. Xiānggǎngde
diànchē, yǒude yǒu liǎngcéng.

Yes. Some of the trolleys in Hong
Kong have two levels.

A: Lúndūnde diànchē, 'shì
bushi yě yǒu liǎngcéng a?

Don't the London trolleys have two
levels, too?

B: Lúndūn méiyou diànchē.
nèrde gōnggòngqìchē, yǒude

There are no trolleys in London.
Some of the buses there have

yǒu liǎngcéng. 'Xiānggǎngde   two levels. About Hong Kong
diànchē ya, yàoshi ni xiǎng   trolleys: if you want to sit
zuò lóushàng, ni děi zài   upstairs, you have to get on
qiántou shàng chē; yíshàng   at the front, and go upstairs
chē, jiu shàng lóu.   as soon as you get on.

A: lóushang, 'shì bushì rén   Is it true that upstairs there are
   'shǎo yìdiǎr?   fewer people?

B: shì.   Yes.

A: 'shì bushì rén dōu bùxǐhuan   Is it that no one likes to go
   shàng lóu?   upstairs?

B: búshi. nà shi yīnwei   No, it's because it's cheaper
   lóuxià piányi, lóushàng guì.   downstairs (and more expensive
                                   upstairs).

                                V

A: nǐ zài nǎr xià chē?   Where do you get off?

B: wǒ zài xiàyízhàn xià chē.   At the next stop.

                                VI

A: ni shàngge yuè, dào 'nǎr   Where did you go last month?
   qù le?

B: diào yú qu le.   I went fishing.

A: qùle yíge yuè?   The whole month?

B: méiyou; jiù qùle sānge   No, just three weeks.
   lǐbài.

A: diàole duōshao yú?   How many fish did you catch?

B: diàole zhēn bùshǎo. zuì   I really caught quite a few. The
   dà de nèitiáo, you qīchǐduō   biggest one was seven feet long.
   cháng.

VII

A: nǐmen sānge rén, cháng   Do you three write home often?
   gěi jiāli xiě xìn ma?

B: wǒmen sānge rén, yíge   One of the three of us doesn't write
   bùcháng xiě xìn; yíge cháng   often; one normally doesn't write;
   bùxiě xìn; yíge shi láile yǐhòu,   and one hasn't written one letter
   'yìfēng xīn, 'dōu méixiěguo.   since she came here.

VIII

A: wo xiàge yuè, dǎsuan qǐng   Next month, I plan to invite a few
   jǐge péngyou chī wǎnfàn. wo   friends to dinner. I wonder if
   bùzhidào tamen dōu yǒu 'gōngfu   they'll all have time.
   méiyou.

B: nǐ qǐng 'wǒ buqǐng? yàoshi   Are you inviting me? If you invite
   nǐ qǐng wǒ, wo 'něitiān dōu   me, I'll be free any day.
   yǒu gōngfu.

IX

A: ni mǎile 'shémma le?   What have you bought?

B: shémma dōu nèmma guì, wo   Everything's so expensive, I didn't
   méimǎi shémma.   buy anything.

X

A: qǐng nǐ ná yìbēi kāfēi lái,   Please, would you bring me a cup
   'xíng buxíng?   of coffee?

B: xíng. ni yào 'táng buyào?   Sure. Do you want sugar?

A: búyào.   No.

XI

A: míngtian, women dào Niǔyuē   We're going to New York tomorrow.
   qu. ni gēn wǒmen yíkuàr qù   Will you come along with us?
   ma?

B: wo. bùnéng gēn nǐmen yíkuàr   I can't go along with you, because
    qu, yīnwei wǒ yǒu biéde shì.   I have something else to do. I
    wǒ děi zìjǐ kāi chē qu.   have to drive in myself.

XII

A: tīng shuō, yào xià xuě le;   I hear it's going to snow; is that
    'shì bushì?   true?

B: wúxiàndiàn shuō, jīntian   The radio says that it'll rain
    wǎnshang xià yǔ; míngtian   this evening and snow tomorrow
    zǎoshang xià xuě.   morning.

A: shi xià 'xiǎo xuě, háishi   Is it going to snow a lot or just a
    xià 'dà xuě?   little?

B: shuō shi yào xià wǔcùn xuě.   It says that there'll be five inches
                                      of snow.

New words

shì, shìqing N (M: -jiàn)[1]   matter, affair
    nèijiàn shì, bùróngyi shuō.   That affair is not easy to talk
                                        about.

    wo yǒu jian shìqing, yào gēn   I have something I'd like to
      nǐ tán.   discuss with you.
    wo yǒu jian shìqing, yào qǐng   I have something that I'm going
      ta zuò.   to ask her to do.
kuàizi N (M: -zhī, -shuāng)   chopstick
    wo jiù yǒu yìzhī kuàizi.   I only have one chopstick.
    zài gěi ta yìshuāng kuàizi ba.   How about giving her another pair
                                        of chopsticks?

dāozi N (M: -bǎ)   knife
chāzi N (M: -bǎ)   fork
dāochā N   knife and fork
    nèijiā fànguǎr, méiyou dāochā   That restaurant has no knives and
      / dāozi chāzi.   forks.

yú N (M: -tiáo)   fish
  nǐ xiǎng mǎi duōshaotiáo   How many fish do you intend to
    yú?   buy?
  ta zuòde tíansuān yú, zhēn   The sweet-and-sour fish that she
    hǎochī.   cooks is really tasty.
Xiǎofāng N   (given name for a little boy; lit.:
                "little square", identifiable as
                a child's name because of "little",
                and as a boy's name because of
                "square")

wúxiàndiàn N   (no-wire electricity:) radio
  wúxiàndiàn shuō, míngtiande   It says on the radio that tomorrow's
    tiānqi hěn hǎo.   weather will be good.
  wúxiàndiàn shōuyīnjī N (M: (radio receive-sound-machine:)
    -jià)   radio set.
diànshì N   (electric view:) television
  diànshìjī N (M: -jià)   television set
  tamen mǎile yíjià xīn   They've bought a new television.
    diànshì.
  háizimen hěn ài kàn diànshì.   Children love television.

yóupiào N (M: -zhāng)   postage stamp
  yìmáo qián de yóupiào   ten-cent stamp / ten cents' worth
        of stamps
  yìmáo de yóupiào[2]   ten-cent stamp
  shízhāng, liǎngmáo (qián) de   Ten twenty-cent stamps and twenty
    yóupiào; èrshizhāng, yìmáo   ten-cent stamps is four dollars
    (qián) de yóupiào; yígòng   altogether, isn't it?
    sìkuài qián, 'shì bushì?

diànchē N (M: -liàng)   (electric vehicle:) trolley car
  wǒmen zuò diànchē dào chéng-   Let's go into the city by trolley.
    litou qu ba.

xìn N (M: -fēng)   letter
  xiě xìn VO   write (letters)
  ta bùcháng xiě xìn.   He doesn't write often.

biéde N[3]	other, remaining
women tán biéde shì ba.	Shall we discuss other things?
nǐ mǎile 'shémma biéde dōngxi le?	And what other things did you buy?
biéde xuéxiào, dōu yǒu nǚlǎoshī.	Other schools all have female teachers.
biéde fànguǎr dōu yuǎn.	The other restaurants are all farther away.
yǒu biéde ma?	Are there any others?
qǐng nǐ gěi wǒ yíge biéde gāngbǐ.	Please give me another (kind of) pen
biéren N[3]	other people, remaining people
bié kàn biéren de xìn.	Don't read other people's letters.
biérende shìqing, dōu bùróngyi zuò.	It's always hard to do the tasks of others.
biérende mǎimai dōu hǎo.	Everyone else's business is fine.
biéren dōu yǒu zhǐ; 'zěmma jiù shi wǒ méiyǒu ne?	Everyone else has some paper; how come I'm the only one that doesn't have any?
xuě N	snow
xià xuě VO	to snow
zuótian xiàle sāncùn xuě.	It snowed three inches of snow yesterday.
shàngyízhàn PW	the last stop (i.e. the stop just before now)
xiàyízhàn PW	the next stop
tamen shi shàngyízhàn shàng de chē.	They got on at the last stop.
women xiàyízhàn xià chē ba.	Let's get off at the next stop.
yǐqián TW[4]	previously, before
yǐhòu TW[4]	afterwards, after, from now on
yǐqián, wo zài Zhōngguo.	Previously, I was in China.
yǐhòu, wo zài Rìběn jiāo shū.	After that, I taught in Japan.
yǐhòu, bié zài tán zhèige le.	Don't talk about it any more, from now on.

yī-jiǔ-qī-wǔ yǐqián	before 1975
yī-jiǔ-qī-liù yǐhòu	after 1976
shínián yǐqián	ten years ago
liǎngge lǐbài yǐhòu	two weeks later
chī fàn yǐqián	before having eaten
xià kè yǐhòu	after class
-jiàn M	(matters, affairs, things)
-shuāng M	(pairs)
bāshuāng kuàizi gòu ma?	Will eight pairs of chopsticks be enough?
-zhǒng M	(kind, variety)
wo bùxǐhuan nèizhǒng huàr.	I don't like that kind of painting.
nèizhǒng chē, hǎo'kāi buhǎokāi?	Is that kind of car easy to drive?
-tái M	(station for transmitting or receiving radio or television signals)
-céng M	(layer, story, level)
nà shi yǐsuǒ sāncéng lóu.	That is a three-story building.
-fēng M	(letters, i.e. items of correspondence)
wo xiěle liǎngfēng xìn.	I wrote two letters.
yīnwei MA[5]	because
suǒyi MA	therefore
yīnwei wo méiyou qián, suǒyi méimǎi nèiběn shū.	I didn't buy the book, because I had no money.
ta yīnwei zhīdao zhèijiàn shì, suǒyi gàosong wo.	She knows about this matter, so she told me.
ta zhīdao, suǒyi wo wèn ta.	She knows, so I'll ask her.
ta zhīdao, wo suǒyi wèn ta.	
xīn A	newly, recently
ta xīn mǎi de yīshang, hěn tèbié.	The dress that she bought recently is odd.
wǒ xīn xué de dōngxi, dōu bújìde le.	I don't remember the things I have just learned anymore.

kèqi SV

    (guest qì spirit:) polite, standing
on ceremony.

  tā hěn kèqi.

    She's very polite.

  bié kèqi (le). IE

    Don't stand on ceremony.

  nín tài kèqi le. IE

    You're too polite. / You're
flattering me.

  wǒ búhuì kèqi. IE

    It's not in me to be (merely)
polite.

búbì AV

    not necessary to, not have to

  ni búbì gěi ta.

    You don't have to give it to her.

  ni búbì mǎi.

    You don't have to buy it.

  búbì kèqi. IE

    It's not necessary to be polite.

  qǐng zuò, qǐng zuò; búbì
    kèqi.

    Please have a seat; make yourself
at home.

  xièxie. -- búbì kèqi.

    Thanks. -- You're welcome.

búbì le. IE

    It's not necessary.

zhēnshi A V

    really is

  ta zhēnshi nemma cōngming.

    She really is that intelligent.

  wo búhuì kèqi; ni chuān de
    neijian yīshang, zhēnshi
    hǎokànjíle.

    I'm not just saying it; the dress
you're wearing is really good-
looking.

háishi A V[6]

    (or) is it?

  háishi 'nǐ jiā yuǎn, háishi
    'tā jiā yuǎn?

    Which is farther away, your home
or his?

  shi Tài Shān gāo, háishi Huá
    Shān gāo?

    Which is higher, Mount T'ai or
Mount Hua?

  'Rìběn jiāotōng fāngbiàn,
    háishi 'Měiguo jiāotōng
    fāngbiàn?

    Which country's transportation is
more convenient: Japan's or
America's?

gěi CV

    for, to

  ta bùcháng gěi ta jiāli de
    rén xiě xìn.

    He doesn't write letters to his
family often.

bié gěi háizimen mǎi táng.　　Don't buy any candy for the
　　　　　　　　　　　　　　　　children.

zhèizhāng huàr, nǐ gěi shéi　　Whom did you paint this painting
huà de?　　　　　　　　　　　　for?

wo shi zuótian gěi ta zuò de　　I cooked for her YESterday.
fàn.

wo zuótian gěi ta zuòle fàn　　I COOKED for her yesterday.
le.

ná V　　　　　　　　　　　grasp, take in the hand; manipulate;
　　　　　　　　　　　　　　bring (with lai); take (with qu)

wo hái bùzhidào zěmma ná　　　I still don't know how to mani-
kuàizi.　　　　　　　　　　　　pulate / use chopsticks.
bié zhèmma ná bǐ.　　　　　　Don't hold the pen(cil) that way.
wo ná qu le, keshi tā búzài　　I took (it) there, but she wasn't
nèr.　　　　　　　　　　　　　there.

— CV　　　　　　　　　　　taking in the hand, with
wo búhuì ná kuàizi chī fàn.　　I don't know how to eat with
　　　　　　　　　　　　　　　chopsticks.

wo zhèngzai xué ná Zhōngguo　　I'm just learning how to paint
bǐ huà huàr.　　　　　　　　　with a Chinese brush.
wo bùcháng ná dāochā chī　　　I don't often eat Chinese food
Zhōngguo fàn.　　　　　　　　with knife and fork.

yòng V　　　　　　　　　　　use
nǐ kéyi yòng wǒde. gāngbǐ.　　You can use my pen.
ni búyòng nǐde gāngbǐ ma?　　Aren't you using your pen?
wo qùnian yòngle hěn duō qián　　I spent a lot of money buying
mǎi shū.　　　　　　　　　　　books last year.

búyòng AV　　　　　　　　　need not
ni búyòng gěi ta.　　　　　　You needn't give it to her.
ni búyòng mǎi.　　　　　　　You needn't buy it.
nín buyòng kèqi. IE　　　　　You needn't stand on ceremony.

yòng CV　　　　　　　　　　using, with
wo búhuì yòng kuàizi chī fàn.　　I don't know how to eat with
　　　　　　　　　　　　　　　chopsticks.

yǒuyòng SV　　　　　　　　useful

méi(you)yòng SV　　　　　　useless

wo zhèngzai xué yòng Zhōngguo bǐ huà huàr.	I'm just learning how to paint with a Chinese brush.
wo bùcháng yòng dāochā chī Zhōngguo fàn.	I don't often eat Chinese food with a knife and fork.
wo yòng Zhōngguo huà gēn ta shuō.	I speak to her in Chinese.
kāi V	drive, open (10); start away (11); open, begin operations
nèige pùzi shi yī-qī-líng-yī kāi de.	That store opened / began in 1701.
kāi mén VO	open a door / gate (10); open (for business)
zhèige shūdiàn, hái méikāi mén ne.	This bookstore hasn't opened yet.
yào V	want (3); order
women yào shémma cài?	What dishes shall we order?
ta méiyào tāng.	He didn't order a soup.
ni xiǎng yào diar diǎnxin ma?	Do you think you'll order some light refreshment / dessert?
huì V	be versed in, know, have learned
wo huì yidiǎr Fàwén.	I know a little French.
guò V[4]	pass, go by, after
guò 'liǎngge xīngqī, ta jiù huí lai.	She'll come back after two weeks.
guò(le) 'liǎngge yuè, ta jiù huí lai le.	She came back after two months.
guò 'liǎngtiān, wǒ lái kàn ni.	I'll come and see you in a couple of days.
guò(le) 'liǎngtiān, wǒ qù kàn ta qu le.	I went to see him after two days.
jiào V[7]	call; tell, ask (someone to do something)

ta jiào ni ne.	He's calling you.
shéi jiào ni ne?	Who's calling you?
ta jiào ni lái.	She's asking you to come.
wo jiào ta mǎi dōngxi qu le.	I asked him to go do the shopping.
wo jiào ta huí qu huàn yīshang qu le.	I told her to go back and change clothes.
diào V	catch (with hook and line)
diào yú VO	to fish
wo bùhěn xǐhuan diào yú.	I don't like to fish much.
ni qùnián diàole 'jǐcì yú?	How many times did you fish last year?
shàng bān VO^8	go to work
xià bān VO^8	get off work
shàng xué VO^8	go to school
xià xué VO^8	get out of school
bàba lǐbàiliù, yě děi shàng bān.	My father has to go to work on Saturday, too.
wo bùzhidào, ta shémma shíhou xià bān.	I don't know when she gets off work.
ta zuótian 'zhōngwu shàng de xué.	He went to school at noon yesterday.
míngtian, wo xià bān yǐqián, ta xià xué.	Tomorrow, she gets out of school before I get off work.
shàng chē VO^8	get on a bus / train / trolley, get in a car
xià chē VO^8	get off a bus / train / trolley, get out of a car
women shémma shíhou shàng chē?	When do we get on the train / ... ?
women dàole Niǔyuē, jiu xià chē le.	We got off the bus when we arrived in New York.

wài. I   Hey! (used to attract someone's
                                    attention); hello? (used in
                                    answering a telephone)
wài; Měizhēn. 'děng yìhuěr.   Hey, Mei-chen. Wait a minute.
wài; nín 'năr a? IE   Hello, (where are you?:) Who is
                                    this?
hǎo shuō. IE   (Fine words:) You flatter me.

Notes

[1]Notice that <u>zuò shì</u> means "have a job, work" (Lesson 7, "New
words", note 6), whereas <u>zuò yíjiàn shì</u> means "do a task, have something to do". <u>shì(qing)</u> "job" has only <u>-ge</u> as its measure; whereas
<u>shì(qing)</u> "task, affair, matter" may have <u>-ge</u> or <u>-jiàn</u> as its measure:
<u>zhèige shì, hěn róngyi zuò</u>. "This task / line of work is easy to do",
but <u>zhèijiàn shì, hěn róngyi zuo</u>. "This task is easy to do."

[2]In phrases denoting the face value or denomination of a stamp
(or a coin, a bond, or paper money), the <u>qián</u> of the money expression
may be omitted. Cf. 8.1.5.

[3]<u>biéde</u> and <u>biéren</u> have indefinite reference ("some other") and
are often translated by a plural in English.

Ways of expressing "other" introduced so far are:

<u>nèi-</u> "that, the other, the other (of two)":

gěi wǒ nèige, 'hǎo buhǎo?   Give me the other one, OK?
nèitiān, wo gēn ta shuō...   The other day, I said to her...

<u>lìngwài-</u> "another, other, different"

gěi wǒ lìngwàiyíge, 'hǎo buhǎo?   Give me another one, OK?

<u>biéde</u> "other (kind)"; <u>biéren</u> "other people, remaining people"

gěi wǒ yige biéde, 'hǎo buhǎo?   Give me one of another kind, OK?
wo lái le; biéren méilái.   I came; the others didn't.

[4]Notice two ways of expressing "after". The first involves the modifier-modified relationship. yǐhòu "time after" is a noun, and it may occur alone in the topic position (as may yǐqián "time before"), in which case it means "afterwards" (and yǐqián means "previously"); but it may also occur in the topic position preceded by a modifying expression. X yǐhòu in topic position means literally "at the time-after of X", where "at" expresses the relationship that the time topic has with respect to the rest of the sentence, "time-after" is the meaning of yǐhòu, and "of" expresses the relationship obtaining between the modifier (X) and the modified (yǐhòu). "At" plus "time-after" plus "of" plus "X" compress, of course, into "after X". (Similarly X yǐqián is "at the before-time of X".)

The second way of expressing "after" involves the verb-object relationship. guò "pass, go by" takes, among other things, expressions denoting amounts of time as its object, so that guò X means "(we) pass X amount of time". Then when this guò X occurs as a time topic, the "at" idea is introduced: "at (our) passing X amount of time", which becomes "after X". Notice that the absence of completed action le indicates non-past; presence of this le puts the action in the past. In past-action sentences, there is an optional verbal suffix -le after guò.

liǎngge xīngqī yǐhòu, tā jiù zǒu.	She'll leave after two weeks.
guò liǎngge xīngqī, tā jiù zǒu.	She'll leave after two weeks.
liǎngge xīngqī yǐhòu, tā jiù zǒu le.	She left after two weeks.
guò (le) 'liǎngge xīngqī, tā jiu zǒule.	She left after two weeks.

[5]When followed by a clause containing the MA suóyi, yīnwei is a movable adverb, occurring before or after any subject in its clause if the subjects of both clauses are the same. (Cf. Lesson 13, "New words", note 2.) In the following sequences, yīnwei, occurring in

the second sentence or clause, is a conjunctive adverb because it
always precedes the subject:

ta 'wèishemma méilái?   Why didn't she come?

yīnwei ta méiyou gōngfu.   Because she had no free time.

ta méilái, yīnwei ta méiyou   She didn't come, because she had no
  gōngfu.   time.

Whereas in the following sequence, yīnwei, occurring in the first
clause, is a movable adverb because it either precedes or follows
any subject:

yīnwei ta méiyou gōngfu, suóyi   She didn't come, because she had no
  méilái.   time.

ta yīnwei méiyou gōngfu, suóyi
  méilái.

    If the subjects of the two clauses are different, yīnwei is
restricted to a position before the subject, and is therefore a
conjunctive adverb.

yīnwei ta zhīdao, wǒ suóyi wènle I asked her because she knows (about
  ta le.   it).

    [6]The pattern which in its fullest form is háishi A, háishi B
may be reduced as follows:

háishi 'Tài Shān gāo, háishi 'Huá Shān gāo?

  shi 'Tài Shān gāo, háishi 'Huá Shān gāo?

      'Tài Shān gāo, háishi 'Huá Shān gāo?

  shi 'Tài Shān gāo.   shi 'Huá Shān gāo?

      'Tài Shān gāo,   'Huá Shān gāo?

    This pattern is used in choice-type questions, (Cf. 1.12.1), and
in the corresponding indirect questions: wo bùzhidào, 'Tài Shān gāo,
háishi 'Huá Shān gāo. "I don't know which is higher, Mount T'ai or
Mount Hua."

[7] jiào and qǐng behave similarly:

wo mei qǐng ta.	I didn't invite him.
wo mei jiào ta.	I didn't call him
qǐng ta chī fàn.	Invite him for a meal.
jiào ta chī fàn.	Tell him to eat.

Notice that tā is a pivot (3.6) in the second pair of sentences.

[8] shàng "ascend" and xià "descend" are functive verbs with relatively limited privileges of occurrence. They form VO combinations, where they correspond to English verbal expressions that are quite various. Expressions introduced so far are:

shàng kè	go to class	xià kè	get out of class
shàng bān	go to work	xià bān	get off work
shàng xué	go to school	xià xué	get out of school
shàng chē	get on a train / ...	xià chē	get off a train / ...

To these may be added:

shàng lóu	go upstairs	xià lóu	go downstairs
shàng chuán	get aboard a ship	xià chuán	get aboard (!) a ship
shàng fēijī	get on a plane	xià fēijī	get off a plane
shàng gōnggòngqìchē		xià gōnggòngqìchē	
	get on a bus		get off a bus
shàng huǒchē	get on a train	xià huǒchē	get off a train
shàng diànchē	get on a trolley	xià diànchē	get off a trolley

wo xīn mǎi de shū zài lóushang;	The book I just bought is upstairs;
qǐng ni shàng lóu qu ná lai.	please go upstairs and bring it (to me).
women xiàle lóu, jiu chī fan.	We'll eat when we go downstairs.

More notes on grammar

14.1 <u>Question words as indefinites</u>. Chinese question words may all function as indefinites. English translations will vary, depending on context, but they may conveniently be referred to the tag meanings given below.

shéi	anyone
shémma	anything
shémma shíhou	anytime
shémma dìfang / nǎr	anywhere
duōshao	any
jǐ-	any
zěmma	anyway, to any degree

14.1.1 <u>Indefinites in questions</u>.

nǐ yào shémma ma?	Do you want anything?
nǐ qǐngle shéi le ma?	Have you invited anybody?
nǐ dào nǎr qù le ma?	Have you been anywhere?

14.1.2 <u>Indefinites after negative adverbs</u>. These sentences are often ambiguous, the indefinite word meaning e.g. "none (at all)" or "none (in particular)"

wo bùchī shémma.	I don't eat anything (special).
wo méichī shémma.	I didn't eat anything (much).
wo bùxiǎng mǎi shémma.	I don't think I'll buy anything (much).
wo méimǎi shémma.	I didn't buy anything (much).
wo búgàosong shéi.	I'm not telling anybody.
women méizhòng shémma cài.	We didn't grow much in the way of vegetables.
wo búhuì zuò shémma cài.	I can't cook much in the way of dishes.

wo méiqǐng shéi.   I didn't invite (much of) anybody.

wo méichī duōshao táng.   I haven't eaten much candy.

wo méichī jǐkuài táng.   I haven't eaten many pieces of candy.

wo méihē jǐshǎor tāng.   I haven't had many spoonsful of soup.

wo méihē jǐbēi jiǔ.   I haven't had many glasses of wine.

wo bùzěmma niàn shū.   I don't study to (much of) any degree.
                                   / I don't study all that much.

wo méizěmma niàn shū.   I didn't study all that much.

ta méizěmma wár.   She didn't play all that much.

ta bùzěmma cōngming.   He's not all that bright.

ta bùzěmma máng.   She's not all that busy.

wo búdào nǎr qu.   I'm not going anywhere (special).

wo méidào nǎr qu.   I didn't go anywhere (special)

ta méigěi shéi xiě xìn.   He didn't write anyone (special).

wo bùgēn shéi shuō.   I won't speak to anyone (about it).

14.1.3 <u>Indefinites in the topic position</u>. When the indefinite
word occurs in the topic position, followed by <u>dōu</u> in positive
sentences, or by <u>dōu</u> or <u>yě</u> in negative sentences, the meaning of the
indefinite is unambiguously universal, e.g. "all" or "none". An indefinite word replacing a post-verbal element (such as a direct or
indirect object) must be transposed in this pattern.

shéi dōu bùchī le.   No one's eating anymore.

shéi dōu chī.   Everyone's eating / will eat.

shéi dōu chī le.   Everyone ate.

shéi dōu méichī.   No one ate.

shéi yě méichī.

shémma dōu xíng.   Anything will do.

shémma dōu bùxíng.   Nothing will do.

nǎr dōu yǒu.   There is (some) everywhere.

nǎr yě méiyou.   There isn't (any) anywhere.

duōshao dōu gòu.	Any amount will be enough.
duōshao dōu búgòu.	No matter how much / many, it won't be enough.
zěmma shuō dōu duì.	Anyway you say it, it's right.
zěmma shuō yě búduì.	Anyway you say it, it's wrong.
ta shémma dōu chī.	She eats everything.
shémma ta dōu chī.	
ta shémma dōu chī le.	She ate everything.
shémma ta dōu chī le.	
ta shémma dōu / yě bùchī.	She eats nothing. / She won't eat anything.
shémma ta dōu / yě bùchī.	
ta shémma dōu / yě méichī.	She didn't eat anything.
shémma ta dōu / yě méichī.	
ta shéi dōu qǐng.	He's inviting everyone.
nǎr wo dōu qù.	I'm going everywhere.
ta něige yě bùxǐhuan.	He doesn't like any of them.
něige tāng, wo dōu méiyào.	I haven't ordered any of the soups.
wo něizhǒng kuàizi yě buhuì ná.	I can't use any sort of chopsticks.

14.2 <u>Negative universals</u>: "<u>Even as little as...</u>". NU-M (O) expressions before <u>dōu / yě</u> bu-/ <u>méi-</u> increase the emphasis on "none". Compare:

wo shémma dōu méigěi.	I didn't give (him) any (money).
wo yíkuài qián dōu méigěi.	I didn't give (him) even as little as one dollar.

The numeral in this pattern is almost always <u>yī-</u> or <u>bàn-</u>

ta yíkuài qián dōu / yě bùgěi.	She won't give even as little as one dollar.
yíkuài qián ta dōu / yě bùgěi.	
ta yíkuài qián dōu / yě méigěi.	She didn't give even as little as one dollar.
yíkuài qián ta dōu / yě méigěi.	

bànkuài qián ta yě méigěi.	He didn't give even as little as half a dollar.
wo yìzhī hǎode yě méiyǒu.	I don't have even one good (pen).
yìwǎn tāng wo dōu bùnéng hē.	I can't even drink one bowl of soup.
wo yìdiǎr yě bùzhidào.	I don't know anything (about it) at all.

14.3 **Time expressions with** yǐqián, de shíhou, **and** yǐhòu.

ta sāntiān yǐqián qù le.	Three days ago, he went (away).
ta shi sāntiān yǐqián qù de.	He went (away) three days ago.
ta sāntiān yǐhòu huí lai.	He'll be back in three days.
ta sāntiān yǐhòu huí lai le.	Three days later, he came back.
ta shi sāntiān yǐhòu huí lai de.	He came back three days later.
jiǔge yuè yǐqián ta huí qu le.	Nine months ago, she went back.
ta shi liǎngge lǐbài yǐqián shàng de xué.	She started school two weeks ago.
wo liǎngnián yǐhòu dǎsuan zài shàng xué.	I plan to go to school again after two years.
yī-jiǔ-qī-sānnián yǐhòu, wo dōu zài Hāfó niàn shū.	I've been studying at Harvard ever since 1973.
wo shàng kè yǐqián chī zǎofàn.	I have breakfast before coming to class.
shàng kè yǐqián, wo chī zǎofàn.	
shàng kè yǐqián, wo chīle zǎofàn le.	I had breakfast before coming to class.
wo shàng kè yǐqián chīle zǎofàn le.	
women shàng kè de shíhou, kàn Zhōngguo bào.	We read (reed) Chinese newspapers during class.
shàng kè de shíhou, women kànle Zhōngguo bào le.	We read (redd) Chinese newspapers during class.

women xià kè yǐhòu, xiūxi yìhuěr.	We rest awhile after class.
women xià kè yǐhòu, xiūxile yìhuěr.	We rested awhile after class.
women shàng chē yǐqián, wo mǎile bào le.	I bought a paper before we boarded the bus / ...
women zuòzai chēshang de shihou, wo kànle bào le.	I read a newspaper while we were riding the bus / ...
women xià chē yǐhòu, wo děngle nǐ le.	I waited for you after we got off the bus / ...
wo chī wǎnfàn yǐqián, hēle yìbēi jiǔ.	I drank a glass of wine before supper.
wo chī wǎnfàn de shihou, hēle yìbēi shuǐ.	I drank a glass of water during supper.
wo chī wǎnfàn yǐhòu, kànle yǐfèr bào.	I read (redd) a paper after supper.

14.4 <u>V</u> <u>O</u> lai / qu. Certain verbs that occur with the directional sentence particles <u>lai</u> "towards the speaker" and <u>qu</u> "away from the speaker" also occur with an object inserted after the verb and before the sentence particle. Thus:

huí lai	come back
huí Měiguo lai·	come back to America
ta shémma shíhou huí Měiguo lai de?	When did she come back to America?
huí qu	go back
huí Zhōngguo qu	go back to China
shàngge yue, tamen huí Zhōngguo qu le.	Last month, they went back to China.

ná lai   bring (here)

women jiào ta ná kāfēi lai ba.   How about if we tell him to bring
                                       some coffee?

ná qu   take (there)

ta ná bǐ qu le.   She took a pen / ... there.

Also:

shàng lai   come up

shàng lóushang lai   come upstairs

ta búyào shàng lóushang lai.   She doesn't want to come upstairs.

shàng qu   go up

shàng lóushang qu   go upstairs

wo zìjǐ néng shàng lóushang qu.   I can go upstairs myself.

xià lai   come down

xià lóuxia lai   come downstairs

ta chī fàn yǐqián, xià lóuxia   She came downstairs before eating.
  lai le.

xià qu   go down

xià lóuxià qu   go downstairs

ta yǐjìng xià lóuxià qu le.   He's already gone downstairs.

14.5 _Reduplication of verbs for casual effect_. In positive
sentences, certain verbs occur in reduplicated form with the addition
of "casualness" to the meaning (see Lesson 5, "New words" note 13).
The second occurrence of the verb is toneless. There is no reduplication of negated verbs. If the original verb is two syllables long,
this is the whole story.

14.5.1 _Reduplication of two-syllable verbs_.

wo děi xiūlixiuli wode chē.   I have to do a little repairing of
                                       my car.

women xiūxixiuxi ba.   Let's take a little rest.

wo děi yùbeiyubei wode gōngkè.   I have to do a little homework.

   14.5.2 <u>Reduplication of one-syllable verbs</u>. If the original
verb is only one syllable long, the reduplicated form may be any of
four different forms. In a non-past situation, it is <u>'VV</u> or <u>'V-yi-V,</u>
with no appreciable difference in meaning.

      14.5.2.1 <u>'VV</u> and <u>'V-yi-V</u>.

wo xiǎng kànkan shū.   I think I'll do a little reading.

wo xiǎng kànyikan shū.

wo děi wènwen ta.   I have to ask her.

wo děi wènyiwen ta.

women xiān shuōshuo ba.   Let's talk it over a bit first.

women xiān shuōyishuo ba.

wo děi xiǎngxiang.   I have to think it over.

wo děi 'xiǎngyixiǎng.*

ni kànkan ba.   Take a look.

ni kànyikan ba.

wo děi huànhuan yīshang.   I have to change my clothes.

wo děi huànyihuan yīshang.

women zài lóuxià tántan, hǎo ba.   How about having a little chat down-
                                      stairs?

women zài lóuxià tányitan, hǎo
  ba.

qǐng ni déngdeng.   Please wait a bit.

qǐng ni 'děngyiděng*

wo míngtian xiǎng dáda qiú.   I think I'll play a little ball
                                      tomorrow.

míngtian, wo xiǎng dǎyidǎ qiú.

*The third tone is restored on the last syllable of the verb
after yi, but the syllable carries less stress than the first.

14.5.2.2 'V-le-V and 'V-leyi-V. In a past situation, le intervenes between the two occurrences of the one-syllable verb.

wo zuótian kànlekan shū.	Yesterday, I did some reading.
wo yǐjing wènlewen ta.	I already asked her.
women zuótian shuōleshuo	We talked that matter over a bit
neijian shì.	yesterday.
wo yǐjing 'xiǎnglexiǎng.*	I've already thought it over.
wo kànlekan.	I've taken a look.
ta huànlehuan yīshang, jiu xià	He changed his clothes and then
lóu. le.	came downstairs.
wo yǐjing gen ta tánletan.	I've already discussed it with her.
wo 'děngleděng tāmen, jiu zǒu	I waited for them and then left.
le.*	
wo zuótian diàolediao yú.	Yesterday I did a little fishing.

*Notice the same restoration of the third tone as mentioned in
the previous section.

In past-time situations, it is always possible to put le alone
between the two occurrences of the verb. Under certain conditions,
it is also possible to have both le and yi between the two occurrences
of the verb. These conditions are: (1) when there is no direct object
following the verb:

tā kànle(yi)kan.	She's taken a look.
wo 'zhǎole(yi)zhǎo.	I looked around (for it).
women yǐjing tánle(yi)tan.	We already discussed (it) / chatted.

and (2) when a measured object follows the verb:

ta kànle(yi)kan nèiběn shū.	She's done a little reading in that
	book.
wo 'zhǎole(yi)zhǎo wo xīn mǎide	I looked around for that dress I had
neijian yīshang.	newly / just bought.

women yǐjing tánle(yi)tan   We already discussed that matter.
  neijian shìqing.

But when an unmeasured object follows the verb, only <u>le</u> alone may
occur:

tā kànlekan shū.   She read a bit.
wo zhǎolezhǎo dōngxi.   I looked around for some things.
women tánletan huà.   We chatted a bit.

Exercises

      Answer the following questions, using question words as indefi-
nites (14.1), or the NU-M (O) "even as little as..." pattern (14.2).

ni gěile ta duōshao qián?
ni míngtian xiǎng dào nǎr qu?
ni huì ná Hánguo kuàizi ma?
ni jīntian gen ta tánguo 'jǐjiàn shìqing?
ni zuótian diàole 'něizhǒng yú?
ni měitian kàn duōshao shíhou de diànshì?
shéi gěi ni xiě le xìn le?
ni xǐhuan chàng 'něiguo gēr?
wo děi 'zěmma zuò?
nǎr yǒu dāochā?

      Answer each of the following questions three times: first using
<u>yǐqián</u>, second using <u>de shíhou</u>, and third using <u>yǐhòu</u>, all three time
words modified by a noun or a clause (14.3).

ta shémma shíhou huí Zhōngguo qu de?
ni měitian shémma shíhou xiě xìn?
ni bàba shémma shíhou xià de bān?
nèijiā shūpù shémma shíhou kāi mén?
ni shémma shíhou zài Gē Dà niàn de shū?

Translate the following:

1. I didn't say anything, because I didn't have anything to say.
2. She's very good at Japanese, so I had her speak in Japanese to the stamp seller for me.
3. No matter how many pairs of chopsticks you buy, it still won't be enough.
4. Have you ever driven a two-level automobile? -- Yes, and it's not easy.
5. I'll buy this one; take the others away.
6. The radio I bought recently is already broken, and no one will fix it for me.
7. Let's get off at the next stop.
8. I don't know why she won't come upstairs with me to look at my stamps.
9. After awhile, we ordered three dishes and a soup.
10. Thanks. -- Don't mention it.
11. Someone as clever as you should be able to learn how to repair a television in a moment. -- You flatter me.
12. It's not necessary for you to get off the bus first.
13. Did she go to France yesterday or the day before? -- Neither; she went back three days ago.
14. Is it true that he'll do anything?
15. I don't think it'll snow tomorrow.

Vocabulary

(Lesson numbers in parentheses)

A

a P   (question particle; 9);
(exclamatory particle; 12)

ài AV   love to, be fond of (7)

Àozhōu PW   Australia (11)

B

bā, bá- NU   eight (4)

-bǎ M   (objects with handles or
something for the hand to grip,
chairs; 4)

ba. P   (at the end of a sentence, softens an imperative; 6)

bàba N   pop, father (9)

báide N   something white,
white (9)

-bǎi M   hundred (6)

Bālí PW   Paris (11)

bàn- NU   half (6)

bàngqiú N   baseball (8)

bào N   newspaper (2)

báyuè TW   August (13)

-bēi M   cup, glass (7)

Běi Dà PW   Peking U. (12)

Běijīng PW   Peking (10)

Běipíng PW   Peiping (10)

-běn M   (bound volumes, books;
4)

běnlái TW   originally (11)

bǐ N   writing implement (13)

biǎo N   watch (3)

biār, biān N   side (10)

-biār, -biān M   (side; 10)

bié AV   (negative second-person
imperative auxiliary verb; 10)

biéde N   other, remaining (14)

bié kèqi (le). IE   Don't stand
on ceremony. (14)

biéren N   other people, remaining
people (14)

Bōshìdùn PW   Boston (13)

bù-, bú- A   not (1)

búbì AV   not necessary to, not
have to (14)

búbì kèqi. IE   It's not necessary
to be polite. (14)

búbì le. IE   It's not necessary.
(14)

búcuò SV   not bad, pretty good (7)

búduì. IE   Wrong. / No. (8)

bùhǎo. IE   No. (5)

bùshūfu SV   (slightly) sick; uncomfortable (12)

bùxíng IE   not acceptable, not OK
(4)

búyào A   (negative second-person
imperative adverb; 10)

bùyídìng A   not necessarily (9)

búyòng AV   need not (14)

bùzěmma A   not so, not all that

C

cài N   vegetable; dish (of food; 7)

Cáo N   Ts'ao (5)

-céng M   (layer, story, level; 14)

chá N   tea (7)

cháng(chang) A   often (9)

cháng SV   long (1)

chàng V   sing (12)

chàng gē(r) VO   sing (12)

Cháng Jiāng N   Yangtze River (5)

chāzi N (M: -bǎ)   fork (14)

chē N   vehicle; car (9)

Chén N   Ch'en (8)

chéng N (M: -zuò)   city (10)

chénzi N   orange (7)

chī V   eat, have (... to eat; 7)

chī fàn VO   eat, have a meal ; (7)

-chǐ M   foot (linear measure; 6)

chū lai V   come out (12)

chū qu V   go out (12)

chuān V   wear (a jacket, shirt, pair of trousers; 9)

chuán N (M: -tiáo)   ship (11)

-cì M   occasion, time (11)

cóng CV   from (11)

cōngming SV   intelligent, bright (9)

-cùn M   inch (6)

D

-dá M   dozen (6)

dà SV   big (5); old (in comparing ages of people; 9)

dǎ bàngqiú VO   play baseball (8)

dǎ diànhuà VO   make a call on the telephone (12)

dǎ lánqiú VO   play basketball (8)

dǎ Měiguo zúqiú VO   play (American) football (8)

dǎ qiú VO   (hit a ball:) play a sport (in which a ball is struck with the hand or with something held in the hand, or thrown; 8)

dǎ wǎngqiú VO   play tennis (8)

dàhòunian TW   three years from now (13)

dàhòutian TW   day after the day after tomorrow (13)

dàqiánnian TW   three years ago (13)

dàqiántian TW   day before the day before yesterday (13)

dào V   arrive (11)

dào CV   to (11); until (12)

-dao VS   to (11)

dāochā N   knife and fork (14)

dāozi N (M: -bǎ)   knife (14)

dǎsuan AV   plan to (11)

dàxué PW   college, university (12)

de P   (follows the modifier in a modifier-modified construction, where the modified element is a noun; replaces the modified noun; 8)

Déguo N   Germany (5)

děi AV   must, have to, ought to (8)

děng V   wait (12)

dì- SP   (ordinalizing prefix, makes an ordinal number out of a cardinal number) the ... -st, the ...-th, etc. (10)

diànchē N (M: -liàng)   trolley car (14)

diànhuà N   telephone (12)

diànshì N   television (14)

diànshìjī N (M: -tái, -jià)   television set (14)

diǎnxin, diǎnxīn N   snack, light refreshment (10)

diànyěngr, diànyǐng N   movie, film (13)

diào yú VO   to fish (14)

diǎr, diǎn N   a little, a bit of; some (7)

dìdi N   younger brother (8)

dìèrtiān TW   the next day (11)

dìfang PW   place (11)

dìxia PW   area underneath (10)

dìyī...IE   First of all ... (10)

dǒng. IE   I understand. (4)

'dǒng budǒng? IE   Do you understand? (14)

Dōngjīng PW Tokyo (12)

Dōngjīng Dàxué PW   Tokyo University (12)

dōngxi N (M: -jiàn)   thing, object (10)

dōu A   in all cases (4)

duì SV   correct, right (11)

duìbuqǐ. IE   Excuse me. (7)

duì le. IE   That's right. / Yes. (8)

-duō M   plus a fraction (of preceding M); and then some (6)

duō SV   many, much (6, 9)

duō, duó, duōma, duóma A   to what extent? how? (6)

-duǒ M   (flowers; 9)

-duǒr, -duǒ M   (flowers; 9)

duōshao N, NU   how much? how many? (6); any (14)

E

Éguo, Èguo N   Russia (5)

èr NU   two (4)

èrlóu N   second floor (10)

èryuè TW   February (13)

érzi N   son (9)

F

Fàguo N   France (5)

fàn N   cooked rice; food; meal (7)

fàndiàn N (M: -jiā)   restaurant (10)

fāngbiàn SV   convenient (11)

-fānglǐ M   square English miles (6)

fànguǎr, fànguǎnzi N (M: -jiā)   restaurant (10)

fángzi N (M: -suǒ) building (10)

fēi V to fly (11)

fēidao V fly to (11)

fēijī N (M: -jià) airplane (11)

fēijīchǎng PW airport (11)

Fēizhōu PW Africa (11)

-fēn M cent (6)

fěnbǐ N chalk (3)

-fēng M (letters, i.e. items of correspondence; 14)

-fèr, -fèn M issue, number, copy (of a newspaper or magazine; 8)

fùmǔ N parents (8)

fùqin N father (8)

G

gāng A just (recently, in the past), was about to (10)

gāngbǐ N pen (3)

gāngcái MA just a moment ago (13)

Gāo N Kao (5)

gāo SV high (1); tall (2)

gàosong, gàosu V inform, tell (7)

gāoxìng SV happy (11)

-ge, -gè M (single person or object; 3)

Gē Dà PW Columbia U. (12)

gēge N older brother (8)

gěi V give (3)

gěi CV for, to (14)

-gei VS to (6)

gēn C and (11)

gēn CV with, accompanying (12)

gēnzhe wǒ shuō. IE Say after me. (1)

gēr, gē N song (12)

Gēlúnbǐyǎ Dàxué PW Columbia University (12)

gōngfu N free time; time (13)

gōnggòngqìchē N (M: -liàng) bus (11)

gōnggòngqìchēzhàn PW bus stop; bus station (11)

gōngkè N school work, homework (12)

-gōnglǐ M kilometer (6)

gòu SV sufficient, enough (6)

gòu A sufficiently, ...enough (6)

gòu le. IE Enough. (6)

Guǎngzhōu PW Canton (10)

guì SV expensive (2)

guìxìng? IE What is your surname, please? (5)

guò V pass, go by, after (14)

-guò, -guo VS (completed action; 12)

-guo VS (at least one occurrence of the action of the verb; 12) guójiā PW   nation, country (11)

Guóxiān N   Kuo-hsien (5)

Guóxīn N   Kuo-hsin (5)

H

Hāfó / Hāfó Dàxué PW   Harvard
  University (12)

hái A   still, furthermore (9)

hái méi ... ne   have not ...
  yet, still not... (12)

háishi A V   or is it? (14)

háizi N   child (5)

Hánguo N   Korea (5)

hǎo SV   good (1); well, healthy
  (2)

hǎo. IE   Fine. (1)

-hào M   (telephone, house,
  room) number (6); day (of
  month; 13)

'hǎo buhǎo? IE   How about it?
  (5)

hǎo shuō. IE   (Fine words:) You
  flatter me. (14)

hǎochī SV   tasty (7)

hǎojǐ- NU   quite a few (10)

hǎokàn SV   good-looking (3)

hǎozǒu SV   easy to travel (10)

hē V   drink, have (...to drink;
  7)

hē jiǔ VO   drink (liquor) (7)

hé N   river (1)

hēide N   something black, black
  (9)

hěn A   very (1); very much (4)

hěn kuài MA   very soon (11)

hóngde, hóngyánsède   something
  (colored) red; red (9)

hóngyè N   red leaves, colored
  leaves (of autumn; 13)

hòubiar, hòubian PW   back (11)

hòunian TW   year after next (13)

hòutian TW   day after tomorrow
  (13)

hòutou PW   back (10)

huà N   speech (4)

huà V   draw, paint (9)

huà huàr VO   draw, paint (9)

Huá Shān N   Hua Mountain (5)

huài le IE   broken, out of
  order, spoiled (9)

huàn V   replace by another;
  change (11)

Huáng N   Huang (5)

huángde N   something yellow /
  brown, yellow / brown (9)

Huáng Hé N   Yellow River (5)

huār N (M: -duǒ)   flower (9)

huàr, huà N (M: -zhāng)   painting, picture (6)

huì V   be versed in, know, have
  learned (14)

huì AV   know how to, can (7);
  learn how to (10)

huí lai V   come back (11)

huí qu V   go back (11)

huǒchē N   train (11)

huǒchēzhàn PW   railway station
  (11)

                    J

jǐ NU   several (ten or under),
  a few (4); any (14)

'jǐ? NU   how many (up to ten)?
  (6)

jiā PW, N   home; family (10)

-jiā, -jiār M   (shops, restaurants; 10)

-jià M   (machines; 11)

-jiān M   (rooms; 11)

jiàn V   see, meet (13)

-jiàn M   (articles of clothing;
  9)

-jiàn M (matters, affairs,
  things); (14)

Jiānádà N   Canada (5)

Jiāng N   Chiang (5)

Jiǎng N   Chiang (5)

Jiànqiáo Dàxué PW   Cambridge
  University (12)

jiāo V   teach (8)

jiào V   be named (5); call;
  tell, ask (someone to do something; 14)

jiāo shū VO   teach (8)

Jiàoshòu N   Professor (5)

jiāotōng N   (mutually pass
  through, go back and forth
  freely:) communication(s),
  transportation (11)

Jiāzhōu PW   California (12)

Jiāzhōu Dàxué PW   University of
  California (12)

jìde V   remember (12)

jiē N (M: -tiáo)   street (11)

jiē V   meet (someone at e.g. a
  railroad station; 11)

jiějie N   older sister (8)

jiěmèi N   (fellow) sister (8)

jiēshang PW   on the street;
  shopping district (11)

jièshao V   introduce (8)

-jíle BF   extremely (11)

jìn SV   near, short (of a route;
  1)

jìn lai V   come in (12)

jìn qu V   go in (12)

jìnbù N   progress, improvement
  (11)

Jīng Dà PW   Kyoto U., Kyōdai (12)

Jīngdū PW   Kyoto (12)

Jīngdū Dàxué PW   Kyoto Unversity
  (12)

jīnnian TW   this year (13)

jīntian TW   today (11)

jiǔ N   wine, liquor, alcoholic
  beverage (7)

jiǔ SV   long (time; 13)

jiǔ NU   nine (4)

jiù SV   old (referring to objects;
  4)

jiù A   only (4); then, afterwards
  (9); right away; then, as a
  consequence (13)

jiǔdiàn N   liquor store (10)

jiǔpù N   liquor store (10)

jiùshi A V   is just, is exactly
(13)

jiǔyuè TW   September (13)

juéde V   feel that, be of the
opinion that (11)

júzi N   orange (7)

K

kāfēi N   coffee (7)

kāi V   drive (10); start away
(11); open, begin operations
(14)

kāi chē VO   drive (an automobile; 10)

kāi mén VO   open the door /
gate (10); open (for business;
14)

kàn V   read (2); look at (9);
think about, have the opinion
that (9); visit, see (11);
visit, look around (13)

kàn qiú VO   watch a sport (8)

kànkan V   take a look and see
(10)

kè N (M: -táng)   class (12)

kě bushì ma? IE   How true! And
how! I'll say! (9)

kèqi SV   polite, standing on
ceremony (14)

kěshi MA   but (4)

kéyi AV   be permitted to, may,
can, will (8)

-kuài M   dollar (6); piece (7)

kuài A   quickly, soon (11); close
to, nearly (13)

kuài SV   fast, quick (11)

kuàizi N (M: -zhī, -shuāng)
chopstick (14)

L

là SV   peppery; hot (7)

la P   (fusion of le and a; 12)

lái V   come (11)

lai P   to here (11)

lánde N   something blue, blue
(9)

lánqiú N   basketball (8)

lǎoshī N   teacher, tutor (8)

Lǎoshī N   (title for a teacher
or tutor; 8)

le P   (at the end of a sentence, indicating a change in state,
9; indicating completed action in
the past, having occurred as of
the present; 12)

le VS   (completed action; 12)

Lǐ N   Lee (5)

-lǐ M   mile; Chinese mile (6)

-li L   inside (10)

-liàng M   (vehicles; 9)

liǎng- NU   two (4)

lǐbài N   week (13)

lǐbàièr TW   Tuesday (13)

lǐbàiliù TW   Saturday (13)

lǐbàisān TW   Wednesday (13)

lǐbàisì TW   Thursday (13)

lǐbàitiān TW   Sunday (13)

lǐbàiwǔ TW   Friday (13)

lǐbàiyī TW   Monday (13)

lǐbiar, lǐbian PW   inside (12)

líng NU   zero; and (6)

lìngwài SP   another, other,
different (11)

lǐtou PW   inside (10)

liù NU   six (4)

liùyuè TW   June (13)

lóu N (M: -zuò)   building of
two or more stories (10)

lóu dǐxia PW   downstairs (10)

lóushàng PW   upstairs (10)

lóuxià PW   downstairs (10)

lù N   road; route, way (1)

Lù N   Lu (5)

lǜde, lǜyánsède N   something
(colored) green; green (9)

lǚguǎn PW (M: -jiā)   hotel (11)

Lúndūn PW   London (13)

M

mǎ N (M: -pǐ)   horse (9)

ma P   (question particle; 1)

mǎchē N (M: -liàng)   horse and
carriage (11)

mǎi V   shop for, buy (2)

mài V   sell; be for sale; sell
for (6)

màigei V   sell to (6)

mǎimai N   business, trade (7)

māma N   mom; mother (9)

màn SV   slow (11)

màn A   slowly (11)

máng SV   busy (2)

Máo N   Mao (5)

-máo M   dime (6)

méi, méiyou, méiyǒu V   not have
(3); there is not (6)

méi, méiyou, méiyǒu A   have not
(12)

měi SV   beautiful (8)

měi- SP   each, every (13)

Měiguo PW   America, the United
States (2)

Měiguo zúqiú N   (American) football (8)

mèimei N   younger sister (8)

méiqián SV   poor, impecunious (8)

Měishēng N   Mei-sheng (5)

méiyìsi SV   uninteresting, no fun
(8)

méiyou guānxi. IE   Never mind. (7)

méi(you)yòng SV   useless (14)

Méizhēn N   Mei-chen (5)

Měizhōu N   America (8)

mén N   door; gate (10)

-men BF   (added to certain nouns
denoting human beings, indicates
plural number; 7)

mén wàitou PW   outdoors (near
the house; 10)

míngnian TW   next year (13)

míngtian TW   tomorrow (12)

míngzi N   name; given name (5)

mǔqin N   mother (8)

N

ná V   grasp, take in the hand;
manipulate; take, bring (14)

ná CV   taking in the hand,
with (14)

nà N   that (5)

ná lai V   bring (here; 14)

ná qu V   take (there; 14)

náli PW   where? (10), anywhere
(14)

nàli PW   there (10)

nán A   be difficult to, be hard
to (8)

nán SV   difficult, hard (8)

nán- AT   male (5)

nánde N   man (8)

nánháizi N   boy (5)

Nánjīng PW   Nanking (10)

nǎr? PW   where? (10); anywhere
(14)

ne P   (following a noun:) And
what about (the noun)? (5); at
the end of a content question:)
And...? (9); (at the end of a
statement: emphasizes action or
condition is continuing at the

time of the statement; 10)

něi- SP   which? (3)

nèi- SP   that (3)

něige N   which? (3)

nèige N   that, the other (3)

něiguó? N   what country? (5)

nèi(yi)tiān TW   that day (in the
past; 11)

nèmma A   in that way (8); to
that degree, so, such (9)

nèmma CA   in that case (13)

néng AV   be able to, can (7)

nèr PW   there (10)

nǐ N   you (singular; 12)

nǐ húidá. IE   Answer. (1)

nǐ shuō. IE   You say it. (1)

nǐ tīng. IE   Listen. (1)

nǐ wèn. IE   Ask the question. (1)

-nián M   year (12)

niàn V   read, study (10)

niàn shū VO   read, study, go to
school (10)

nǐmen N   you (plural; 2)

nín N   you (singular, polite; 2)

nín tài kèqi le. IE   You're too
polite. / You're flattering me.
(14)

niú N (M: -tóu)   cow, ox, cattle
(9)

niúchē N (M: -liàng)   oxcart (11)

Niújīn Dàxué PW   Oxford University (12)

niúròu N   beef (11)

Niǔyuē PW   New York (10)

nóngchǎng N   farm (9)

nǚ- AT   female (5)

nǚde N   woman (8)

nǚér N   daughter (9)

nǚháizi N   girl (5)

O

o. I   Oh. (10)

Ōuzhōu PW   Europe (11)

P

pángbiār, pángbiān PW   area

  nearby, next to (10)

píjiǔ N   beer (7)

péngyou N   friend (4)

-pǐ M   (horses; 9)

piányi SV   inexpensive (3)

-píng M   bottle (7)

píngguo N   apple (7)

pùzi N   shop (10)

Q

qī, qí- NU   seven (4)

-qiān M   thousand (6)

qián N   money (3)

qiānbǐ N   pencil (3)

qiánbiar, qiánbian PW   front

  (12)

qiánnian TW   year before last

  (13)

qiántian TW   day before yester-

  day (13)

qiántou PW   front (10)

qìchē N (M: -liàng)   automobile

  (9)

qìchēzhàn PW   bus stop; bus

  station (11)

qǐng V   request, invite (3)

qīngcài N   vegetable (7)

qìshuěr, qìshuǐ N   carbonated

  soft drink, soda pop (7)

qiú, qiúr N   ball (8)

qīyuè, qíyuè TW   July (13)

qù V   go, go to (11)

qu P   to there (11)

qùnian TW   last year (13)

R

rén N   person (5)

rènshi V   be acquainted with,

  recognize, know (8)

Rìběn N   Japan (5)

róngyi SV   easy (7)

róngyi A   be easy to (8)

ròu N   meat (7)

S

sān NU   three (4)

sānyuè TW   March (13)

shān N   mountain, hill (1)

-shang L   surface, top, above

  (10)

shàng bān VO   go to work (14)

shàng chē VO   get on a bus /
   train / trolley, get in a car
   (14)

shàng kè VO   go to class (12)

shàng lai V   come up (14)

shàng qu V   go up (14)

shàng xué VO   go to school (14)

shàngbiar, shàngbian PW   surface, top, above (shàngtou; 12)

shāngdiàn N (M: -jiā)   store
   (10)

shàng(ge)lǐbài TW last week (13)

shàng(ge)yuè TW last month (13)

Shànghǎi PW   Shanghai (10)

shàngtou PW   surface, top,
   above (10)

shàngwu TW   forenoon, morning
   (11)

shàngyízhàn PW   the last stop
   (i.e. the stop just before now;
   14)

shǎo SV   few, little (in amount;
   10)

-shǎor M   spoonful (7)

shéi N   who? whom? (5); anyone
   (14)

shémma N   what? (5); any, anything (14)

shēng V   be born (13)

shēngrì N   birthday (13)

shí NU   ten (4)

shì N   job (7); (M: -jiàn)
   matter, affair (14)

shì V   be (5); mean (8); be true
   that (11)

shì. IE   It is so. / Yes. (7)

'shì bushì? IE   Is that so? (7)

shì de. IE   Yes. (11)

shí'èryuè TW   December (13)

shìqing N   job (8)

shìqing N (M: -jiàn)   matter,
   affair (14)

shí'yīyuè, shí'yíyuè TW   November
   (13)

shíhou, shíhour TW   time (12)

shíyuè TW   October (13)

shū N   book (2)

-shuāng M   (pairs; 14)

shūdiàn N   bookstore (10)

shūfu SV   comfortable (12)

shuǐ N   water (7)

shuǐguǒ N   fruit (7)

shuō V   speak (4); say (5);
   talk about (10)

shūpù N   bookstore (10)

sì NU   four (4)

sìbiār PW   on all four sides, all
   around (10)

Sītú N   Szut'u, Seeto (5)

sìyuè TW   April (13)

suān SV   sour (7)

-suǒ, -suǒr M   (buildings; 10)

suǒyi MA   therefore (14)

T

tā N   he, she (2)

-tái M   (stations for transmit-
   ting or receiving radio or

television signals; 14)

tài A   too, excessively (2)

Tài Shān N   Mount T'ai (5)

Tái Dà PW   Taiwan U., T'ai Ta (12)

Táiběi PW   Taipai (10)

tàitai N   wife, lady (5)

Tàitai N (abbr. Tt)   Mrs. (5)

Táiwān Dàxué PW   (National) Taiwan University (12)

tāmen N   they (2)

tán V   chat, discuss (12)

tāng N   soup (7)

táng N   sugar; candy (7)

-táng M   class (as a period of time) ; 12

-tàng M   (journey, trips; 13)

tèbié SV   odd; uncommon (11)

-tiān M   day (11)

tián SV   sweet (7)

tiānqi N   weather (11)

-tiáo M   (long things; 3)

tīng shuō... V   (I) hear that... (10)

tóngjī N   same airplane (11)

Tóngxué N   Student, Fellow Student (5)

tóngxué N   fellow student (8)

Tóngzhì N   Comrade (5)

-tóu M   (certain domestic animals, vegetables; 9)

tóu- SP   the first... (10)

W

wài! I   Hey! (used to attract someone's attention); Hello? (used in answering a telephone; 14)

wàibiar, wàibian PW   outside (12)

wàiguo N   foreign; non-Chinese (9)

wàitou PW   outside (10)

wán V   play, have fun, have a good time, play with (13)

-wǎn M   bowl (7)

-wàn M   ten thousand (6)

wǎnfàn N   supper (12)

Wáng N   Wang (5)

wǎngqiú N   tennis (8)

wǎnshang TW   evening (12)

wár V   play, have fun, have a good time, play with (13)

-wèi M   (respected persons; 5)

wèishemma? MA   for what reason? why? (8)

wèn V   ask (5); ask about (8)

wènwen V   make a few inquiries of (5)

wǒ N   I (2)

wǒ búhuì kèqi. IE   It's not in me to be (merely) polite (14)

wǒ kàn ... IE   (as I look at it ...) in my opinion (9)

wǒmen N   we (2)

wǔ NU   five (4)

wúxiàndiàn N   radio (14)

wúxiàndiàn shōuyīnjī N (M: -jià)
  radio set (14)

wǔyuè TW   May (13)

wūzi N (M: -jiān)   room (10)

X

xià bān VO   get off work (14)

xià chē VO   get off a bus /
  train / trolley, get out of a
  car (14)

xià kè VO   get out of class (12)

xià lai V   come down (14)

xià qu V   go down (14)

xià xué VO   get out of school
  (14)

xià xuě VO   to snow (14)

xia yǔ VO   to rain (12)

xiàbiar, xiàbian PW   bottom,
  below (12)

xià(ge) lǐbài TW   next week (13)

xià(ge) yuè TW   next month (13)

xiàyízhàn PW   the next stop (12)

xiān A   first, beforehand,
  earlier (11)

xiǎng V   think (6)

xiǎng AV   have it in mind to,
  intend to (6)

Xiānggǎng TW   Hong Kong (10)

xiàngpiār N (M: -zhāng)
  photograph (9)

xiānsheng N   gentleman, husband (5); teacher (6)

Xiānsheng N (abbr. Xs)   Mr.
  (5)

xiànzài TW   the present, now (9)

xiǎo SV   small (5)

Xiǎofāng N   Hsiao-fang (14)

xiǎohár, xiǎoháizi N   child (5)

Xiǎojie N (abbr. Xj)   Miss (5)

Xiǎopíng N   Hsiao-p'ing (8)

xiàtou PW   bottom, below (10)

xiàwu TW   afternoon (11)

xiàyízhàn PW   the next stop

-xiē M   a few; a small amount
  of, some (6)

-xiē NU   a few; a small amount
  of, some (6)

xiě V   write (8)

xiě zì VO   write (8)

xièxie. IE   Thanks. (2)

xǐhuan AV   like to (7)

xǐhuan V   like (3)

xìn N (M: -fēng)   letter (14)

xīn SV   new (4)

xīn A   newly, recently (14)

xíng IE   acceptable, OK (4)

xìng V   be surnamed (5)

xìng N   surname (5)

'xíng buxíng? IE   would it be
  all right? OK? (4)

Xīngǎng PW   New Haven (10)

xīngqī N   week (13)

xīngqīèr TW   Tuesday (13)

xīngqīliù TW   Saturday (13)

xīngqīrì TW   Sunday (13)

xīngqīsān TW   Wednesday (13)

xīngqīsì TW   Thursday (13)

xīngqītiān TW   Sunday (13)

xīngqīwǔ TW   Friday (13)

xīngqīyī TW   Monday (13)

xiōngdì N   brothers (8)

xiūlǐ V   repair, fix (9)

xiūxi V   rest (11)

xué V   study, learn (8)

xué AV   study how to, learn
how to (8)

xuě N   snow (14)

xuésheng N   student (6)

xuéxiào N   school (6)

Y

ya? P   (question particle; 9)

yánsè N   color (9)

yào V   want (3); require (6);
order (14)

yào AV   want to (4); be about
to, be going to (10)

yàoshi MA   if (13)

Yàzhōu, Yàzhōu PW   Asia (11)

yě A   also, too, either (2)

Yélǔ PW   Yale (12)

yèzi N   leaf (of a tree, etc.;
13)

yī, yí-, yì- NU   one (4); as
soon as, once (9)

yíbàr, yíbàn N   half (6)

yìdiǎr N   a little, a bit of;
some (7)

yídìng A   definitely, certainly (9)

yídìng yào   must, have to (9)

yíge NU-M   one (4)

yígòng A   altogether, ... in all
(6)

yǐhòu TW   afterward, after, from
now on (14)

yìhuěr, yìhuǐ TW   a little while
a moment (12)

yǐjing A   already (12)

yíkuàr A   together (12)

yíkuàr PW   together, one place
(12)

yìlóu PW   first floor (10)

Yīngguo PW   England (4)

-Yīnglǐ M   English mile (6)

Yīngwén N   English language (4)

yīnwei CA   because (13)

yīnwei MA   because (14)

yìqǐ A   together (12)

yìqǐ PW   together, one place (12)

yǐqián TW   previously, before
(14)

yīshang N (M: -jiàn)   article of
clothing; dress (9)

yìsi N   meaning (8)

yīyuè, yíyuè TW   January (13)

yǐzi N (M: -bǎ)   chair (4)

yòng V   use (14)

yòng CV   using, with (14)

yǒu V   have (3); there is (6)

you? I   Hey! (10)

yǒu jìnbù SV   improved (11)

yǒu (yì)diǎr A   a bit (12)

yǒu yitiān... IE   One day...
  (10)

yǒude N   some (5)

yǒumíng SV   famous, well-known
  (8)

yǒupiào N (M: -zhāng)   postage
  stamp (14)

yǒuqián SV   rich, wealthy (8)

yǒurén N   some people (5)

yǒuyícì TW   at a certain time,
  once (11)

yǒuyìsi SV   interesting, fun
  (8); cute, appealing (activities of children, small animals,
  etc; 10)

yǒuyòng SV   useful (14)

yú N (M: -tiáo)   fish (14)

yǔ N   rain (12)

yuǎn SV   far; long (of a route;
  1)

yuànyi AV   want to (7)

yùbei V   prepare (12)

yuè N   month (13)

-yuè M   (in names of months;
  (13)

Z

zài V   be located at (10)

zài A   again, then (in the
  future; 7)

zài A   be in the process of
  (10)

zài CV   (located) at (10)

-zai VS   at (10)

zài jiā VO   be at home (10)

zài shuō. IE   Say it again. (1)

zàijiàn. IE   See you later. (5)

zǎo SV   early (2)

zǎofàn N   breakfast (12)

zǎoshang TW   morning (12)

'zěmma! MA   How come...?! (10)

zěmma A   in what way? how? (8);
  anyway, to any degree (14)

zèr N   (written) character,
  letter, word (8)

zhàn N   station (for buses
  trains, etc.; 11)

-zhàn M   (station, stop; 11)

-zhāng M   (flat objects, tables;
  4)

Zhāng N   Chang (5)

zhǎo V   look for; call on (10)

Zhào N   Chao (5)

zhè N   this (5)

zhèi- SP   this (3)

zhèige N   this (3)

zhèli PW   here (10)

zhèmma A   in this way (8); to
  this degree, so, such (9)

zhēn A   truly (1)

Zhèng N   Cheng (5)

zhèngshi A V   is just (during),
  is exactly (during; 13)

zhèng hao. IE   Just right. (6)

zhèng(zai) A   just (now) exactly,
  right in the process of... -ing
  (10)

zhēnshi A V   really is (14)

Zhēnzhēn N   Chen-chen (5)

zhèr PW   here (10)

-zhī M   (stick-like things; 5)

-zhī M   (certain domestic
   animals; 9)

zhǐ N (M: -zhāng)   paper (6)

zhīdao V   know (5)

Zhījiāgē PW   Chicago (11)

zhǐpù N   stationery store (10)

-zhǒng M   (kind, variety; 14)

zhòng V   plant, grow (9)

Zhōng-Měi BF   China-America (10)

zhōngfàn N   lunch (12)

Zhōngguo PW   China (2)

Zhōngguo huà N   Chinese language
   (4)

Zhōngwén N   Chinese language (4)

zhōngwǔ TW   noon (11)

zhōumò N   weekend (13)

zhū N (M: -zhī)   pig (9)

zhù V   reside, live; live at
   (11)

Zhū Jiāng N   Pearl River (5)

zhuōzi N (M: -zhāng)   table (4)

zhūròu N   pork (11)

zhùzai V   live at (11)

zì N   (written) character,
   letter, word (8)

zìjǐ N   oneself (9)

zǒu V   take (a route / road)
   (10); depart (12)

zuì A   the most..., the more...
   (9)

-zuò M   (large, immovable objects;
   mountains; 5)

zuò V   do (7)

zuò V   sit; use...as a means of
   conveyance (11)

zuò CV   by (a means of conveyance; 11)

zuò cài VO   prepare a dish (7)

zuò fàn VO   cook (a meal);
   cook rice (7)

zuò mǎimai VO   be in business (7)

zuò shì VO   to work (7)

zuótian TW   yesterday (12)

zuòzai V   sit at (10)

INDEX

Items both in the "Notes" and "More notes on grammar" sections as well as the more important items in the "Pronunciation" section are included here. References after each item are to the relevant page.

a (question particle) 167

abbreviations xxv

adjective and noun clauses
  with de 169-74

adverbs 7; (fixed) 52;
  (movable) 52,297; 105;
  (conjunctive) 270,298

affricates 65,66

"after" 297

ài (use of) 126

apicals 68; apical affricates
  and spirants 69

appositive relationship 61

attributive 75

auxiliary verb 51,52; (review
  of) 129

ball games 146

bàn (half) 101

-biān, -biār (as suffix) 243

bound form 21; 150-51

break, the 4,5

"brother" and "sister" 145

calendar years 104-05

cháng and chángcháng 167

choice-type questions 11,12

color nouns 165,166

comparison (with hěn) 10; (equal
  comparison) 277

compound descriptive phrases
  (hǎochī, etc.) 196

completed action (le) 244;
  (negated) 245, (and non-content
  questions) 245; with gùo) 246;
  (action completed at any time)
  247

conjunctions 223

co-ordinate compound 105

co-ordinate relationship 11,12;
  (with conjunctions) 223

counting (in tens of thousands)
  103; (money) 103,104; (styles
  of) 104-05

co-verb 194-95   (zùo, cóng, dào
  (with lái and qù) 224,225

dào 225-27, 244

de (subordinating particle),
  (constructions ending in) 203-
  04; (review of) 204 declarative
  intonation pattern 1

descriptive sentences 9,36

direct object 22

directional sentence particles
(with certain verbs) 304-05
displaced stress 4
dōu 52; (use of) 53-57
doubling 305-08
dorsals 68
dozen 105
duìbuqǐ (use of) 129
duō, duó, duōma, duóma
(question words) 106
duōshao and jǐ 101-02 (use
as indefinite) 300-02

embedded sentences 78-79
English meanings 7
exclamatory intonation
pattern 196
experiential suffix -guo 252

finals (free-standing) 69;
(analysis of) 88
frontals 68
functive sentence 22; (with
specific phrases as objects)
36

gàosong (use of) 128
-ge (general measure) 34
gěi 39,105,302
given names 75,76
grammatical notations xxv
-guo (names of countries) 76
guò (pass, go by, after) 297
-guò, guo (completed action)
246

-guo (at least one occurrence of
the action of the verb) 252

haishi 298
hǎo-verb compounds (compound
descriptive phrases) 196
hái méi ... ne 248

idiomatic expression 8
if 270
imminent action 227
imperative sentence 112
indefinites (in questions) 300;
(after negative adverbs) 300,
301; (in the topic position)
301,302
indefinite small number (xiē) 104
indirect object 39
indirect statement 78,79
initials, (plain vs. aspirate) 30,
31; (spirant) 65; (retracted) 68
interjections 197
interrogative intonation pattern
1; 22
intonation pattern 1

jǐ? ("how many?") 101-02, 300-02
jiā (use of) 195
jiào and qǐng (compared) 299
jíle ("in the extreme") 211,223
jiù 167,227,270
juéde (as compared to xiǎng) 223

kuài (as an adverb) 223,270

labials 67
lái and qù ("V to here/
   there") 225,226; (with
   purpose clauses) 226
le (with yí/yì 167,168;
   (changed status) 168;
   (with huài, etc., and tài)
   168; (with xiànzài) 175;
   (future change of status
   and imminent action) 227;
   (immediately) 227; (and
   object-less functive verbs)
   247,248; (sentence particle
   le with co-verbs and purpose
   clauses) 249
lǐ (Chinese miles, kilometers,
   etc.) 105, 112-13
lìngwài, (other) 222
localizers 194
location and existence 197-200;
   (existence) 200,201;
   (compared) 201,202; (with
   modification) 202,203

measurement 110; (indefinite,
   of the type "two or three")
   111
measures 34; (lone measure)
   104; (measures which add
   meaning) 125
medials 88
-men (pluralizing suffix) 125
modifier-modified relationship
   8-9

"Mom" and "Dad" 167
movable adverbs 52

names and titles 74,75
names of countries 76
naming 83
nasals 66,67
ne (question particle) 82-83;
   (uses of) 204-06
negative adverbs: bù-/bú- 12
negative adverb méi 37,245
negative universals (pattern)
   302-03
non-past le 250
noun-noun construction 22
nouns 7
nouns (modification) 146-48
nouns (omission of) 149
number 50
number-measure-noun phrases 50

objects 22 (2.5)
object as topic 53
or 11-12, 298 (1.11)
occupation or trade phrases 150

partial inclusion 76; (nouns of) 84
particle 8, 10
parts of speech (general classification of, abbreviations for) xxv
past tense (with le) 244, 250, 251
pattern displays (explanation of) 9
pīnyīn alphabetic writing,
   transcription, spelling xii

pivot 38,39; (with yǒu and
méiyǒu) 113-14
place words 193, 194
prices (giving) 106; (totaling)
107; (unit pricing) 108;
(apiece) 109; (grand totals)
109
pronouns (personal) 21

punctual and non-punctual
verbs and verbal expressions
174,175

qǐng (request) 38; 165; (as
contrasted with wèn) 165
quasi-quotes 112,113
question (choice-type patterns)
11,12; 298; (in functive
sentence) 23-26; (three
kinds) 80; (indirect) 81;
298; (with ne) 82,83;
(polite) 83
question particle a 167
question words 79
question words as indefinites
300

range, see intonation patterns
reduplication of verbs (for
casual effect) 305-08

shàng and xià (compared) 299
shì and shìqing (compared) 296
shì...de (for past action)
252-53

simple descriptive sentence 9;
(with specific phrases) 36
simple sentences with ma 10
socially charged dialogs 20,22
sound borrowings 124,125,243
specifiers 34
specification 34-36
square measure (mile) 105
stative verb-noun construction 58
stative verb-noun expression 148,
149; (with de) 149; (with noun
omitted) 149
stative verbs as adverbs 152
stress 4,15
stress in two syllable phrases 15
suffixes (verbal) -zai and -dao 225
surnames (Chinese and foreign) 74,
75; (one syllable) 151
syllable 30; 88; 91
subordination 8-9

telephone style of numbers 104-05
time expressions with yǐqián, -de
shíhou, and yǐhòu 303-04
time words (time when) 167
tones 1-4; (neutral at end of
sentence) 15; (half-fourth tone)
17; (tone weakening) 50
tóng- (use of) 221-22
topic-comment relationship 8; (the
"topic-comment" comment) 53
tóu- and dì- (compared as prefixes)
195
titles (see names and titles)

universities (names of)
  243,244

verb (functive) 22; (stative)
  7
verbal suffix 105,252
verb-object phrases (translation of) 126,127; verb-
  object phrases which behave
  like stative verbs) 146
verb-object relationship 22
verbal prefix yǐ (with le)
  251-52
verbs which take sentences as
  objects (review of) 130,131

when clauses 253, 254
word-making 222
worth of 148

xiǎng, 113; (compared to juéde)
  223
-xiē (indefinitely small
  number) 104
xué (study) (use of) 153

"yes" and "no" 7
yǐdiǎr (a little) 124
yǐjing (already) (adverbial use
  of) 248
yīnwei (because) (use of) 297,
  298
yuànyi (want, desire) (use of)
  126

zài (use of) 126
zhèi and nèi (as "the") 60; (after
  pronouns) 61
zìjǐ (self) (use of) 166